# Eleven Blunders that Cripple Psychotherapy in America

# Eleven Blunders that Cripple Psychotherapy in America

## A Remedial Unblundering

Nicholas A. Cummings
William T. O'Donohue

Routledge
Taylor & Francis Group
New York   London

Routledge
Taylor & Francis Group
270 Madison Avenue
New York, NY 10016

Routledge
Taylor & Francis Group
2 Park Square
Milton Park, Abingdon
Oxon OX14 4RN

Printed in the United States of America on acid-free paper
10 9 8 7 6 5 4 3 2 1

International Standard Book Number-13: 978-0-415-98963-3 (0)

### Library of Congress Cataloging-in-Publication Data

Cummings, Nicholas A.
  Eleven blunders that cripple psychotherapy in America : a remedial unblundering / Nicholas A. Cummings, William T. O'Donohue.
    p. ; cm.
  Includes bibliographical references and index.
  ISBN 978-0-415-98963-3 (hardbound : alk. paper)
  1. Psychotherapy--United States. 2. Psychotherapy--Practice. I. O'Donohue, William T. II. Title.
  [DNLM: 1. Psychotherapy--economics--United States. 2. Psychotherapy--trends--United States. 3. Practice Management--economics--United States. 4. Practice Management--trends--United States. 5. Psychology--economics--United States. 6. Psychology--trends--United States. WM 420 C9717e 2008]

  RC480.5.C86 2008
  616.89'14--dc22
                                              2008001564

**Visit the Taylor & Francis Web site at**
**http://www.taylorandfrancis.com**

**and the Routledge Web site at**
**http://www.routledge.com**

# Contents

# Preface: The 50-Minute Hour in the Nanosecond Era

This has been a difficult book to write. No one wants to dwell on past mistakes, and if that were the only reason for this book's existence, it would never have been written. We were compelled to address our colleagues in the psychology field because after half a century we are still repeating the same errors. The world has moved to an era in which change occurs with lightning speed. The Internet not only provides vast information at our fingertips, but has escalated the exchange of ideas beyond anyone's imagination. Political and cultural debates that heretofore would have required a generation of attention now get tossed off in weeks. We call this the nanosecond era, and within it our 50-minute hour is struggling for survival.

Whether it will survive is a matter of whom you ask. Traditionalists and humanists say it must. In an era of unprecedented scurrying we need a mechanism for reflection. Others say this is not the determinant, that society has grown impatient and moves at a rapid pace. People still love nostalgia, but as a pleasant reminiscence, not as a way of life. Just as once-dominant psychoanalysis collapsed seemingly overnight, its remnant, the 50-minute hour, will inevitably meet the same fate. The new medications with ostensibly fewer side effects are quick, and therefore preferred. And, even granted there might be some side effects, these are regarded as much less severe than the worst side effect of all: the snail's pace of psychotherapy.

We believe in the importance of behavioral interventions. However, if these are to prevail, psychologists must transcend their 20th-century mentalities and innovate evidence-based treatments that are not only effective but also meet the needs and requirements of the new era. Psychotherapy's decline has paralleled the ascendance of the biomedical revolution, and no amount of lamenting and gnashing of teeth will bring back the golden era of psychotherapy, which, believe it or not, was in the 1950s. Ever since that dizzying climb, we have been sliding downhill like hapless snowboarders, a plunge that began escalating in the 1980s.

To get to this unfortunate state, psychology has had to ignore a plethora of harbingers and a number of well-meaning warnings. Were we to witness this behavior in our patients, we would therapeutically call it to their attention. But as to our own future, we psychologists have shown an unquenchable denial, and there are not enough bad times to break through it. This prompted an earnest and concerned colleague, writing anonymously as The

Shrinker in the *Clinical Practitioner* e-newsletter (April 2007), to speculate, "Psychology may be worth saving, but can the same be said for psychologists?"

We are determined to try again, for at least one last time, to awaken the profession to its continued precipitous decline before it is too late. The senior author, calling upon his more than half century as a psychologist, has identified 11 blunders that continue to cripple psychotherapy. He believes that if solutions are possible, they must come from the emerging generation of psychologists. His co-author is just such a mid-career, successful psychologist with fresh, youthful vision. He has written the "Unblundering" section following each of the 11 blunders. In these he proffers new ideas and innovations, not merely as solutions in themselves but as vehicles to stimulate thinking and actions that will lift psychology from the mire of an outmoded 20th-century purview.

Not only because it may be the 11th hour, but also because professional psychology seems well buttressed against insight, at times these chapters may be a bit in your face. We apologize in advance if anyone is offended; this is not our intent. But if readers are angered enough to do something constructive, short of assassinating the authors, our purpose will have been achieved.

The book begins by describing the political and economic savvy of the pioneers who created from seemingly nothing the profession of psychology after World War II. It then moves on to a series of blunders that are bound by the common thread of impeding the profession and preventing the changes needed to meet exigencies of progress. As the premier psychotherapy profession, psychology seems to have rested on its initial successes, unable to rise to the rapidly evolving challenges of a changing society.

Blunder 1 describes how and why we lost the savvy that we inherited from our founders. Lacking a strong scientific basis for practice, psychotherapy substituted the authority of gurus, Blunder 2. Blunder 3 traces our economic downfall as we ignored the harbingers of healthcare industrialization and passed under the control of business interests. Perhaps Blunder 4 is psychotherapy's perennial downfall: Our insistence that we are not a health profession separates us from a $2 trillion health conglomerate, relegating mental health to a tiny underfunded carbuncle on a huge healthcare industry that continues its rapid growth. Blunder 5 describes the singular failure of the profession to own its own training, while Blunder 6 delineates the ways in which our antibusiness bias has remanded psychotherapy to relative poverty while all other health professions are prospering. Our public relations fiascos, some of which rise to the level of disasters, are the subject of Blunder 7. In Blunder 8 the reader will see how political correctness has usurped science and professional integrity in psychology. Unable to change to meet varying consumer requirements, psychotherapy has embraced Blunder 9, which is to invent diagnoses and create patients where there are none. Diversity is a stellar achievement of psychology, but Blunder 10 tells how we turned that success into a fetish and a substitute for our inability to respond constructively to the decline of practice. Finally, Blunder 11 addresses our desperate need to obtain prescription authority to rescue the psychotherapy profession.

All this is woven together in the "Afterword," which looks again at our fixation with the 50-minute hour, and discusses whether psychotherapy can change rapidly and sufficiently enough to prevent a descent into irrelevancy or even extinction.

The format of this book does not include citations within the text. Rather, citations are included in the "Endnotes" section after each chapter. This accords academic and professional readers needed references without distracting the attention of lay readers.

Finally, it should be noted that each of the 11 blunders was written so it could stand alone. This resulted in required repetitions here and there, for which we apologize.

# *Acknowledgments*

The authors are grateful to Janet L. Cummings, PsyD, for her contributions to Blunder 11 and its unblundering. Dr. J. Cummings is not only a master psychotherapist and co-editor of *Clinical Strategies for Becoming a Master Psychotherapist* but also an expert in psychopharmacology, and has taught the subject at the graduate school and postdoctoral levels for a number of years. In addition, she has co-authored several other clinical books. She is also the daughter of the senior co-editor of this volume.

The authors gratefully acknowledge the assistance of Joanne Freeman, whose editorial expertise was essential to the editing and shaping of this volume.

# Introduction: Our Founders
# Were Economically Savvy

Imagination is more important than knowledge.

—**Albert Einstein**[1]

This profound statement from the genius who opened seemingly limitless horizons in the science of physics is certainly applicable to the founders of the modern psychotherapy movement. With more imagination than psychological knowledge, they created a profession where there was none. In so doing, they had to possess an intuitive appreciation of economics despite having no formal training in finance or entrepreneurship. Unlike the celebrated millionaire and even billionaire college dropouts who created the Silicon Valley and the subsequent electronic information revolution half a century later, our founders were essentially unsung and largely forgotten heroes. They parlayed the paucity of psychotherapy science and professionalism extant at the time and buoyed their meager understanding of business with audacity, determination, an unshakable conviction they were right, and downright brashness. Only one of our founders became a millionaire, and it is because he went the extra mile into entrepreneurship. This important aspect escaped his colleagues, who, having founded the new profession of psychological practice, concluded the economics of the job were completed.

Young colleagues graduating in psychology and social work in the 21st century only fleetingly appreciate that licensure, societal acceptance, third-party reimbursement, and an extended scope of practice are relatively recent and hard-won victories, without which they would not be able to make a living today. One need only visit countries like Japan, Australia, and Israel to see what it could have been like in the United States. In such countries either psychotherapy does not exist as an independent practice or the remuneration is very low.[2] Thus, the few psychotherapists are so poorly paid that in Israel they went on strike, not a very effective one since their consciences did not allow them to abandon their patients. During a recent speaking trip to Japan, my co-author met an excellent master's-level psychologist who earns the equivalent of $9 an hour from the national healthcare system.

Before World War II there were only a few psychologists in independent practice. They were scattered throughout the country and, with a few exceptions, were women with master's degrees who were seeing children. In a chauvinistic male psychiatric profession, women without a medical degree treating children was somehow acceptable while nonphysician males seeing adults was threatening. Psychiatrists were few in number; most had European accents, and they congregated in large metropolitan areas, principally New York, Chicago, and Los Angeles. Many were descriptive psychiatrists, often employing electric shock or hospitalization as their major forms of treatment, while those with the European accents were mostly Freudian and occasionally Jungian analysts.

World War II changed all that. The numbers of practitioners exploded, fueled by a surging, almost insatiable demand for psychotherapy. The manner in which it all came about was so inadvertent that it could not have been anticipated. The Veterans Administration (VA) and the newly formed National Institute of Mental Health (NIMH) scurried to funnel millions of dollars into training funds, not only for psychiatrists but psychologists and social workers as well. The consensus was that there would never be enough psychiatrists, and psychologists and social workers would be needed to fill the mental health positions in our public institutions, which were largely unfilled since most psychiatrists favored private practice.

What spurred this surprising upsurge in demand for psychotherapy? During World War II, William Menninger, co-founder with his brother Karl of the famed Menninger Clinic in Topeka, Kansas, was appointed chief psychiatrist for the U.S. Army. General Menninger reasoned that if psychological interventions could be provided immediately in the battalion aid stations near the front lines, the degree of exacerbation and chronicity of combat-related neuroses would be markedly reduced. However, most psychiatrists, and especially those trained in Europe, were beyond military age. In order to train personnel young enough to be deployed to the front lines, he established the School of Military Neuropsychiatry at Mason General Hospital on Long Island, New York. He recruited and drafted from academia young master's-level psychologists and social workers and put them through basic military training. After several months at the new military neuropsychiatry school, they were assigned to battalion aid stations overseas. Menninger also brought select combat officers back from the front for two- to three-month crash programs on treatment—what this author, who participated in one of these, named "psychological first aid"—to be administered during combat.

General Menninger's well-conceived program was an enormous success. Psychological interventions on the front lines and in the battalion aid stations and field hospitals were heralded in books and portrayed in movies. They instantaneously captured the public's admiration and acceptance. Interest in psychotherapy skyrocketed. Those who could afford it sought psychoanalysis, or at least psychoanalytically oriented psychotherapy. Many others took advantage of low fees accorded patients who served as psychological "guinea pigs," needed to provide training for the swelling ranks of psychoanalytic trainees and for other forms of psychotherapy. So convinced was NIMH of a shortage of

trained professionals that it launched the paraprofessional movement, thus muddying forever the definition of what discipline
was entitled to perform psychotherapy.

The unfortunate answer is now almost everybody. This has
resulted in a glut of professionals, as well as paraprofessionals
who have now escalated themselves into professionals (e.g., counselors, substance abuse counselors, marriage/family therapists,
school psychologists, nurse practitioners, pastoral counselors,
all of whose psychological training is on a master's-degree level),
confusing the public by providing services of alarmingly varying
quality, scope, and effectiveness.

The NIMH's plan that psychologists and social workers graduating with the help of federal training stipends would populate
the grossly understaffed public institutions went awry, at least as
far as psychology was concerned. Chafing under the domination
of the psychiatrists who controlled these state and federal government agencies, the newly minted postwar psychologists opted
to exit them and entered the private practice of psychotherapy in
droves. Social workers, on the other hand, felt less rivalry with
psychiatry, got along well in the public institutions, and did not
begin migrating to independent practice in large numbers for at
least three decades after psychologists had done so.

The manner in which this was accomplished was a combi-
nation of serendipity and imaginatively seizing an opportunity.
In the late 1940s and early 1950s training in psychotherapy in
APA-approved doctoral clinical training programs was woefully

inadequate. Purposely unknown to their graduate faculty, many clinical psychology students made side arrangements with highly respected psychiatrists for in-depth training in psychotherapy. These students harbored a secret wish to someday independently practice psychotherapy, secret because the few students who naively disclosed this wish quickly found themselves out of the program.

This training with prominent psychiatrists continued after graduation, since both psychiatrist and psychologist were benefiting. The mentor psychiatrists became dependent on the psychological testing provided by their nonmedical trainees. Strange as it may seem now that psychological testing referrals have sharply declined, in the 1940s through the 1960s it was unthinkable to begin psychotherapy without administering and interpreting a battery of psychological tests, including the Wechsler-Bellevue Intelligence Scale, Rorschach, Thematic Apperception Test (TAT), Bender-Gestalt, and Machover Draw-a-Person (DAP). Since these tests were a necessary prerequisite to treatment, and since psychologists were the only mental health practitioners so trained, psychological testing became the first solid economic base for psychologists in the private sector.

It did not stop there, however. The same psychiatrists who were training psychologists in psychotherapy were also providing the patients for their trainees. In time a collegial working relationship between psychiatrist and psychologist developed with sufficient trust that the psychiatrists began giving these psychologists their ever-increasing patient overflow. So, without licensure, malpractice insurance, societal recognition, or third-party reimbursement, hundreds of newly minted postwar psychologists were practicing psychotherapy in private sector psychiatric group practices in which all these deficiencies were covered by a psychiatric umbrella. Psychologists had an economic private sector base, but it was tentative and unstable, and the honeymoon was destined to be short lived.

As collegial as psychologists and psychiatrists were on a local level, storm clouds began to gather as the American Psychiatric Association (ApA) grew uneasy with the burgeoning encroachment on its domain. The national organization began to pressure its members to avoid such relationships with psychologists, who, turning to the academically oriented American Psychological Association (APA) to intercede in Washington, DC, found a totally disinterested and even hostile ear. Psychological associations were forming in the more populous states, but these, too, were academically oriented and were not of much help.

The two largest enclaves of privately practicing psychologists, New York and Los Angeles, formed local associations, the first such in the nation. The New York Society of Clinical Psychology (NYSCP) and the Los Angeles Society of Clinical Psychologists (LASCP) were attempts to represent practicing psychologists whose efforts were often undercut by their own national and state organizations. Members of these groups saw licensure as an imperative, public education as important, and influencing the

APA as a necessity, but essentially they were not attuned to the business nuances of their plight. Nor did they understand fully that they alone would have to surmount the economic impediments confronting them. These realizations came with the birth of the Dirty Dozen.

It was during a forgotten era following World War II that the Dirty Dozen came into being. This aggressive, indefatigable group of newly minted PhD psychologists, eventually numbering 14, used near-guerilla tactics against seemingly insurmountable odds to create the economic base upon which their successors have flourished. They donated their time, paid their own expenses, and suffered disdain from the academically dominated psychological establishment. Under the leadership of Rogers Wright, whom they affectionately called "psychology's Attila the Hun," they cajoled the APA into making licensure, third-party reimbursement, malpractice insurance, national advocacy by the APA itself, and a host of other issues matters of policy that made the practice of psychology economically possible. The nearly three decades during which this battle was waged have been chronicled by this author and Rogers Wright, but few realize that without the intuitive economic appreciation possessed by the Dirty Dozen, the practice of psychotherapy would never have survived beyond its initial 20 years.[3]

In the late 1950s and early 1960s, health insurance that included liberal mental health benefits was becoming popular, particularly in New York and California. Claims administrators for these early policies, who did not know the difference between psychologists and psychiatrists, were inadvertently reimbursing for the services of both. Thus, psychologists in independent practice fared well.

Soon came the crackdown, however. Reimbursement was limited to psychiatrists, and although psychologists felt somewhat of a pinch, in those early days most patients were paying out of pocket. Psychiatrists' usual charge was $15 per session, with some, especially in New York, as high as $20—a tidy sum in those early days. Psychologists competed by offering services at $10 a session, which was my fee when I first entered independent practice in 1948. Prospective patients would phone, ask if I were a psychiatrist, and when told I was a psychologist, would object until they were told that they would receive equally competent psychotherapy for one-half the cost. Two out of three callers would then agree to a trial session, after which more often than not they would continue.

Private practice remained frightening, however. Malpractice insurance was not available for psychologists until the mid-1960s, and one lawsuit with an adverse judgment could take the remainder of one's life to pay off. I was one of the first five independent practitioners in San Francisco who met monthly to discuss ways to build our practices. Actually, these were hand-holding sessions in which we not only bolstered each other's confidence but also discussed methods of caution and protection in our fledgling and scary practices.

It was Len Small, a New York psychologist calling himself the NCLC (National Clinical Liaison Committee), who began mailing out to anyone he thought might read it a laboriously hectographed (long before copy machines) newsletter. He repeatedly pointed out that soon every American would have some kind of health insurance, that psychotherapy paid out of pocket would vanish, and that if psychology were not eligible for third-party reimbursement, it would end as an independently practicing profession. He acquired a small initial group of converts, including Milton Theaman and Max Siegel, who established a reimbursement committee within New York's psychological association; Melvin Gravitz, who established a similar group in Maryland; and Rogers Wright, who did the same with LASCP in California.

Wright became an avid activist of the NCLC; he and Small turned it into a highly visible group through its expanded *NCLC Newsletter.* They soon pressured the APA into forming an insurance committee, naming Theaman as its chair. Health problems precluded the continued involvement of Len Small, who was the first to warn of the precarious economic base of psychological practice. While the APA board of directors agreed to appoint an insurance committee, insurance was regarded as sufficiently unimportant to occupy the mandate of an entire committee.

Thus was born the ad hoc Committee on Insurance and Related Social Developments (AHCIRSD), affectionately pronounced "accursed" by its members. This was the APA's first committee of practicing psychologists, and no one on the board of directors had anticipated how active this group would be. Theaman, Gravitz, and Wright, initially appointed to the AHCIRSD, soon were joined by Nick Cummings, who had just made public his medical cost offset studies demonstrating that psychological interventions reduced medical and surgical costs to an extent far exceeding the cost of providing the targeted psychological interventions. This research figured prominently in negotiations with insurance companies and the federal government. In 1968 AHCIRSD became a standing committee, the Committee on Health Insurance (COHI), with Cummings as its first chair. COHI was able to speak for the APA, but therein lay one of its limitations: It could not push advocacy with the intensity needed to move the laggard APA itself. By necessity, the Dirty Dozen took the offense.

The development of nonmedical psychotherapy in America is essentially a saga of how psychology practice was established. (Social work followed very similar footsteps 20 years after psychology, overcoming the opposition of the National Association of Social Work (NASW) in a struggle not unlike that experienced earlier in psychology.) The Dirty Dozen identified two seemingly obvious goals. First, psychology needed to secure an economic basis, including reimbursement from third-party payers in the private sector and eligibility to participate as providers in the government health sector that was just beginning to take shape. Second, nationally supporting structures needed to be created, including licensure or certification in every state, the availability of professional liability insurance, and the establishment of professional and ethical standards of practice that would give practicing psychologists credibility with society. All of these required a concerted effort on the part of the APA, which failed to come through in a number of crucial situations.

## Shooting Ourselves in the Foot With Medicare

A major test arose when in 1965 the Congress of the United States passed Titles 18 and 19 of the Social Security Act, otherwise known as Medicare and Medicaid. The then Department of Health, Education and Welfare (DHEW) sent letters to all the healthcare societies seeking recommendations for implementation during open hearings to be held over a several-week period. The Dirty Dozen instantly realized the economic importance of this new program, correctly predicting that one day it would become the largest healthcare system in America.

After contacting DHEW secretary Joseph Califano, they learned to their dismay that the APA had never responded to his invitation to testify.[4] Secretary Califano related his strong conviction that psychology ought to participate in this program, and further stated that he was mystified by the APA's disinterest and even discourtesy in not replying to his letter. Several Dirty Dozen members flew to Washington and met with Mr. Califano on a Friday. In an amicable and productive meeting, the Dirty Dozen made the case for professional psychology's inclusion as

Medicare providers. Califano stated he would include psychology if he received a letter of support from the APA before the conclusion of the hearings on Monday. Fortunately, the APA board of directors was having its regular meeting that very weekend, giving us the opportunity to obtain APA approval in time to meet the deadline.

Four members of the Dirty Dozen were waiting outside the conference room in the APA building the first thing Saturday morning. They immediately requested the opportunity to present the case to the board and were refused, the ostensible reason being that the agenda was already overloaded. They persisted that day and the next, and were steadfastly refused by APA president Jerome Brunner. Finally, early on Sunday afternoon when the board was beginning to wind down, Nicholas Hobbs, the president-elect, came to hear directly from us what this was all about. Within minutes he grasped the importance of the matter and persuaded Brunner and the board to grant us the 15 minutes we had begged for.

As we were being seated, one board member made a statement that has remained seared in my memory for more than 40 years: "I want you to know in advance that I do not intend to lift one finger to put another nickel into the pocket of a private practitioner." Suddenly it struck me that our opposition in APA was not based on economic ignorance as I had thought. It was competition within the psychotherapy field itself that had realized the best way to prevent a profession from developing is to cut off its livelihood. Our enemy had defined itself.

Rogers Wright spoke eloquently and persuasively and, supported by president-elect Nick Hobbs, persuaded enough board members to agree to the requested letter to DHEW. It was decided I would remain in Washington and spend Sunday night writing the letter for APA president Brunner's signature the first thing Monday morning. The letter would then be hand-delivered to Secretary Califano, who would be informed to expect it. To make the case for inclusion of psychologist providers in Medicare, in addition to arguments of therapeutic efficacy I concentrated on the economic aspects that I knew from our meeting were important to Secretary Califano. I cited my own research findings at Kaiser Permanente—that 65% of primary care visits involved patients who had only psychological problems or a physical disease that was exacerbated by emotional stress, and that targeted psychological interventions significantly reduced this incidence. Mr. Califano had expressed a keen interest in what his own department, after two dozen replications by NIMH, would name the "medical cost offset phenomenon."

Once assured by the executive director's administrative assistant on Monday morning that Dr. Brunner would be in soon to sign the letter, I headed back to San Francisco, satisfied that the Dirty Dozen had done its job well. Several months later I received a call from Brunner's secretary saying, "I have this letter addressed to Secretary Joseph Califano. What exactly do you want me to do with it?" My heart sank. The letter had never been sent. I spoke with Mr. Califano, but of course the deadline had passed and psychology was not a provider within Medicare. When told what had happened, Califano was incredulous, saying, "Sounds like psychology shot itself in the foot."

Twenty-five years later, Representative Fortney "Pete" Stark invited the APA to participate in the Congressional Medicare Reform hearings he was chairing. Ironically, the APA asked me to testify. Accompanied by Bryant Welch, the first head of the APA's newly formed Practice Directorate, I again concentrated my testimony on the economic advantages of including psychologists. Representative Stark was duly impressed with the studies I provided, citing three years of data from psychologists' first managed mental health contract for Medicare, which included several hundred thousand seniors in Florida. Late by only a quarter of a century, psychologists finally became providers in the Medicare program.

## No You Don't! Not Again!

The Dirty Dozen had learned a costly lesson: Never trust anyone to follow through. After the 1965 Medicare fiasco, we turned to the private sector, laboriously meeting with health insurers, one after another, and largely to no avail. The two companies that agreed to recognize psychologists comprised less than one-tenth of 1% of the market. The industry consensus at the time was that psychotherapy was too ethereal to be covered by insurance, and furthermore, no one could predict its duration or outcome. One actuary told me that estimating the length of psychotherapy was like asking, "How long is a piece of string?"

Although COHI had mounted a campaign to persuade private sector insurers to recognize psychology, I was repeatedly cautioned by the APA that its committees were deliberative, not action bodies, and that we were to desist from any further such meetings. COHI and the Dirty Dozen, between which there was considerable overlap, ignored these restrictions. In going ahead, we always had to pay our own travel expenses and also lost income when we took time away from our practices. Medical cost offset and the fact that I had written the first prepaid psychotherapy insurance benefit for Kaiser Permanente in 1959 caught their attention, but in the end actuarial skepticism about psychotherapy prevailed—at least until Red Halverson, the CEO of Occidental Life, entered the picture.

Rogers Wright had discussed our economic data with Halverson, who became very interested. At his request I had a series of meetings with him in Los Angeles. He became convinced of the efficacy of psychotherapy, but his company was not in the mental health insurance business. However, he designed what he called a shortcut to get us to our goal, and put me in touch with H. Paul Brandes, attorney in the California Insurance Commissioner's office. The three of us came up with a legislative plan. Whenever the insurance code referred to payments to physicians, a state legislature would need to insert by amendment only three words after the word *physician*: "which includes psychologists." Abruptly terminating the fruitless visits to insurance companies, COHI arranged for a full-day insurance workshop the day preceding the 1968 APA convention in San Francisco.

COHI had worked diligently with state psychological associations to form its counterpart in every state, and 38 insurance chairs attended the workshop at which Paul Brandes and Red Halverson delivered a course designed to launch the new legislative campaign. The attendees were electrified and went home to do their work, while attempts to turn this new legislative campaign into APA policy failed miserably in the council. However, COHI—working with the Dirty Dozen in defiance of the APA—was able to pass the legislation in New Jersey within 6 months and in California within 12. Not too much later it had been passed in six states.

My successor as COHI chair, Dirty Dozen member Jack Wiggins, had dubbed the campaign "freedom-of-choice legislation," emphasizing the patient's right to choice of treatment and provider. This made the amendment even more palatable for state legislators by shifting the emphasis away from psychologists' prerogatives to patient rights, and even the APA eventually adopted the campaign as official policy. Shortly after Herbert Dorken succeeded Wiggins as chair of COHI, he announced "23 skidoo." This meant that the insurance industry, finding it too expensive to differentiate claims arising in the 23 freedom-of-choice states from those originating in the other 27, decided to implement inclusion of psychologists in all 50 states. The APA publicly claimed victory, and the Dirty Dozen smiled knowingly. The economic foundation of psychology practice was strengthening for the first time.

### The Struggle for Advocacy

Even under the best circumstances, a small splinter group like the Dirty Dozen, acting on its own, could not sound a strong voice. Both the public and private sector naturally looked toward psychology's national organization to speak for the profession. Unfortunately, in the 1960s and 1970s the APA was an academic/scientific body that was devoid of representation from practitioners. The APA executive officers (not called CEOs at that time) knew well who their employer was, and strongly opposed and openly deflected and even thwarted the efforts of professionals.

It became apparent to the Dirty Dozen that the APA had to be revamped. Feeling it had little choice, the Dirty Dozen mounted campaigns of harassment, constantly challenging APA executives' decisions and authority. It got to the point that the executive officers would bolt at the sight of us, using their office back door to escape into the hallway and down the elevator. When we caught on to this, I would appear at the administrative assistant's front desk, refusing to be brushed off and vowing to remain in the waiting room the entire day while I openly discussed my purpose with every visitor who appeared in the waiting room. The only solution was for the executive officer to be out of the office, so he quickly attempted an escape through the back door, only to find Rogers Wright waiting for him in the hallway.

The polarization between the APA power structure and the professionals who were disenfranchised rose to such a crescendo that three executive officers were either forced out or their tenures curtailed. Even the Dirty Dozen felt that this struggle could not continue at such a contentious level without destroying psychology. However, the APA remained intransigent until Charles Kiesler was appointed executive director in 1975, largely through the insistence of Wright and Cummings, who by that time had been elected to the APA's board of directors.

In seeking to revamp the APA, the Dirty Dozen was expressing essentially five goals: (1) support for mandatory state credentialing, with an APA-approved model licensure and a definition of psychologists for purposes of insurance reimbursement; (2) capability within the APA to interact with the Health Insurance Association of America (HIAA) and the individual insurance companies comprising it; (3) a national conference on the broad issue of appropriate training for practicing psychologists; (4) a monthly periodical devoted to news, information, and topics of interest and importance to practitioners; and (5) APA's active participation in public policy and political arenas. In short, the Dirty Dozen was asking the APA to become a national advocacy organization for psychology.

An increasing number of practicing psychologists coalesced around these issues, all of which eventually came to pass. However, early on it was apparent that the goal of a national psychology advocacy organization would remain elusive for years. It was time for another shortcut, the type of tactic at which the Dirty Dozen excelled. On a Friday night three members met in Long Beach, California, vowing not to exit until they had formed and implemented a national advocacy organization. By late Saturday afternoon the organizational structure and the bylaws had been drawn up. On Saturday night and all day Sunday they telephoned 500 practicing psychologists, one by one inviting them to become members of the board of governors by contributing $500 each. By Sunday evening the Council for the Advancement of the Psychological Professions and Sciences (CAPPS, not to be confused with a later and different group called CAPP) was established. Soon we had an office and an executive officer in Washington, DC. It is interesting to note that CAPPS made more presentations on Capitol Hill in its first year than the APA had done in its entire history.[5]

The APA cried foul and, embarrassed that it had been so deftly bypassed, formed a task force to resolve the issue directly with CAPPS. Unwittingly it was named the Committee on Relations between APA and CAPPS (the acronym CRAPACAPPS was reformulated as "crap on CAPPS," something the APA quickly learned it could not do). As a now-active and respected national organization that had gained the ear of both government and insurers, CAPPS definitely had the upper hand. The APA gave in to a plan to form the Association for the Advancement of Psychology (AAP) under APA auspices if CAPPS agreed to go out of business. The APA expected us to be demoralized by this compromise; instead, the Dirty Dozen was delighted because the plan all along was that APA itself, not another organization, should advocate for practice. To add to the victory, Wright, the head of the Dirty Dozen, was appointed AAP's first executive officer, a position he held for a number of years with great success.

Throughout the years that the Dirty Dozen vaulted at the academically controlled APA, it worked hard to elect practitioners to the Council of Representatives, the board of directors, and the presidency. Practicing psychologists had grown in numbers and voted for the candidates for the Council of Representatives as proffered by the Dirty Dozen. In 1977 Ted Blau was the first of five members of the Dirty Dozen to serve as president, with Nick Cummings the second in 1979.[6] It was under the latter's term that past-president George Albee declared at the conclusion of the council meeting, "The room has tilted." He was metaphorically describing how the power in the Council of Representatives had shifted from the older, academically oriented APA divisions that sat in the front of the room to the newer ones that had been formed around practice issues and were traditionally seated farther back in the room.

It must be emphasized that the type of advocacy launched with CAPPS, as well as the earlier AHCIRSD and COHI, was done on behalf of the economic viability of all psychology. It was not the political/ideological advocacy for which the APA has become known. These economics included such important issues as training stipends and research grants in academia, as well as reimbursement and scope of practice for professionals. Among ourselves, we constantly referred to the importance of what we alternately termed lifeblood or, more prosaically, bread-and-butter issues.

How did 14 young psychologists with no training in finance or entrepreneurship acquire such an appreciation of economics? We were all "depression babies." The Great Depression dragged on from 1929 to 1940, and at its peak nearly half the population was unemployed. Bread lines stretched for blocks and hunger was everywhere. These were the years in which we were molded into young men with the ethic that a man's first duty is to put bread on the table for his family. In choosing the new, not-yet-established profession of psychology, we were risk takers and innovators, and our intuitive commitment to economic security and stability was in every pore of our bodies.

Thus, the first task was to ensure the economic stability of the profession we were creating from the bottom up. Our contemporaries, young men and women with similar backgrounds, understood our message, followed our lead, and together we founded an economically stable practice of psychology. Sadly, with our success, we became complacent and unprepared for the economic decline that was to come. The influx of baby boomers that followed never experienced the Great Depression and were shielded from stark economic realities by depression-baby parents determined that their children would have better lives. We were soon to lose the economic savvy so important to the founders of our profession.[7]

## Endnotes

1. The quotation from Albert Einstein is in three-time Pulitzer Prize winner Thomas L. Friedman (2005), *The World Is Flat* (p. 441), New York: Farrar, Straus and Giroux.
2. The Sunday, September 16, 2007, edition of the daily newspaper *The Australian* carried a story by its medical reporter Clara Pirani, "Medicare for Mental Health Displaces Counsellors." In Australia there are only about 1,200 psychologists, while there are 17,000 counselors. She writes, "People are waiting up to 16 to 20 weeks for an appointment with a psychologist." Australia has universal government-sponsored healthcare. A recent rule termed Better Access to Mental Health, designed to increase access, has worsened the situation because it so often restricts referral to psychologists only, not counselors. The intention was to improve care because counselors are not equipped to treat the more serious conditions, such as bipolar disorder. This is just an example of how far behind us Australia is.
3. The three-decades-long struggle by the Dirty Dozen to establish psychology practices that defined the field is chronicled extensively in R. H. Wright & N. A. Cummings (Eds.) (2001), *The Practice of Psychology: The Battle for Professionalism*, Phoenix, AZ: Zeig, Tucker and Theisen.
4. The Department of Health, Education and Welfare (DHEW) was changed to the Department of Health and Human Services (DHHS) when education received its own cabinet post. Joseph Califano, known for his foresight, executive, acumen, and impartiality, was appointed secretary of DHEW by President

Jack Kennedy. He continued under President Lyndon Johnson and is regarded as an early architect of many extensive federal health programs, particularly Medicare and Medicaid.

5. The founding of CAPPS took place at the Long Beach, California, home of Rogers Wright, who joined Nick Cummings and Ernest Lawrence in rolling up their sleeves and doing the necessary work to get this entity started. The full story of the founding of the AHCIRSD, COHI, and CAPPS, as well as several other early organizations, is described in J. L. Thomas, J. L. Cummings, & W. T. O'Donohue (2002), *The Entrepreneur in Psychology: The Collected Papers of Nicholas A. Cummings* (Vol. 2), Phoenix, AZ: Zeig, Tucker and Theisen.

6. Five members of the Dirty Dozen (whose names are preceded by an asterisk) became APA presidents, and one also was its CEO for 13 years. The Dirty Dozen members were *Theodore H. Blau, *Nicholas A. Cummings, *Raymond Fowler (also CEO), Melvin Gravitz, Ernest Lawrence, Marvin Metzky, C. J. Rosecrans, S. Don Schultz, A. Eugene Shapiro, *Max Siegel, Robert D. Weitz, *Jack G. Wiggins, Rogers H. Wright (chair), and Francis Young.

7. Economic aspects of psychology practice intuitively understood by the founders but neglected by their successors are the subject of N. A. Cummings (2006), "Treatment and Assessment Take Place in an Economic Context," in S. Lilienfeld & W. O'Donohue, *18 Great Ideas of Psychological Science*, New York: Routledge (Taylor & Francis).

# 1 We Lost Our Economic Savvy

Thanks to the strong base founded by the Dirty Dozen and its many adherents in the preceding decades, psychology practice enjoyed an economic boom during the 1980s and into the 1990s. Then things began to unravel. We overcame seemingly insurmountable odds by doing everything economically right, so what went wrong? Will Rogers said it best many years ago: "Even if you are on the right track, you'll get run over if you just sit there." In short, we sat on our laurels, basking in relative prosperity, and we got run over.

Professional psychology had been the underdog from its inception, and when we were on top we thought our practices were safe and secure, a status we regarded as well earned. Did not professionals now control the APA? Had not psychiatry remedicalized, becoming a prescribing and hospitalizing profession and leaving psychology to become the preeminent psychotherapy profession? Were we not licensed in every state, enjoying third-party payment for our services, along with the respect of society? Was not our APA finally speaking with a strong professional voice, commanding attention from the media that now included psychology in its press coverage? Yes, we had arrived, and after decades of hard-fought struggles, we deserved to enjoy it. And that we did, but only for a relatively brief period.

Despite gathering storm clouds, we ignored the warnings. In failing to dodge the meteor that metaphorically killed our dinosaur practices, two truisms emerge: First, no one can blame us for wanting to enjoy our success, turning a deaf ear to those who warned of the impending end to our hard-won prosperity. But the price of complacency has been high. We are now the lowest-earning doctoral health profession.[1] Second, when the hit in incomes became a reality, professional psychologists were running the APA, and we cannot blame our academic/scientific colleagues for the sudden, precipitous decline in psychological practice. This time it was the practitioner, not the academic, who was the economic illiterate.

As one of five invited opening keynote speakers at the 2002 competency conference held in Scottsdale, Arizona, I lamented that the trend for decades in psychology has been to add more and more requirements and credentials without ever defining competency. I predicted that if we did not change course, we would soon become the most credentialed and least paid doctoral profession in healthcare. Sadly, statistics revealed just two years later that we had achieved that dubious goal even more rapidly than I had anticipated. According to the Medical Management Association survey of median incomes for 2004:

- Psychologists are, indeed, the lowest-paid doctoral health profession in America.
- Pharmacists make more than psychologists.
- Podiatrists make more than psychologists.
- Optometrists make considerably more than psychologists.
- Nurse practitioners have substantially higher incomes than psychologists.
- Forty percent of occupational therapists are paid more than 30% of psychologists.
- Mental health networks for managed care largely reflect master's-level fees.

Other health professions have suffered sudden, precipitous declines but have recovered. After widespread fluoridation of drinking water markedly decreased dental cavities, dentists found their practices languishing. The American Dental Association (ADA) was able to turn this around, and now many dentists make more than physicians. The APA can learn an important lesson from the ADA, and the way the dental turnaround was accomplished is extensively discussed in Chapter 9. In the 1980s there were predictions that psychiatry was about to become extinct. So severe was the economic plight that residency positions were going begging and were often filled by either foreign students or the bottom of the medical school classes. Guess what? Psychiatry is on top, charging as much as $350 per session, with a mean of more than $200, while patients must wait weeks for first appointments. Again, for the benefit of the APA, how the ApA orchestrated this turnaround is delineated in Chapter 12.

## Nursing, a Model for Economic Innovation

It has been so many decades since nursing became a profession that few people are cognizant that it was founded as a paraprofession. The "nurses" that patients see running about in doctors' offices and hospitals are most frequently not registered nurses (RNs), but non-RNs who go by names, such as vocational and practical nurses. RNs are busy running things in positions of considerable responsibility, to say nothing of the master's-degreed nurse practitioners (NPs), who are now high in the healthcare pecking order. From humble beginnings, nursing has insinuated itself in all aspects of medicine. Nurses often perform duties once reserved for physicians, such as prescribing medications, conducting physical examinations, handling prenatal/postnatal care, and even delivering babies with additional training. At the recent World Health Care Conference in Washington, DC, nurses were found on every cutting-edge program, and often they were in charge.

A frequent lament in psychology Internet chat rooms is that nurse practitioners with master's-level degrees have incomes substantially higher than doctoral-level psychologists. This did not happen gratuitously; it was hard fought and well planned over several decades. I was privileged to be at Kaiser Permanente in the early 1960s when that health plan was one of the first to elevate nurses with master's degrees to practitioner status, where they were widely accepted by patients and constituted a natural physician extender.

After years of acrimony, most of the United States has licensed nurse practitioners who did not stop at just being physician extenders. They have expanded boldly and rapidly, and for years they have been performing most of the services in urgent care centers—often referred to as docs-in-a-box—especially in rural areas and in those states in which a shortage of physicians still exists. Now they have expanded to group practices in lucrative areas, including Manhattan. Patients have accorded them wide acceptance, citing the fact that nurses spend more time with them and are less aloof than physicians.

Have you noticed the miniclinics that are popping up in retail stores such as Wal-Mart, shopping centers, and some large drug stores?[2] True, they offer limited service, but the nurse practitioners who staff them offer immediate, less expensive care, and early studies suggest they may be bringing down health costs. In addition, patients enjoy immediate service. Although an increasing number of primary care physicians are attempting to offer same-day service, this often requires hours in the waiting room. This is in contrast to the in-and-out healthcare of the new shopping mall miniclinics, which cost a fraction of what it takes to operate an urgent care center. More than half of these facilities do not even have a physician on call, referring patients needing more complex attention to doctors. They insist they are not replacing any part of the healthcare system, but complementing it. This author considers nursing the "poster profession" for expanding its economic base while enjoying wide patient acceptance. In addition to increasing their incomes, nurses are making care more affordable and accessible, and even reducing overall health costs.

## DISEASE MANAGEMENT SHOULD HAVE BEEN OURS

As psychology nears the tipping point at which it will be composed largely of women, some critics have attributed its lack of entrepreneurship to the feminization of the profession. The bias that women tend to be less entrepreneurial than men is belied by nursing, a largely feminine profession and one of the most innovative in the field of healthcare. In fact, as it advances economically, nursing is attracting a greater number of men, the opposite of what is occurring in psychology.

A decade after World War II the government and some of the private sector, especially HMOs such as Kaiser Permanente, began to put increasing emphasis on prevention, employing patient education about lifestyle risks and teaching day-to-day management of chronic medical conditions. Thus emerged "educational nursing," a new expertise that grew steadily in large health systems. In 1978, Kate Lorig, a brilliant and innovative nurse who is now at Stanford, took it one step further. She designed an arthritis self-help course that rapidly proved its utility and became the prototype for other courses in such chronic diseases as diabetes and asthma. Chronic disease management was born and by the 1990s had grown into a huge industry in which nurses are prominent.

I was privileged to meet Lorig at a chronic disease conference in the early 1990s, and we discussed the lack of psychological components to existing disease management protocols. She agreed that such variables as noncompliance are essentially behavioral and require behavioral interventions. She relayed her frustration with the disinterest of psychologists in chronic disease management, pointing out that all the cognitive techniques applicable to disease management protocols were developed by psychologists. She challenged me to do something about it. Thus, in 1997 I published the template expanding psychological understanding and behavioral interventions in psychoeducational programs in chronic diseases (such as arthritis, asthma, diabetes, emphysema and other pulmonary blockages, hypertension, and ischemic heart disease) and population management of chronic psychological conditions (such as borderline personality disorder, bipolar depression, protracted agoraphobia, and schizophrenia).[3]

I and the co-author of the book, my psychologist daughter, began to attend disease management conferences, where we spoke, conducted workshops, and were even invited to participate in planning sessions. However, we were unable to interest our psychologist and psychotherapist colleagues to join us. Even though by the late 1990s psychotherapy practice had begun to wane, the official stance of our national organizations was that this dip was temporary, and the boom era of the 1980s would soon be renewed.

Eventually nurses, who had preempted the field and remained willing to bring in psychology, gave up all efforts to interest psychologists. This gigantic, multi-billion-dollar industry could have been our province. Instead, we decided through the two APAs and NASW to attack the waning of our mental health practices politically rather than entrepreneurially.

## NURSES AS MANAGERS

Nurses have upgraded their status so effectively that they see themselves as managers in a number of endeavors. Miniclinics, independent group primary practices, and disease management are just three examples. The newest example attests to the forward-thinking leadership in American nursing today. In February 2006, the U.S. Department of Labor announced that one of the fastest-growing sectors through 2012 will be emergency management. The hurricane season of 2005 and its attendant difficulties in appropriate response, plus a series of other disasters, have drawn attention to the need to ensure rapid and expert response to disasters.

Months before this announcement, and in response to the perceived need following Hurricane Katrina, the Adelphi University School of Nursing in Garden City, New York, designed and implemented a master's degree program in emergency nursing and disaster management. Several other schools of nursing announced they would also implement such a master's degree program to be available in the fall of 2006. The timeliness and speed of response by nursing is a model for all healthcare.[4] It should be noted that nursing no longer hesitates to see itself in healthcare managerial and entrepreneurial roles, so do not be surprised if one day your employer or boss is a nurse practitioner.

### Parity: Much Ado About Nothing

One of the most successful political campaigns ever conducted by psychology and psychiatry is the legislative effort that within a short time enacted parity laws in 44 states and the federal government. This remarkable achievement mandated equal expenditures for both physical and mental health, thus providing a political solution for an economic problem. However, while parity is touted as a quick solution to inequity, it is well known that access to and benefits for mental health services lag far behind those accorded for physical health. Legislatures cannot dictate economic laws, and this widely heralded political triumph has been much ado about nothing.[5] A smaller percentage of the total health budget is being spent on mental health today than before the enactment of parity laws.

It was long ago discovered with dismay that rent controls, rather than increasing the availability of low-cost housing, drastically reduced it. Landlords, realizing they could no longer meet expenses and property taxes, merely walked away from them. The wholesale abandonment of buildings created neighborhoods resembling bombed-out war zones—for example, a large part of the Bronx in New York. Furthermore, investors avoided building new units in rent-controlled areas, further reducing the availability of housing. In a similar manner, the managed care companies and the insurance industry, fearing runaway costs for mental health, put in place more draconian requirements to qualify for mental healthcare than for physical health. Rent controls for housing, price controls for goods and services, along with parity laws for mental health are prime examples that political dictates do not trump economic realities.

In spite of this, the drive to renew the federal parity law and to enact such laws in the 6 states that do not have them continues with vigor. The reason for this is simple: In the end, the rapid enactment of these laws makes mental health advocates appear to be successful and justifies continued contributions from rank-and-file practitioners who are frightened by their dwindling practices. No one seems to be asking, "But where's the beef?" and our paid advocates end up looking like heroes. All those who have monetarily supported parity drives in the past might ask if it would not be more productive to expend time, effort, and funds to innovate and create new economic opportunities for psychotherapists rather than continuing the futility of politically mandating them.

### Not to Worry, We Have More to Offer

High on the list of economic woes is the glut of psychotherapists that continues to grow in the face of dwindling numbers of referrals. Swelling the ranks that originally were limited to psychiatrists, psychologists, and social workers are psychiatric nurses, master's-level counselors, marriage and family therapists (MFTs), addiction counselors, and pastoral counselors. The patchwork of state licenses and certifications is baffling to the public, which eventually provided the all-inclusive term *therapist*. Whenever someone is interviewed on television or radio and is introduced as a therapist, I wonder what the legitimate profession is, if any at all, because most state laws permit the use of the term *therapist* if the person who is unlicensed does not claim the title accorded any of the string of licensed professions.

In 1996 APA president Dorothy Cantor announced there were 650,000 licensed or otherwise credentialed psychotherapists in the United States, a figure that health economists regarded as well over the number required at the time to meet the demand for services. Since then, demand has dropped while the number of psychotherapists has increased. Common sense would say that eventually there must be a tipping point, as happened in law. After decades of an increasing oversupply of lawyers, with some earning millions while others avoided unemployment by staffing disdained positions in public defender and county prosecutor offices, applications to law schools significantly declined in 2004 and took even more of a dip in 2005. Why has this not happened in the psychotherapy professions?

Graduate school–bound young people who either avoided science and math or had their high schools and colleges adroitly avoid these basics for them are limited to seeking professions that do not require numerical skills or scientific literacy. Unfortunately, those lacking these basics far outnumber those who are proficient in them. Consequently, pharmacy, a profession that is booming (with pharmacists earning substantially more than psychologists and very much more than social workers), is crying out for qualified applicants. Meanwhile, social work and counseling programs are attractive, serving the hordes of students whose choice is dictated by their having previously avoided the tough courses.

Academically oriented doctoral psychology programs require mathematical and social science abilities, but this can be circumvented by the many professional schools that deemphasize science and do not even require a dissertation. Even among the more stringent doctoral clinical psychology programs, the dirty little secret is that they are admitting applicants with SAT scores so low they would never have been considered for admission a decade ago. The silent, under-the-radar decline in applicants may have begun, as brighter or more scientifically prepared students choose the hot business schools that feature entrepreneurship, or seek careers in new technologies that are changing the face of our world.

Those entering psychotherapy training programs have an additional handicap: They come with an antibusiness bias that precludes their going into the business schools and MBA programs that are attracting bright young people and launching many into the kinds of successful entrepreneurships that elude psychotherapists. The belief that *business* is a bad word is reinforced by their professors in graduate school, thus depriving the psychology graduates from finding solutions to the economically ailing profession they are entering. This will be discussed in detail in Chapter 7.

## A Solution Missed: The California Model

California was one of the first states to enact state statutory recognition and regulation of psychology, but it was a certification act. Years later when it upgraded its original 1957 law to licensure, it also added the provision that licensed psychologists could employ two psychological assistants—master's-level psychologists who would supervise and bear responsibility for their work. Any activity by the psychological assistants (PAs) had to be signed off on by the employing licensed psychologist. Maybe the then psychological leadership in California had the prescience that someday master's-level counselors would be direct competition, or perhaps they were emulating physicians who, having lost control over nurse practitioners, were creating the occupation of physician assistants who would be more under their control.

When elected to the APA board of directors in the mid-1970s, this author saw PAs as an ultimate solution to a problem that was still latent but would be a major one within a short time. Several colleagues and I set out through a series of editorials in the newly established *APA Monitor* (later renamed *Monitor on Psychology* and transformed into a magazine from the original newspaper format) to convince the APA to amend its model psychological licensing law to incorporate the concept of the psychological assistant. We argued that whereas master's-level psychologists at the time had no home and no statutory recognition, they would follow the path traversed by other paraprofessionals before them and eventually become independently licensed. This was the time to bring them in-house and under our employment and supervision, which not only would preclude future competition but also would limit the number since each licensed psychologist could employ only two. The concept was resoundingly defeated. The prominent professional psychologist who led the opposition calmed any fears in his fellow council members that someday master's-level psychologists would be serious competition, by stating, "Not to worry, we have far more to offer."

Fast forwarding 30 years, we have not convinced the marketplace that we do, indeed, have far more to offer. The majority of psychotherapy conducted in the United States is by social workers, who have accommodated to managed care far better than have psychologists. Further, a startling feature of managed care networks is that they have far more master's-level providers listed than doctoral-level ones—often a ratio of as much as five to one. Consequently, fees are gauged at the predoctoral level. Thus, although all providers are suffering from the low fees universally paid by managed care, doctoral psychologists are taking the biggest hit since most networks do not differentiate between doctoral- and master's-level providers when it comes to payment.

If they do, the differential is more token than substantial. These are results of the law of supply and demand, which applies as equally to labor as it does to goods.

Most psychologists are aware that if a product is in short supply the price escalates. On the other hand, a glut of goods sharply reduces costs, resulting in a buyer's market as sellers seek to unload the surplus. However, these same psychologists are not aware that the same laws of supply and demand also apply to services. Since master's-level providers are willing to work for less, and since there are far more providers than needed, fees are set accordingly and doctoral psychologists listed on the network can take it or leave it. Because we have not proved that "we have far more to offer," there is no hue and cry from the patients that they are being deprived of better-trained doctoral psychologists. To the consumer, they are all therapists. For those who pay the bills (government, insurers, managed care, HMOs) it is a buyer's market.

One of the most frequent pleas I hear from young colleagues is: "All I want is an income commensurable with the years I spent getting my PhD. Why does a nurse practitioner on a master's level make twice as much as I do?" The answer is a simple supply-and-demand relationship: There is a glut of psychologists who do whatever it is that master's-level psychotherapists do just as well, according to those who pay the bills, while there is a shortage of nurse practitioners who perform services that no one else but even more costly physicians can render. Maybe, as they say, "that just isn't fair." But there are no fairness police that preside over our economy, assigning pay scales in accordance with degrees of training and levels of education. Buyers will always seek to gain the most value for their dollar, and often seeking the lowest price is the way to achieve this. There is only the brutal law of supply and demand. My somewhat pathetic mortar-carrying bricklayer patient may be illustrative here.

A bricklayer with many years experience in the trade moved to a new area where he found that an oversupply of bricklayers made it impossible for him to get a job. While on a waiting list for openings, he went to work carrying mortar up the scaffolding to the bricklayers, a minimum wage job in sharp contrast to high-paying bricklaying. He insisted, unsuccessfully, that even though he was carrying mortar, he should be paid bricklayer wages, or at least something near that level, because he was a journeyman bricklayer. He resented being told that when you carry mortar you are paid as a laborer, and when you lay bricks you are paid as a tradesman.

As time dragged on without an opening, he became increasingly disgruntled, eventually falling from the scaffolding and sustaining a severe injury, an accident that might well have been related to his anger and dissatisfaction. Now on disability, he complained unsuccessfully that he should receive tradesman scale payments, not those of a laborer. He did not manifest the course of improvement expected of his injury, and worker's compensation referred him to me, suspecting depression. He refused to listen to reason or to take responsibility for failing to investigate or anticipate that in warm climes far less brick buildings are constructed, therefore requiring a smaller bricklaying force.

My patient was not a very intelligent man, mitigating his refusal to understand the economics of the situation. But what of PhDs who are capable of understanding supply and demand, yet refuse to do so? If we continue to deny economic realities, how can we ever arrive at economic solutions? So we remain a part of networks that pay on a predoctoral level, and even feel glad to have a job. Do we resign ourselves and fall back on parity legislation and other ineffective political attempts at a solution? Do we live with the vain hope that eventually the consumer will realize we have far more to offer even without our ability to demonstrate it? Or do we innovate as have nursing, dentistry, and medicine, creating endeavors heretofore never dreamed of that are tantamount to wealth creation? Nurse practitioners running miniclinics in malls is just that sort of wealth creation. As nurses move up on the scale of responsibility and management in these innovative ventures, they create new jobs for non-RNs. Entrepreneurship not only redistributes resources, but actually creates wealth.

Because of my speaking out on economic issues, a surprisingly large number of colleagues are eager to tell me their plight. Their stories are sad, and also discouraging in that in the 10 to 15 years since the decline in psychotherapy began, we have yet to formulate a viable economic solution—with the possible exception of one, which will be discussed in Chapter 12. Recently my spouse and I were having lunch at a delightful deck restaurant overlooking the water at Marina del Rey, California. Our server, a woman in her early 30s, surprised me by asking, "Aren't you Dr. Nick Cummings?" She turned out to be a psychologist who had graduated with her PhD three years earlier. She was trying to build a private psychotherapy practice, had applied to several managed care networks, and had two patients she saw on her days off from waiting on tables. She considered herself lucky, since a friend who had graduated with her and was also serving tables at the same restaurant had no clients. Besides, the tips were more remunerative per hour than either of her patients, to whom she had given a reduced fee. Later my wife expressed sadness for her plight and was further saddened when I informed her that I was inundated with stories even more unfortunate than this, such as a colleague who after 20 years found his practice had dried up along with his livelihood. This is not to mention the number of both younger and older colleagues who have left the field altogether.

There are rumblings within APA that the solution is to curtail the numbers of psychologists graduated by our clinical doctoral programs, especially those by professional schools that are essentially supported by tuition and require large classes to keep the revenue stream sufficient. Since the APA exercises some oversight in approving doctoral programs, this would seem an immediate solution. But psychologists seem to forget that fees are being suppressed not merely by too many doctoral psychologists but by the far greater number of master's-level psychotherapists. Where once we might have had control over master's-level counselors, it is now totally beyond our control. We need to innovate new endeavors for psychotherapists until potential students, as is happening in law, realize that becoming a psychotherapist is less than an economically stellar choice.

## The Need to Innovate Practice

Psychologists and other psychotherapists have done as well as might be expected through stopgap measures. But this limited or temporary relief is a far cry from a long-range solution, as the following examples show.

*Out-of-pocket fee-for-service practice* has attracted a substantial number of psychotherapists who have quit managed care networks and rely on clients who can or prefer to pay for their own healthcare. By freeing themselves from managed care, they can ostensibly charge fees above network scales. The caution here is that success in seeing only paying clients is inversely proportional to the number able and willing to handle self-payment, which will eventually reach a saturation point. Rand and other studies suggest that the number of patients who are willing to forego their benefits and pay out of pocket is somewhere between 5% and 7% of the covered population. In other words, this solution is dependent upon the timidity of most practitioners to venture out of insurance or managed care reimbursement, leaving a lucrative opportunity for those who have the courage. Taking this step has been touted in a series of books and workshops. If there were a large migration to practices limited to paying clients, soon competition would begin to impact on fees. Strictly speaking, this type of practice is not a viable solution for the psychotherapy profession as a whole.

*Coaching* is an endeavor that has become popular among certain sectors in America, principally among individuals who need or wish to have expert advice in making life choices. It is the antithesis of classical psychotherapy, which requires neutrality on the part of the therapist, encouraging the patient to set his or her own goals without being told by the therapist what to do. So far coaching has been far more remunerative than psychotherapy for those who have a knack for the role, but therein lies the pitfall. There is no statutory regulation of coaching, and prominently successful coaches run the gamut from well-trained doctoral psychologists to charismatic but lesser-trained persons to outright flimflam artists. How long this cash cow will last is anyone's guess since it has many attributes of a fad. In any event, it is not a solution to the economic woes of psychotherapy since it is not psychotherapy. Those psychotherapists who become coaches are actually opting out of psychotherapy and competing with individuals with a wide range of backgrounds.

*Neuropsychology* has been a growth area, with substantial fees attached to neuropsychological testing because of the time involved. These in the past have ranged upward of $2,000, but with more psychologists joining the ranks, fees have had to come down. One large managed care company typically has a flat fee of $750, prompting many neuropsychologists to employ lesser-trained individuals to administer the time-consuming tests while the psychologist interviews the patient, interprets the test findings, and signs the report. The most lucrative clients for neuropsychology are tort lawyers, who not only pay well but may also require the psychologist's testimony in court, again at a substantial fee.

The latter merges into *forensic psychology*, a relatively new field that has grown impressively in the last decade. A few forensic psychologists also have law degrees and are in demand, but not as much as renowned authorities who have established the ultimate expertise. One example is Lenore Walker, who wrote the first book on battered women and who has traveled the country testifying on behalf of women who have killed their violent, abusive husbands. Within forensic psychology is another interesting niche, advising lawyers on the selection of jurors; however, this expertise is relatively rare and limited. Lawyers can retain forensic psychologists for a variety of purposes. Some psychologists have acquired the reputation of providing testimony so regularly that they are known as either plaintiff or defense psychologists. Once such a reputation is acquired, usefulness decreases. Most forensic psychologists, however, are involved in a wide range of more prosaic activities, providing a livelihood outside psychotherapy.

*Health psychology*, which has taken a back seat in the past to the interventions deemed more glamorous by psychotherapists, is finally commanding more attention, especially because of the initiatives of recent APA president Ronald Levant.[6] Whether psychotherapists, and particularly health psychologists, will seize the opportunity to innovate creative delivery systems that will expand the profession is the subject of a later chapter.

Psychotherapists often demonstrate ingenuity as they carve out personal careers in highly individualistic endeavors such as counseling the growing numbers of women who need fertility treatment. In essence, these esoteric niches will do little to ameliorate the surplus of psychotherapists that currently stymies the economic growth of the profession. Why is psychology practice in Hawaii the notable exception? Because social workers have only recently been licensed, and all other psychotherapy professions that usually follow them are not yet licensed in that state, psychologists have little competition. It should not be surprising, then, that psychologists in Hawaii command literally three times the hourly fee that is the median in provider-glutted California.

Mental health practitioners, like the academicians who taught them, think of the economy as a zero-sum game. This fallacy would hold that the pie is only one size, and if someone gets a bigger piece, someone else must get a smaller one. In psychotherapy practice this means that there is a finite number of patients, and we need to increase access so they can receive our services. This overlooks the possibility that many of these people may not want our services for various reasons, ranging from not finding them attractive to finding them actually offensive. Others may be responding to cultural and religious prohibitions, while still others think all behavioral interventions require 15 minutes or less to resolve in the manner of such media icons as Dr. Phil and Dr. Laura; thus, they are disappointed by and resistant to the long haul often necessary. There is also the growing distrust of psychotherapy, eroding the once near-hero worship of psychologists and psychiatrists in the post–World War II era. In meeting these challenges, let us take our inspiration from the other health professions that have created delivery systems where once there were none, expanding their professions to new horizons and demonstrating that we are no longer inadvertent slaves to the zero-sum game.

### Blunder 1: Summary and Conclusions

Within a remarkably short period, we lost the economic savvy of the founders who in the decades post–World War II carved a new and prosperous profession where there had been nothing. The seemingly insurmountable odds confronting these early clinical psychologists, later emulated by social workers and counselors, served to make our founders more economically savvy, while prosperity rendered their successors economically complacent. Blunder 1 can best be described as the failure to either limit the growth of psychotherapy with more stringent training, especially in areas of science, or encompass nondoctoral personnel within the doctoral profession. Failure to do so has created a glut of psychotherapists. In order to absorb the surplus, we must expand the profession into innovative endeavors patterned on lessons from dentists, nurses, physicians, and the healthcare fields other than mental health.

The incomes of psychotherapists are estimated to remain static over the next decade, even as the Department of Labor anticipates a healthcare boom during that period. The greatest growth will come in professions with severe shortages, such as pharmacy, whose excellent median income is anticipated to grow by more than a third in the next decade. The median income of nurses, who not only are in short supply but also are expanding innovatively, is expected to rise 27% during that same period.

## Unblundering

The first step in correcting the current plight of psychology is for us to realize that economics do matter. We as a profession need to come to the collective realization that economics is important and does not just take care of itself. We have been bludgeoned by our economic illiteracy and our laissez-faire attitude. If we continue along this path we will take an even greater beating.

What is involved in the attitudinal shift? We need to:

- Deal with our ambivalence regarding money and business.

- Gain an education in and an appreciation of basic health-care economics. We must become literate in trends, problems, and opportunities at a macro level.[7]

- End spending time and effort in emotionally satisfying but futile and expensive efforts, such as suing managed care.

## DEALING WITH OUR AMBIVALENCE TOWARD MONEY AND BUSINESS

Most of us entered this profession to help others. Taking money from them seems inconsistent, since how does an empty pocketbook help another? Wouldn't they really be better off if they could keep all their money and just receive all our help? We want to be magnanimous and "give away" psychology. If we could function like this, we could feel really good about our mission of helping others.

Third-party reimbursement seems to solve the problem for us. We can offer our services for free, or nearly free (small co-payment), and have some faceless company send us money. Because this third-party payer is not a person (we did not enter this profession to help companies but rather people), we can then adopt the attitude that they ought to pay us a lot.

Problem solved? Not really, for two main reasons. First, someone has to put cash into these third-party payers. They cannot simply print money. The biggest third-party payer is the federal government, through Medicare, Medicaid, and the Department of Defense (the government pays for about 50% of all healthcare). We know who ultimately has to pay—all of us through taxes. Although this solution has some appeal because it diffuses the sense that any one individual is being charged, people still pay. Employers appear to pay for the premiums charged by these third-party payers. But a strong case can be made that it is really the employees who are paying, albeit indirectly. My employer looks at the total costs involved in employing me. If it is $50K, the employer does not care if it is $45K in wages and $5K in benefits such as health insurance, or just $50K in wages. Employers have to write the same size check, although they may prefer health insurance because they do not have to pay taxes on that amount. Additionally, if it makes me healthier, it may make me a better worker.

So someone has to pay. And we have to realize that often it is the person in front of us. We cannot get off the hook by pretending our patients do not pay and that we function in a quasi-charitable manner. If we want significantly higher payments from the third-party payer, we must realize that they will pass these increases on to the employer, who will pass them on to the employees by lower raises or higher co-payments. Economics never goes away.

There is another important aspect to this: How comfortable and guilty do we feel about money? Do we care about it too much? How much is too much? What is an acceptable income and what is greedy? What is a fair way to earn more money, and what are illegitimate ways? Why are the fair ways legitimate? Is profit always bad? Are nonprofits always good?

The authors think that psychologists' attitude toward money is similar to the American public's attitude toward sex in the 1940s and 1950s. There is, at a minimum, much ambivalence involved. We like it, and we feel guilty about liking it. We wonder if we can like it too much, and we believe there are a lot of illegitimate ways of getting it. We think it can be a source of evil, although at the same time we know we enjoy it and that it is necessary. Psychologists are confused about money but not about sex.

In the last several decades there has been a sexual revolution, much of it led by psychology. We now have constructs such as "healthy sexuality" and "sex positive." People can talk very openly about their sexual desires, even statistically unusual ones. We believe sexual minorities have rights. But we have made little progress regarding our attitudes toward money and business. There is still a lot of guilt, disgust, and conflict toward this "secret pleasure." We need to get our attitudinal house in order.

## WHY ARE BUSINESSES AND MONEY GOOD?

### *Money: Several Reasons Why It Is Good*

- Obviously, it is a necessity. We need money to survive.
- It can allow us to pursue pleasures in life—vacations, estates for our children, and so on. We psychologists know that life does not have to be all work and no play.

- Intelligent planning about money can alleviate much anxiety. It can help to pay for our children's college, our retirement, our healthcare when old.

- An intelligent outlook about money results in its playing a smaller role in our lives. If we make the right financial moves, we can focus on other issues rather than being stuck at "How do I pay my bills?"

- We can give it away and help others. Note that the Bill and Melinda Gates Foundation has provided billions of dollars in healthcare for Third World peoples. Warren Buffet recently endowed another $30 billion to his foundation. The Rockefeller, Ford, and Robert Wood Johnson Foundations, just three more among many, are examples of wealthy individuals giving back and doing good in very significant ways. America is a generous nation that is involved in charity at many levels.

- Excess money finds innovation. Psychologists are rarely cognizant of this important aspect. It is relatively wealthy individuals with money to risk in entrepreneurial endeavors that create new products and services, and consequently millions of jobs for the rest of us.

### Businesses: Several Reasons Why They Are Good

- Businesses meet needs or perceived wants; otherwise, they would not exist. If no one wanted computers, Apple and Dell would go out of business. We deal with businesses because we perceive them as improving the quality of our lives. What would we be if all business went away? Hunters? Gatherers?

- Businesses create jobs. They put food on the table and pay for all the other activities of the employee.
- Businesses create wealth. Many psychologists, not understanding economics, see wealth as a zero-sum game: There is only so much to go around and the pie must be distributed equitably. Wrong! This view connotes economic illiteracy; businesses can create wealth by increasing the number of pies.
- Successful businesses are always looking to provide better value to the customer; they need to do this to survive in the competitive marketplace. Consumers benefit immensely from this competition. For example, we now have better cars than we had 30 years ago because of the fierce competition in the automotive industry.

I witnessed an interesting phenomenon while I was in high school (I graduated in 1975) and in college at the University of Illinois. Some of my friends were really into computers. We in psychology felt kind of sorry for the computer "nerds," who seemed to be out of touch with things. Some were so introverted and into programming that they had a difficult time ordering a pizza. We psychology students would pat ourselves on the back for our people skills and our practical problem solving. We had excellent life skills and felt concern for our geeky computer science friends.

In the last two decades, those nerds have created companies valued at hundreds of billions of dollars. They have created amazing products that make our lives better, more productive, and pleasurable. They have created jobs that put bread on the table for hundreds of thousands of individuals. And what have we done? How many jobs have we created? How many individuals can have a comfortable retirement because of their investments in our companies and our stocks? How well paid are our employees? How many kids rely on our paychecks to put them through college?

Mental health professionals certainly have a social mission. We want to make the world a better place. We must realize that creating or growing successful businesses is a way to do this. There are myriad opportunities; we are not selling something no one wants, such as trephaning machines or orgone boxes. People want to get over their depression, people want to change their lifestyle, and people want to help their autistic child. But why have we, in contrast to computer science majors, been so poor at seizing opportunities to create businesses that more effectively deliver our products?

## GAINING AN EDUCATION AND APPRECIATION OF BASIC HEALTHCARE ECONOMICS AND BUSINESS

What follows is a brief introduction to healthcare economics. It is meant as a teaser to help promote interest and further reading, such as the excellent book by David Dranove, *The Economic Evolution of American Health Care.*

The United States is experiencing a healthcare crisis. The crisis can be explained along several dimensions, but the primary one is escalating costs that are multiple times the rate of inflation for other dimensions of the crisis (e.g., access, quality, the uninsured). Here is the crisis in a nutshell: In 1960 we spent 5% of the gross domestic product (GNP) on healthcare. This allowed, of course, 95% to be spent on all other goods and services. Bear in mind that most people would rather spend money on vacations, autos, education, roads, food, clothes, and boats. In that previous era they got their druthers 95% of the time. In 2005 we spent 15% of GNP on healthcare, or a total of $1.5 trillion. So, proportionally, there is much less money for goods and services.

If your eyes have not glazed over, there is even more bad news. The rate of increase is accelerating; the healthcare budget has been increasing at two, three, and even more times the rate of inflation in the general economy. If this does not cease, we will be spending more than 25% of the GNP on healthcare in the year 2030.

Note that this does not just mean that we have less money to spend on goods; it signals a crisis for the entire American economy. In a globally competitive environment our goods are more expensive because the employers' healthcare costs have to be filtered into the price of the goods and services produced. It is estimated that every American car has $1,700 of healthcare costs in its price. In contrast, every Japanese car has only $800. This is a significant competitive advantage for the Japanese.

Why are these healthcare costs increasing? There are several reasons:

*Advances of medical technology*: Feeling a bone to determine if it is broken is cheap but imprecise. X-rays, which include the cost of the reading by a radiologist, are more expensive but also more precise. CAT scans increase the diagnostic accuracy and substantially increase costs. MRIs allow 15% more detail, but are more than 150% costlier than CAT scans.

*Prescription drugs cost more*: Every year sees an impressive increase in the number of more effective drugs that usually have less side effects. However, these come at higher prices. The drug companies must pass on the cost of developing a drug, which has now exceeded $5 billion even for drugs that fail to receive FDA approval. In 1990 there were four prescription allergy drugs at an average cost of 98 cents per dose. In 2005 there were 17 such allergy drugs, costing an average of $3.41 per dose.

*The aging population*: Better public health, safety, and medicine are increasing life expectancy, producing a huge demographic shift. The elderly utilize a significantly greater amount of healthcare. In 1998, Florida, which has the highest mean age, spent $60,000 per capita in healthcare, while Utah, with the youngest population (median of 26.7 years) spent only $2,000 per person.

*Chronic diseases*: In the United States, 40% of all healthcare costs are attributable to chronic diseases such as diabetes, COPD, asthma, hypertension, and pain. Many of these patients are treatment noncompliant, while others have problematic lifestyles that contribute to poor health, further increasing costs. Additional factors are their mental health (e.g., depression, stress) and substance abuse comorbidities.

*Other economic facts*: Behavioral care is only 5% of the entire healthcare budget, rendering us small potatoes in an escalating cost picture. It is our task to demonstrate to the other 95% of healthcare that behavioral health interventions add value. Much of our medical dollars are not being spent wisely because they ignore the psychological distress that manifests itself through physical symptoms, or the emotional factors and lifestyles that exacerbate illness. Demonstrating that cost-effective behavioral interventions delivered within a primary care setting can save millions in medical and surgical costs would grow our services appreciably. This would create more jobs, open business opportunities, and significantly raise the current low-income level of our profession.

## KEEP ABREAST OF ECONOMIC TRENDS
## TO CREATE OPPORTUNITIES

We need to learn about and pay attention to economic trends that can open our eyes to opportunities. Consider the following:

- All those paying into healthcare want to contain costs. There are numerous business opportunities relating to decreased cost if these also maintain quality.

- "Pay us more" and "We are not paid enough" are out-of-touch messages in the current crisis environment. It is like someone asking for a match when the building is on fire. We need to move away from this self-centered lament and instead learn what our customers want. We need to address how we can decrease costs while delivering more effective services.

- There are enormous opportunities in providing valued services to the elderly. However, psychology has done a poor job of orienting toward this growing demographic segment, making this another missed opportunity.

- There are huge economic opportunities in treatment adherence and chronic disease management. Even though this should have been our province, we let it slip through our fingers and into a non-psychology-dominated market. There are still vast opportunities if we heed the advice of Dr. Michael Balint, who stated that "physicians need to become more like psychologists and psychologists need to become more like physicians."[8]

## ENDING FUTILE AND EXPENSIVE EXERCISES

Suing managed care may alleviate a specific problem, such as a company that is slow to reimburse provider claims; however, it does nothing to improve the overall economic decline of psychotherapy. Managed care is dying in itself, inasmuch as consumers have not liked the restrictions it placed on access to care. Managed care did work for a while in that it tethered accelerating costs for a time. One healthcare economist estimates that managed care saved the nation $300 billion. Now we again are witnessing 15% rises in premiums, which simply cannot be sustained economically. We need to work to find solutions.

The APA has spent millions of dollars suing managed care. Nothing has come of this other than correcting a grievance here and there and perhaps creating some emotional satisfaction. What we have not realized is that managed care was just an attempt to respond to the healthcare crisis. It may not have been the best solution, but what did we offer in its stead? We as a psychotherapy profession must use our creative skills to help resolve this crisis. Such a path would result in an improved, vigorous profession, not just a reactive one.

APA spent millions on parity legislation, now in 44 states and the federal government. Yet, if anything, the percentage of the national healthcare budget that is spent on mental health and substance abuse has decreased since parity.

## Endnotes

1. Who is getting rich from America's ailing health system, and who is not, is detailed by Nathan Vardi (2005), "Moore's Law," *Forbes*, November 28, pp. 116–126. The article covers the year 2004 and cites the Medical Management Association's survey of average incomes for various healthcare professionals. Not surprising, it is lawyers, not healthcare practitioners, who are getting rich from our health system.

2. Wal-Mart got a lot of publicity when it opened several miniclinics in its stores and announced the intention of expanding the process to others. This is only a small fraction of the hundreds of miniclinics that have sprung up in such places as supermarkets, drug stores, and shopping malls, with hundreds more in the planning stage. See Unmesh Kher (2006), "Get a Check-up in Aisle 3," *Time*, March 20, pp. 52–53.

3. For a reading of the early psychological adaptations of psychoeducational models for chronic disease and population management, see N. A. Cummings, J. L. Cummings, & J. N. Johnson (1997), *Behavioral Health in Primary Care: A Guide for Clinical Integration* (especially pp. 325–346), Madison, CT: Psychosocial Press. For more current adaptations, see N. A. Cummings, W. T. O'Donohue, & E. V. Naylor (2005), *Psychological Approaches to Chronic Disease Management*, Cummings Foundation for Behavioral Health: Healthcare Utilization and Cost Series, Vol. 8, Reno, NV: Context Press. The pioneering work of Kate Lorig in the disease management of arthritis is still available in a newer edition: K. Lorig & J. Fries (1990), *Arthritis Helpbook* (3rd ed.), Reading, MA: Addison-Wesley.

4. The U.S. Department of Labor projections, along with the new nursing school master's degree programs in emergency disaster management, were extensively reported by *USA Today* and at USAToday.com, March 21, 2006.

5. Major examples of failed efforts to legislate economics are poignantly presented by Thomas Sowell (2003), *Applied Economics*, New York: Basic Books. For an exposition of the failure of parity legislation, see Ira Carnahan (2002, January 21), "Asylum for the Insane," *Forbes*, pp. 33–34.

6. Ronald Levant served as president of the APA in 2005. One of his four initiatives was the expansion of psychology as a health profession and its integration with primary care. See R. Levant (2004), "21st Century Psychology: Toward a Biosocial Model," *Independent Practitioner*, *24*, 128–139. Whether his well-intentioned thrust takes root, or whether it fades as presidential initiatives tend to do, remains to be seen.

7. An excellent source for readings in healthcare economics is David Dranove (2000), *The Economic Evolution of American Health Care, From Marcus Welby to Managed Care*, Princeton, NJ: Princeton University Press. The healthcare statistics cited in the "Unblundering" section are from Dranove.

8. The quote from Dr. Michael Balint is from his classic work, M. Balint (1957), *The Doctor, His Patient and the Illness*, New York: International Universities Press.

# 2  We Turned Our Charismatic Leaders Into Gurus

While some may regard this chapter as somewhat irreverent, it is not meant to be so. Certain features may be accentuated or even exaggerated to make our main point: that we created our gurus because we needed them. Since the psychology profession had no scientific base, we had nothing else with which we could prove to the world that our work was psychotherapeutically credible and worthy of respect other than to quote the Great One, be it Sigmund Freud, Carl Jung, Karen Horney, B. F. Skinner, Carl Rogers, or Albert Ellis. It worked, and the public followed us in worshipping at the shrines of those we had elevated to near sainthood.

While it all may have begun with their individual genius, our gurus became victims of our adulation, driving them deeper into narcissism, encouraging them to permit no dissension from the faith as they had written it and to demand of us even more adulation. The alternative would have been to turn to research to prove the worth of our techniques, but there was none—at least of the kind that would aid the weary practitioner struggling with the problems of patients.

The end game of this kind of hero worship resulted in what many years ago I termed psycho-religions, challenging the generally accepted, face-saving, and euphemistic name "schools of psychotherapy" (e.g., Freudian psychoanalysis, neo-Freudian psychoanalysis, Jungian analysis, Adlerian therapy, Kleinian analysis, behavior therapy, cognitive behavior therapy, interpersonal therapy, transactional analysis, humanistic therapy). Post–World War II practitioners did not invent the psycho-religion game; they learned it from their professors in graduate school. The 1930s saw the rapid development of schools of experimental psychology, with a burgeoning interest in learning theory that was based on rat maze and pigeon-pecking experiments.

By the time I and the swelling ranks of my fellow World War II veterans began our psychology training, hard lines had developed among such giants as Clark Hull, Kenneth Spence, Wolfgang Kohler, Edward Tolman, and B. F. Skinner. It was a period in which these giants suffered no demonstrable publication lag, and the literature was replete with back-and-forth experimentation designed to refute the opponent's last publication. We knighted our leaders, and instead of moving forward from where they stood, we followed their writings religiously and tried to emulate their work.

This behavior has all the attributes of secularized religiosity, perhaps a bit surprising in a profession that often prides itself in being outside the realm of religion. The belief system of all religions, secular or sectarian, demands intellectual and behavioral conformity from its followers. Decades ago Eric Hoffer, the so-called longshoreman philosopher, called such adherents true believers. The leaders, in essence, are sectarian high priests and rabbis, and the price paid is that the psycho-religion is unquestioned and, as such, resists change and progress. It is okay to question and even denigrate other psycho-religions, but not one's own. Such conformity fosters splinter groups among those who would question the group's tenets.

Once the master had died, orthodox Freudian psychoanalysis reached a zenith of conformity never to be seen again to that extreme in the field of mental health. Every practicing psychoanalyst had hanging in his office a portrait of Sigmund Freud. It was always the same photo, taken at the height of his career, sporting a well-trimmed beard and frock coat. Freud smoked five cigars during every workday, and he had his tailor sew a series of five vertical pouches inside his breast pocket to hold them. Yes, his male followers all had their tailors replicate the five pouches on the inside of their coats. As if by obligation, all psychoanalysts took off the entire month of August, vacationing in locations designated by the ranking psychoanalysts. Curiously, their patients did not collapse during that month, and there was no appreciable rise in psychiatric hospitalization or emergency room admissions. One year the two top psychoanalysts at the San Francisco Psychoanalytic Institute moved from the city to suburban homes in Woodside. Within two years all San Francisco psychoanalysts were living in Woodside. These are examples of the degree of conformity that existed, none of which even came close to that demanded of trainees, who strove for years to demonstrate their faith. I recall one close friend who was in his 18th year of training and had no idea when he would be knighted a full-fledged psychoanalyst. Earlier in his training he had sometimes questioned what he was told, labeling himself a problem; even after years of penance, his heretical self was still not considered recovered.

In contrast, I experienced a rare bit of heresy from my own training analyst, Erik Erikson, who cut short my psychoanalysis. In a control training session I described an extremely aggressive, accusatory patient I was seeing and wondered why he was still being so obnoxious in spite of many hours of psychoanalysis. Was I doing something wrong? What was I missing? Erikson knew the patient from my previous descriptions and replied philosophically, "Nick, when you take a schmuck and psychoanalyze him, you end up with a psychoanalyzed schmuck." I was shocked since, as a novitiate in the psycho-religion of psychoanalysis, I was a true believer. He hit me with an even greater heresy a few weeks later when he announced he was terminating my analysis after only one year. I was shocked, erroneously thinking I had failed my training. He explained I was doing well but that if we continued my analysis I would become a highly success-ful, albeit stodgy and insufferable psychoanalyst. However, if we terminated now, I would go on innovating for the rest of my life. I challenged his conclusion, but he won in the end. He was also right.

At the time I did not realize that if more psychoanalysts had been as heretical as Erikson, perhaps the course of events would have been different. But Erik Erikson was an unusual psychoanalyst. At first he was in disrepute among the schools of psychoanalysis, tolerated only because his training analyst had been Anna Freud herself. Before he died, however, all the psychoanalytic psycho-religions claimed him and his genius. Mr. Erikson, as he insisted he be called because he did not have a doctorate and would not accept an honorary one, had no university mental health training. He was a watercolorist who came to the attention of Anna Freud when she was on a holiday on the south coast of France. She was amazed that the children on the beach preferred to talk to this man hour after hour instead of building sand castles or chasing the waves. She told him he had the greatest child rapport she had ever seen and invited him to come to Tavistock in London and train to become a child psychoanalyst. He shrugged his shoulders, saying he might as well because his paintings were not selling. Thus, he became one of the most unusual and reluctant psychotherapist gurus of all time. Erikson did not have an impact until it was much too late to influence the cult of hero worship. The preponderance of our profession continued its worshipping ways, neglecting the development of a therapeutic scientific base, changing only by spawning new psycho-religions that, in turn, demanded their own orthodoxy in lieu of scientific credibility.

But we flourished, helped by the sincerity, self-assurance, and often arrogance of our leaders, who tolerated no deviation. We were often secretly rebellious, however, like adolescents who are both in awe and envy of the parent. As an ardent follower of my own particular gurus, I was catapulted into recognizing this ambivalence several decades ago during dinner in Washington, DC, with a group of prominent psychoanalysts. One of the dinner group arrived late and breathlessly declared that one of the nation's leading psychoanalysts had just died of cancer. After we had expressed our sadness, someone asked what the nature of the cancer was. Our informant's eyebrows rose up well into his forehead as he whispered in a conspiratorial tone, "It started with cancer of the rectum and spread." All eyebrows were raised correspondingly, heads nodded, and all of us knew what everyone was thinking, although no one uttered a word: Our exalted colleague was an anal retentive personality. After all, had not the deceased promulgated the knowledge that fighting one's domineering mother by fecal retention during toilet training leads to a lifelong personality of anal retention that culminates in rectal cancer? No proof, but the guru had spoken, and he was now hoisted on his own petard.

There was the incontrovertible "knowledge" that such a disease was caused by the character formation of anal retentiveness operating over many years. We had learned our lessons well, but we also knew deep down that none of this had ever been proven. To acknowledge this would be heresy, something even the deceased would have condemned. And so we, too, became victims of our own orthodoxy and hero worship as we passed this victimhood on to our patients. Thus, without a shred of research evidence, pregnant women who had extreme morning sickness were said to have an unwanted pregnancy and unconsciously were trying to expel the fetus by vomiting. Childhood autism was caused by "refrigerated parents who can't thaw out." And without any research on the matter, we all believed it. The wheezing of the asthmatic was nothing more than a suppressed sob in the face of domineering parents who would not allow the child to cry.

But where would we be without these ill-begotten theories since there was no other foundation, scientific or otherwise, that made possible the passing of fees from the patient to the doctor? So we minions, having become dependent upon the guru for both our self-worth and our livelihoods, fostered and exaggerated the powers of the Great One in whose steps we followed, in an unconscious replication of the fraud perpetrated by the Wizard of Oz and his followers. There was no scientific evidence, but out of this sleight of hand we built a respected and lucrative profession. In the words of Mel Brooks as he spoke to an assembly of psychiatrists and psychologists in the movie *High Anxiety*, "And so our great leader, Sigmund Freud, gave us not only th'

to embrace him—at least for his day in the sun. Psychotherapists remain loathe to transcend the guru era, so it is not surprising that new gurus enter the pipeline as the older ones fade or die.

With the guru narcissism that pervades the field of psychotherapy, it is no small wonder that many of our early analytic patients during an era when there was no health insurance were wealthy narcissists. Who else would and could pay a stiff out-of-pocket fee for four to five sessions a week over several years to talk solely about himself while an ostensibly prestigious psychoanalyst doted on every word? Upper-class parties often evolved into discussions of "my psychoanalyst said such and such," with each socialite vying to brag about how much his or her analysis cost. To be sure, if you were willing to see a psychoanalyst in training, the fee was quite nominal, but even then only a narcissist would get off on talking about himself or herself hour after hour, year after year, while having a doctor's undivided attention. Unless, of course, the analyst was dozing, something the patient would not know because the doctor sat behind the couch and was expected to be silent 99% of the time anyway.

Narcissism reached its zenith, for both patients and gurus, during the human potential movement of the 1960s and 1970s. Self-exploration and turning inward, often with the use of LSD, was expected of both patient and psychotherapist. Seminars for therapists readily admitted that psychotherapy was as much for the benefit of the psychotherapist as it was for the patient. The thinking that "we also learn about ourselves from our clients" was supposed to justify therapist self-exploration while the patient was paying for the session. This level of self-indulgence was the hallmark of the Esalen Institute, which I termed Club Narcissus, where gurus and penitents intermingled in hot tubs, tolerating boring self-revelations for the privilege of soon boring others. Club Narcissus was replicated all over the United States.

For a time, there was an economic boom for psychotherapists as much of the nation fell into a state of perpetual self-exploration. It has been termed America's narcissistic era, lining the pockets of psychotherapists and spawning Esalen clones and questionable ashrams. The glut of psychotherapists had not yet materialized, so there seemed no end to the vast number of patients, resulting in waiting lists for those seeking services with preferred psychotherapists. People quietly waited, sometimes for months, until the guru of choice had an opening. Frederick Perls delighted in reminding people that before this era he was known as "crazy Fritzy," and that this was now the "era of the crazies." Inevitably people had enough, and the backlash came in the 1980s. The psychotherapy economy began to show signs of its eventual crash as waiting lists evaporated and those gurus who had been riding high scrambled to regain respectability.

A little recognized fact is that the human potential movement signaled the beginning of the economic decline of psychoanalysis. This is not to suggest that most persons undergoing psychoanalysis did not benefit, or that they were there because they were narcissists. However, those that were narcissistically inclined found greener pastures in the human potential movement, which promised more effective, quicker results than the prolonged nature of psychoanalysis.

The 1980s saw self-indulgent self-exploration disappear almost as rapidly as it had appeared in the 1960s. Further, the 1980s ushered in managed behavioral care in response to the seemingly endless costs of psychoanalysis, the excesses of the human potential movement, and open-ended psychotherapy in general. This was a devastating economic sea change from which none of these modalities has ever fully recovered to anything resembling its former economic stature. Managed care stopped paying for traditional psychoanalysis, as well as psychotherapy, without proof of a demonstrably effective treatment plan. And no psychotherapist today would dare ask to be reimbursed for the intended goal of patient self-actualization, a previously prominent term that has all but disappeared from psychotherapeutic parlance.

At the present time there are strong movements pushing psychotherapy toward evidence-based treatments (EBTs). But there are equally strong forces opposing evidence-based practice. Lagging behind medicine, it will take some time before psychotherapy becomes an evidence-based profession, shedding its reliance on pronouncements by its leaders and gurus. Debate rages in the literature, with one side arguing that opposition to evidence-based treatment is indefensible, while the other, equally vocal side states that much of what goes on in psychotherapy does not lend itself to the scrutiny of strict experimental techniques. One side says protocols and guidelines are imperative; the other objects that manualization would stymie the flexibility needed in individually complex and diverse cases. Both sides could not be more right and more wrong at the same time. Eventually our research tools will be expanded to better accommodate EBT research, but for now the majority of practicing psychotherapists feel threatened by impending EBTs.

This was evident at the 2005 Evolution in Psychotherapy Conference that brought together 9,000 psychotherapists to Anaheim, California. The largest assemblage of psychotherapists in history created an unparalleled enthusiasm. Brilliantly planned and executed by the Milton H. Erickson Foundation, participants were enthralled to see all their living gurus present, up to and including the venerable 92-year-old Albert Ellis, who spoke from his wheelchair. I made six presentations by invitation,[1] and realized as I stood before audiences of 2,000 or more that I was one of the gurus, though a minor guru at most; there were the stars and then the second string of "state-of-the-art faculty" such as me. As I looked into the enthusiastic faces, listened to the buzz in the corridors of the convention center, felt the excitement of the attendees, I realized this gathering was an antidote to the despair they had been feeling. The eager faces seemed to cry out: "All the Great Ones are here, and surely psychotherapy is alive and well. Surely I shall learn something from them, and this conference will rehabilitate my sagging practice."

Tens of thousands of the gurus' books were sold, all hopefully bearing knowledge that would improve one's practice. But looking beneath the veneer of enthusiasm I could see the concern for the profession. Nonetheless, their pervasive preference for psychotherapeutic techniques, the hallmark of gurus, was evident when my colleague and I presented a several-hours-long nuts-and-bolts workshop on how to deliver behavioral care within the primary care setting. The attendance was roughly one-tenth of that in my other five, more guru-like presentations. The imperative economics of practice and EBTs are boring and far less stimulating than a succession of exciting new techniques proffered by psychotherapist heroes.

Every generation has the opportunity, if not the obligation, to honor its giants. Our error lay in getting stuck on the orthodoxy of the individual theories instead of concentrating on verifying and refining the techniques. It has become fashionable to dethrone those we previously idolized, especially such icons as Sigmund Freud and B. F. Skinner. These postmortem attacks are brutal and unfair, but idolatry is often followed by a period of dethroning, constituting a kind of abrogation and sanitizing of our previously blind hero worship.

We need to go beyond both the idolatry and its subsequent dethroning to create a strong foundation for a profession that is at a critical point. Do we, as David Barlow advocates, designate evidence-based therapies as "treatments" eligible for reimbursement in healthcare, while traditional modalities retain the title of psychotherapy?[2] Or do we go the way of Scott Miller, who insists that evidence-based interventions are flawed and that professional verification is required?[3] Or, more likely, do we need a combination of the two? Psychotherapy cannot continue as it has without accelerating its decline. The first step, however, is to outgrow our guru creating.

I saw signs of the era of the guru weakening in 1980, and said so as I was chairing a meeting of MRI presenters before a large audience in San Francisco. A widely acknowledged and respected psychotherapy idol, a member of the panel, openly took issue with me. He referred to the vast and ever-increasing horde of psychotherapists, most of them subdoctoral and poorly trained, who always come to these conferences hoping to hear something from the experts that will cause their practices to flourish. He concluded somewhat cynically, "So there will always be a good livelihood for us experts." I was taken aback; the audience was not. The idol was right. As 9,000 enthusiastic attendees in Anaheim proved in 2005, the guru era is far from over.

## Unblundering

Focusing on interesting personalities is, of course, quite tempting, particularly to psychologists. However, we suggest there are two better foci: (1) our customers and (2) our problem-solving effectiveness.

## A RENEWED FOCUS ON OUR CUSTOMERS

Instead of focusing on what some charismatic character says we ought to do, we should focus on increasing our understanding of what our customers (clients, patients) want and need. We have generally violated important business precepts such as "stay close to your customers" and "exceed your customers' expectations."

Instead, we have given our customers what we want to give them, which sometimes is what some charismatic leader says they should want. One can get away with some of this in healthcare inasmuch as patients come to us and trust us to give them what is best for them. The economist Kenneth Arrow has called this "the shopping problem." Before buying many goods we seek a lot of information in order to make informed decisions based on our interests. Thus, when we buy a car we find out about the various prices, reliability, and depreciation. We look for sales rebates and discounts, we test drive the vehicle, and finally we make our decision by weighing all of these factors.

But we often cannot shop in the same way for medical and psychological services. We may not understand what our problem is. Are we a little sad, or are we suffering from major depressive disorder, dysthymia, or bipolar depression? We often need an expert to tell us what the problem is. Even when we know our diagnosis we may have little knowledge regarding the best course of action (e.g., watchful waiting, medication, cognitive behavior therapy, Rolfing, inpatient treatment). Individuals are usually much more informed and depend on others much less when buying a car, television, or choosing a restaurant. The Internet, with such sources as WebMD, is beginning to change this, but most people still depend heavily on the healthcare practitioner.

This does not mean that the client's trust is always well placed. Given the wide variability of treatment recommendations and variability in diagnosis, we have what quality control experts such as W. Edwards Deming call a lot of "unwanted variation." Our mental health system is far from what Deming describes as "in statistical control."[4] Rather, outcomes are unpredictable because the process also is unpredictable.

A root cause of this has already been discussed in this chapter: We have blundered by falling into psycho-religions. Even if there are only 15 gurus (dead or alive), one would have to assume at least 15 different processes (and even more, as there are some clever "integrationists" or "eclecticists" who create interesting combinations and permutations of these therapies). Another part of the problem is that we often think more is better than less. When you ask a computer nerd what is wrong with your computer, he or she tends to give lengthy explanations, replete with technical terms and much detail. We feign interest and nod attentively, hoping that he or she will just fix the damn computer as soon as possible. Customers want efficient problem solving, not long, technical therapeutic explanations. Are we therapy nerds?

One of the worst things psychoanalysis has accomplished is to create a legacy of ineffective therapies and invalid projective tests. It has also set an anchor on how long therapy should last, and that an individual treatment consists of the 50-minute hour. Psychoanalysts often prescribed three and four visits a week for decades, with a mere 500 sessions regarded as "quick therapy." With such an anchor the more modern approaches, such as cognitive behavior therapy (CBT), which relied on 12 to 18 sessions, were regarded as efficient. And they were, in comparison.

But should this be the end of the story? Twelve hours is a long time to work on a problem, and maybe we should consider other anchors. A primary care physician walks into a room and often has our problem diagnosed and treatment initiated in 15 minutes! And the body is very complex, indeed. What about this anchor—15 minutes —as an inspirational goal?

The key dilemma is that we know little about what our customers want because we have not been close to them. For example, a customer who wants relief from migraine headaches may be told that this is merely symptom treatment that will not cure the deep-seated root psychological problem. We must ponder the answers to two major questions: First, who are our customers? Second, what do we know about what they want?

## WHO ARE OUR CUSTOMERS?

Various funding organizations have done a better job of answering this than we as a profession. The term they often use is stakeholders. We know some parts of the answer: Our clients are certainly our customers. But we have largely missed other customers. These might be employers, the government, and some large healthcare organizations that we have been spending our time suing instead of wooing. Such managed care organizations as Magellan, United Behavioral Health, and others are our largest customers. But seemingly the only place we have tried to be close to them is in a court of law when we are suing them! We may not like that they have lowered our hourly wage, and we may not like the length of time they take to pay a claim, but suing a large customer is generally not a good business development strategy.

## What Do Our Customers Want?

Another quality improvement principle is to partner with customers to identify win-win situations. We have not done this with insurers, health plans, or managed care organizations. These are important customers controlling the purse strings that contain our incomes, and we have virtually no productive relationship with them. We do not know what they want, what their problems are that we can jointly work on, and whether they are satisfied or dissatisfied with our services. If we worked with these folks we would see a lot of opportunities for us to grow in more healthy economic directions. For example, had we been closer to these organizations 20 years ago we would have recognized that they were looking for effective chronic disease management programs. Had we been closer to them we would have anticipated that employer assistance programs (EAPs) were about to take off. What opportunities are we missing now? This question should be a paramount one for our leadership, but the APA is focusing on other issues, many of them political, like gay adoption. We are not close to these customers, but nurses and physicians are and they now control the hundreds of millions of dollars in the disease management industry.

We also know very little about what our individual therapy clients want. What is brief to them? What do they think about e-health such as telephonic contacts? Do they like Web-based solutions such as Dr. Martin Seligman's authentichappiness.com for depression at a cost of $9.95 per month? According to one report, 10,000 persons are monthly subscribers. What do they want in our waiting rooms? What type of scheduling do they prefer? One hour twice a week, two hours once a week, half an hour, sessions every other week with intermittent telephone contact? Like the hospital sponge bath that comes at 5:00 A.M., schedules more often fit the provider's convenience than the patients' needs.

Finally, we have to realize that the answers are not static. What customers want this year may not be what they want two years hence. Developments and opportunities are evolving rapidly, and the profession needs to pay close attention. Additionally, we must remain committed to increasing the value proposition one offers. How satisfied are our customers with the effectiveness, convenience, and price of our services? We must remain close to customer needs and wants to see priorities emerge, and then work together with them to provide ever-increasing value and satisfaction in the products we offer. It is of concern that too much of our practice is like Freud's of a century ago. We still see one patient for 50 minutes, and for many problems there is little documented change. This is not a good value proposition for our payers.

**Solution:** We need to know all our clients, understand their problems, and work to construct products that give them high value and satisfaction. We should focus on customers, not charismatic leaders. If you are having trouble with such terms as *customer, product, value, provider,* and *quality assurance,* you are not ready for the 21st century.

### Endnotes

1. The concept of turning our charismatic leaders into gurus because we lacked a solid scientific base for psychotherapy was the subject of an invited address by the senior author, "My Sixty Years as a Psychotherapist: Triumphs, Disappointments and Future Challenges," at the Evolution of Psychotherapy Conference, Anaheim, California, December 9, 2005. A DVD is available from the Milton H. Erickson Foundation, 3606 North 24th St., Phoenix, AZ 85020.

2. David Barlow has proposed that only evidence-based therapy, to be called treatment, should be eligible for reimbursement by healthcare third-party payers, leaving traditional psychotherapy to continue as it has, financed only by those who are willing to pay out of pocket. See D. H. Barlow (2004), "Psychological Treatments," *American Psychologist, 59,* 869–878.

3. Scott Miller takes strong exception to what he calls Barlowism, actively questioning the drive for empirical support in his Baloney Watch. See http://www.talkingcure.com/baloney.asp?id=97.

4. W. Edwards Deming developed his famous 14 points to transform management practices. At first ignored in the United States, he was espoused in Japan where his principles resulted in the quality control systems that enabled the Japanese auto industry to soar past the American Big Three: General Motors, Ford,

and Chrysler. Thereafter, American manufacturers began to pay close attention to his science of improvement, which he named Systems of Profound Knowledge.

# 3 Don't Worry; Managed Care Is a Passing Fad

The history of the past two centuries, the era in which most of the world's scientific achievements and technological advancements have taken place, is strewn with the carcasses of successful industries that ignored the signs of impending drastic economic shifts. This has been especially true in the United States, the cradle of modern entrepreneurship, where innovations successively usher in new industries that replace the old. This is often a painful process since it is the propensity of innovation to replace, often wrenchingly, the heretofore successful industry or methods that have become obsolete.[1] The consequences to those displaced include loss of jobs, wiping out of fortunes, and declining property values. One need only compare the booming Silicon Valley, where cybernetics came of age, with depressed Akron, which failed to keep up with changes in the economics of the tire manufacturing industry. The price of a three-room bungalow in Silicon Valley will buy a stately mansion once belonging to one of the rubber barons of Akron.

Most of the endeavors that failed to heed the harbingers of economic change disappeared altogether, and others are plugging along on a very limited basis. A few belatedly got their acts together, adopted technological advances, and are once again doing well. The solo practice of psychotherapy is an early 21st-century casualty. Although it no longer is flourishing as it did in the 1980s, it continues to limp along with a diminished clientele, yielding lower incomes for its practitioners. In 2005, U.S. Labor Department statistics listed psychology as the lowest paid of the doctoral-level health professions, a prediction this author made at the 2002 Competencies Conference held in Phoenix, Arizona.[2] But rather than taking until 2010, we fell into these doldrums within only two years.

It is possible to continue in this depressed fashion almost indefinitely, as even the buggy whip industry that once laughed at the dangers posed by the invention of the automobile continues to sell a few whips to a small number of consumers, including lion tamers and fetishists. It remains to be seen whether the delivery of psychotherapy will continue to limp along, or disappear altogether. Ideally, it will reinvent itself and once again become a rising star, both in healthcare and in the economy. For this reason it is important to ferret out what got us to the present state, and how other declining endeavors reinvented and are once again on top. There are lessons to be learned, and the survival of psychotherapy may depend on practitioners understanding and acting upon them.

Another 19th-century miracle was the telegraph, which made instant communication possible to all parts of the nation. Rivaling the railroad companies for stupidity, the telegraph companies decided they were in the telegraph business, when in reality they were in the communication business. Seeing that the telegraph wires already spanning the continent could be easily modified to accommodate the telephone, Alexander Graham Bell attempted to sell his invention to the telegraph companies. The response was an emphatic rejection, in essence saying that they saw no future in the telephone. Where once they could have owned the telephone, Western Union and Postal Telegraph have become archaic little companies through which one can wire money to a distant recipient. With healthcare booming and mental health rapidly declining, it is startling to hear our colleagues insist that we are not part of the healthcare system. If ever a lesson were almost overwhelmingly obvious, this one is it. Yet it continues to escape psychotherapists, who insist that we must resist the "medical model."

More stupid sagas continue into the 20th century. The giant IBM did not comprehend that it was in the information business, not the mainframe business. This decision resulted in the myopic declaration that Americans would never want an electronic machine in their homes. Along came Steve Jobs and Michael Dell. The personal computer was soon an affordable reality, and the information age was in full swing as the PC became almost as common in every home as a television set. Down plunged

IBM's stock. Similarly, Xerox pioneered efficient dry copiers and was inordinately successful for decades since it essentially had the copier market to itself. Not realizing that it, too, was in the information business and not just the copier business, Xerox looked on as companies like Ricoh, Sharp, and Kyocera transformed the simple copier into a computer, a scanner, a fax, a desktop publisher, and a host of other functions that reflected they knew they were in the information business. Xerox adapted too late, and the once undisputed giant is now lagging in the industry.

Ah, say psychotherapists, one-on-one individual psychotherapy is a face-to-face and very personal endeavor that cannot be delivered otherwise. They may further point out that even most of our group practices are actually several solo practitioners dispensing individual 50-minute hours under one roof and merely sharing overhead and other expenses. This is short-sighted; successful alternatives to solo practice already exist, and new approaches are being refined and are poised for implementation.

The first such example was American Biodyne, founded and totally managed for 10 years by psychologists responsible for the mental health of 14.5 million covered lives in 39 states. It flourished for 10 years by seeing 75% of its patients in 68 targeted group protocols. These were products of years of research, refined by additional years of field testing, such as in the Hawaii Project described later in this chapter. Experience demonstrated that these targeted group therapies for 68 specific conditions were not only cost-effective but superior in psychotherapeutic effectiveness to individual sessions. American Biodyne was eventually engulfed by the Magellan Health Services, a corporate giant run by business interests rather than by health professionals. It has typically abandoned direct services and has morphed into a care management company that may even be gravitating away from behavioral health to medical and surgical care management. But the Biodyne technology exists, and one day an innovative psychologist will rediscover, update, and successfully resurrect it.

For emerging technologies, look at Inflexxion, a rising psychology-driven company in Massachusetts that is creating all kinds of interactive electronic systems. Another new psychology-driven company, CareIntegra, has created a series of behavioral health portals for returning veterans, their families, and their health professionals. These offer a glimpse into forthcoming virtual interventions, already termed "telehealth," that have received amazing early public acceptance. The CareIntegra portals prepared for TriWest experienced a surprising 9,751 hits the first month they were up. Anyone complacent enough to think that computer models of psychotherapy with well-researched algorithms are not on the horizon will eventually find ignominy along with the railroads, the telegraph, IBM, Xerox, and other follies of the past.

Psychology Caught Unaware: The
Industrialization of Healthcare

Within 10 years of the enactment in 1965 of Medicare and Medicaid, the health system began to chafe under the inflationary
spiral that is inevitable when the federal government launches
a huge entitlement program without proper economic planning
or appropriate constraints. Concerned, the federal government
enacted a series of belated programs designed to slow down the
escalation in healthcare costs. The first of these came in 1975
when the HMO Empowerment Act was signed into law. Federal start-up grants encouraged the proliferation of health main-
tenance organizations, heretofore an essentially California and
Minnesota phenomenon. The U.S. Senate Subcommittee on
Health, chaired by Senator Edward Kennedy, was impressed
with the success of the Kaiser Permanente Health Plan, which
for decades increased services, maintained high quality, and
enjoyed unprecedented patient satisfaction and loyalty, all the
while substantially lowering costs. Senator Kennedy hoped this
model would be the eventual entrée into universal healthcare.

The HMO Empowerment legislation, however, was the first
impetus behind the industrialization of healthcare. Little did the
government realize that the HMOs it helped launch would bear
scant resemblance to the Kaiser model or the Jackson Hole plan
that sprang from it. This latter is a well-conceptualized economic
model that captured the imagination of a Democratic congress
determined to begin solving our growing healthcare crisis. It was

promulgated by a group of the nation's leading health economists (e.g., Paul Ellwood, Alain Enthoven,[3] and Stuart Altman),
who met regularly in the Wyoming town that gave it the name
Jackson Hole Group. Called by its authors managed competition, this model was an ingenious and sound response to spiraling healthcare costs. Despite misinformation from corporate
healthcare to the contrary, managed competition has never been
tried and was not appropriately written into the HMO Empowerment Act of 1975.

Healthcare continued to spiral upwards and was soon more
than twice the rate of inflation for the rest of the economy by
1985 when Congress enacted, literally at the 11th hour, Diagnosis Related Groups (DRGs). This created hospital reimbursement
ceilings for nearly 400 diagnoses. If the hospital's costs exceeded
these ceilings, different for each diagnostic category, it lost money,
whereas if the costs were less, the hospital made a profit. This was
the second and more drastic of all the programs to tether healthcare costs, and it inadvertently furthered the industrialization of
healthcare. Nonprofit hospitals, used to reimbursement guaranteed at cost plus 15% by the government programs, began to fail
and were bought by for-profit corporate hospital interests that
dominate the hospital industry to this day.

A third and little noted occurrence that pushed the gate wide
open for healthcare industrialization was a series of high court
decisions striking down laws prohibiting the corporate practice

of medicine, making health boycotts illegal, and overnight subjecting medical societies and healthcare to antitrust laws.

A fourth thrust, and the one most directly affecting mental healthcare, resulted from the government's inability to write DRGs for psychiatric diagnoses. After repeated tries, it abandoned DRGs for mental health and turned the cost containment of mental health over to the private sector, which was made possible by the courts vacating the laws banning the corporate practice of medicine. Managed behavioral care was born, and the rest of the scenario is well known, but still largely misunderstood by psychology.

## The Initial Idealistic Response

Even though psychology is not known for its ability to read economic signs and discern their potential impact on practice, the 1980s were an era of such unprecedented prosperity that psychotherapists had no inclination to heed warnings. Psychology had come of age. The last state to enact statutory recognition of psychology practice was Missouri in 1979. Social workers were unlicensed in most states, and master's-level psychotherapists had not even begun their licensure campaign. Psychiatry announced its determination to remedicalize, all but abandoning psychotherapy.

It was not long before psychiatrists practicing psychotherapy were all over age 50, as psychiatric residencies paid only lip service to what they disdainfully began to call talk therapy. Insurance companies had extended third-party reimbursement to psychologists, and the public demand for psychotherapy was not only enormous but seemingly accelerating. Psychiatric hospitals were a Wall Street growth industry, and the large chains of for-profit hospitals that had emerged were hospitalizing an increasing number of patients, especially adolescents, all of whom were referred upon discharge to outpatient psychotherapy. Psychologists, and very few others, were there to receive them as well as the ever-increasing hordes that clamored for psychotherapy. We were turning out psychologists at an unprecedented rate, most of whom were jumping into private practice. We were fat cats and had no stomach for a message that this prosperity was not infinite. My warnings made me nothing short of the turd in the punchbowl.

To me the economic signs were unmistakable. I had extensive discussions with John McMillan, PhD, a staff officer at APA who had been in government service and was surprisingly (for a psychologist) attuned to the economic harbingers. Both of us were impressed by former APA president George Albee's insistence that as long as we practice in the house of medicine we are foolish to think that we could be equal to our physician colleagues. George was adamant that psychology must create its own house. John and I decided that the time was right to begin planning psychology's house. John even had a name for it: Blue PSI (Psycho-Social Insurance). In 1975 I incorporated Blue PSI and pulled together a group of psychologist leaders in California to help me. It ended in utter failure, one of the very few of the many organizations I have founded that did not survive.

I made two tragic mistakes. The first was that I inadvertently assembled the gang that could not shoot straight. Recruiting two members of the Dirty Dozen who were also past presidents of the California State Psychological Association, Rogers Wright and Ernest Lawrence, seemed the way to go as these were seasoned doers. But the Dirty Dozen had essentially finished its mission, was content to rest on its laurels, and had no appreciation that winning is only the beginning; the hardest part is maintaining.[4] Other members of the group proved to be unhelpful or downright antagonistic.

The second and even more fatal mistake was the assumption that we could sell a psychosocial model when industry and the government pay only for healthcare. There were no investors, marketing was a complete bust, government was disinterested, and in 1977 Blue PSI was disbanded. This entire concept incorporated the best and the worst in psychological ideals: that psychology could have its own house and treat clients outside of healthcare. It eventually became apparent that psychology, indeed, could have its own house but only within the health system because that is what Americans want. I could have used my years of experience at Kaiser Permanente, where I wrote the nation's first comprehensive psychotherapy insurance benefit and discovered the medical cost offset phenomenon, to create such a system. However, we needed a vehicle to demonstrate that psychologists, not physicians, could administer and deliver a comprehensive and extensive mental health plan. After all, Kaiser was a prepaid medical/surgical system, my superiors were all physicians, and the psychologist who served as chief of mental health did not necessarily play first violin in its orchestra. The world would require proof that psychology could run its own house.

The idea of an innovative demonstration project, especially in the Medicaid system that already was spinning out of control, interested the federal government, and in 1978 we were able to begin dialogue on a prospective, randomized, and controlled demonstration project with the Medicaid population in San Francisco. As fate would have it, Jerry Brown, later to be known as Governor Moonbeam, had just been elected governor of California. His administration promptly replaced Blue Shield as the fiscal intermediary for MediCal (the name of that state's Medicaid program) with a new, then obscure Texas company that through its incompetence and lack of fiscal experience brought the state's computers to a grinding halt. It was taking 18 months to process claims, patient records could not be tracked, and MediCal was at a standstill.

It was then that I first met its founder, Ross Perot, who had been chosen by Governor Brown himself and had the backing of Beverly Meyers, the state's medical director. The situation was so bad that we could not randomize the population and keep single mothers and their own children intact. Herbert Dorken, PhD, whom I recruited as scientific director, had been director or assistant director of mental health in two states and one Canadian province. But even he, with all his political and administrative savvy from a previous high-level post in California, could not solve the dilemma. California eventually did clean up the mess, but only after Ross Perot had for three years refined the company that made him a billionaire on the backs of the California taxpayers.

Herb and I were just about to give up the project when we got a call from Pat DeLeon, PhD, a psychologist in Senator Daniel Inouye's office, asking whether we would be willing to do the research demonstration in Hawaii. In time we arrived at a three-way contract (not a grant) among the Health Care Financing Administration (HCFA) in Washington, DC, the State of Hawaii, and the Biodyne Institute. The project began in 1981 and encompassed the 36,000 Medicaid recipients and the 91,000 federal employees in Hawaii. First we had to create from the ground up a new delivery system, including the intensive training of all providers in the innovative treatment methodology that later became known as the Biodyne model. The Biodyne centers, as they were called, were inordinately successful throughout three years of delivery of clinical services, as well as during the four-year follow-up. Through medical cost offset resulting from Biodyne's intensive outreach and interventions, the government recouped its initial investment in the new system within 18 months, with the savings continuing to accrue for several more years to the end of the follow-up.[5]

HCFA was delighted, and the Hawaii Project resulted in far-reaching changes in the entire Medicaid system. During this period, Congress passed unrelated legislation encouraging research findings emanating from government funding to be translated into the private sector. With the strong encouragement of the director of the Centers for Disease Control (CDC), we moved ahead, incorporating American Biodyne in 1985. We had proven that psychologists could run their own health system, and even trump the existing system.

### The Clarion Call: The Locust Is Coming

Even before my APA presidency in 1979, and certainly beyond it, I spoke about the opportunities that the evolving health economy would be according the profession of psychology, and in 1985 my colleague Luis Fernandez, PhD, and I published an optimistic list of possible practices that went far beyond the confines of our singular solo practice of psychotherapy. It became apparent, however, that this optimistic message was falling on deaf ears. In 1986 it was decided to get real and warn our colleagues that hard times were coming unless we owned the industrialized mental health delivery systems that would soon arrive to destroy our solo practices. The term *managed care* had not yet been invented, so I described what was coming and called it a "locust that would sweep across the land."[6] I also described the

run a successful company and do it on the clinical premise that healthcare costs are saved by the delivery of effective, quality care, but we bested Wall Street itself in our business acumen while maintaining our clinical integrity.

## What of the Future?

With my departure in 1994 the company was swallowed up by one of the giant healthcare corporations that now control healthcare in America, and the concept of a psychology-driven company combining both business success and clinical integrity has vanished, hopefully not forever. However, it is difficult to be sanguine in the face of a profession that still does not fully comprehend the industrialization of healthcare or genuinely appreciate its role in its own demise. Just before the year 2000, discussions among the APA board of directors began to reflect the inkling that perhaps Nick Cummings had been right all along. It goes to demonstrate the prophets of one generation can become the reactionaries of the next. But it is most perplexing and disheartening to witness the intransigency of a profession that purports to be an agent of change for its patients and society at large, but paradoxically not for itself.

## Unblundering

It is reasonable for psychologists to be angry at managed care. Managed care has been the harbinger of some very bad news. It has seemingly driven down psychologists' hourly reimbursement. In addition, some managed care companies frustrate the practitioner by imposing time-consuming (and hence expensive) paperwork and taking a long time to pay claims, thus taking advantage of the financial "float" by paying back in cheaper dollars. However, there are important caveats:

1. We have to realize that managed care came into existence not to be evil and to give us a hard time. It came into existence because of a legitimate crisis: Healthcare costs have been increasing at multiples of the rate of inflation in the general economy. As of this writing, that rate is 14% annually, a doubling of costs every five years. Entities that pay these costs can no longer afford to do so. Think about it. If today's premium is $3,600, in five years it will be $7,200, and in five more years it will reach $14,400. Payers wanted some control.

2. There is research and theory to suggest that when there is no third party looking at a transaction between a healthcare professional and a patient, more money is spent— perhaps more money than is necessary. Theoretically, this is called demand inducement by economists. Dranove[7] describes demand inducement in physical medicine, but similar points can be made regarding mental health:

   Inducement theory rests on four key points. First, inducement arises because the indications for many medical interventions can be vague, so that a physician may be unable to decide which of several interventions best serves the patient's interest. Second, given such clinical ambiguity, physicians who are reimbursed on a fee for service basis might recommend the most costly intervention. Third, in extreme cases of inducement, physicians might even ignore unambiguous clinical indications to pursue financial goals. Fourth, to the extent that hospital managers (of for profits and nonprofits) want to keep their beds filled, they have no reason to object to inducement. If inducement theory is true then HMOs have a powerful justification for replacing fee for service reimbursement with capitation. (p. 33)

Is there empirical evidence for demand inducement? The answer, unfortunately, is yes. It has been found, for example, that the demand for surgery is higher in regions with more per capita surgeons. One research report found that a 10% increase in the supply of surgeons leads to a 3% increase in the demand for surgeries. Other research has found that a decrease in Medicaid payment rates for surgery results in an immediate increase in the number of surgeries. This has been interpreted as physicians' attempts to preserve income levels by increasing the number of procedures. There is other such evidence. For example, physicians who own imaging labs send more patients for imaging than those who do not own such labs. The reader is referred to Dranove for other examples and a more thorough exposition of this issue.

We have to beware of the psychotherapy practice of "updiagnosing" for the alleged reason of doing our patients a favor. This practice involves giving a patient that does not deserve it a reimbursable diagnosis so that the third party will pay instead of the patient. We rationalize that this is for the benefit of our patient, but the therapist who is paid also benefits, especially if the patient could not otherwise afford treatment. Insurers provide coverage for "medical necessity," not for "it could be of benefit." This is why most policies do not cover Viagra.

3. We must accept the notion that purchasers are always looking for a better value for their dollar. We all like to get a deal, and some of us bargain hard. One of the functions of managed care is to get a better deal (i.e., lower prices) from professionals. Practitioners do not like this, but those on the purchase side (employers, government) do. We need to learn ways of giving managed care companies more value other than by cutting our reimbursement rates.

4. Managed care companies compete against one another to get contracts. Price is often the most important factor, as all companies can generate roughly equivalent networks. Because we are unable to differentiate ourselves on product features or quality, purchasers often buy on price alone. This is the worst of all possible situations for sellers (i.e., the psychotherapist, in this case). Margins are squeezed and therapists are angry and frustrated.

A better position is one in which purchasers are relatively price insensitive because they value and want a certain product. People do not buy a Lexus because it is the cheapest but because it is an upscale, superior product. Behavioral health has become a commodity much like gasoline; one buys simply on price. However, what happens when the price of a commodity is lowered again and again? Gasoline price wars, which we have not seen for several decades, will result in some companies going out of business. Therefore, it behooves psychotherapy to reorganize itself in more productive delivery modes and to do it soon, since we have not yet come close to the bottom of the downward spiral.

5. Like it or not, managed care worked for a decade or more. Some have estimated that it saved the healthcare economy upwards of $300 billion. It did not lose favor because of practitioner opposition; it lost popularity with consumers because of its restrictions on access. But for a time it did stem the tide of increasing costs. By the way, it is important to note that those who benefited the most from managed care were not the managed care companies but employers and the government.

## WHAT CAN BE DONE?

The key to unblundering is not to slay the messenger but rather to develop innovative solutions to the core problem. Expensive lawsuits such as those brought by the APA are not the solution. They are generally beating up the messenger, and while this may feel good, it is not a successful long-term strategy. Neither are the legislative triumphs that brought about our toothless parity laws.

Remember: The problem is the ever-increasing cost of healthcare. If they are to have a brighter future, mental health professionals need to develop strategies, products, and research relevant to this question. My co-author has provided some important insights along these lines. Cummings has astutely pointed out that mental health and substance abuse constitute only 5% of the healthcare budget. The good news is that we are not receiving a lot of the cost-cutting attention because we make only a small contribution to the spiraling costs.

Second, we can actually expand our share of the healthcare budget by providing cost-effective solutions to the other 95% of contributors to the budget. We need to do this for two major reasons. One is the Willie Sutton principle. When this legendary bank robber was asked why he robs banks, he replied, "Because that's where the money is." Second, we need to do this because we actually have a lot of skills for making people healthier and thus reduce demand for medical services.

One such solution is integrated behavioral and primary care. In essence, such integrated care attempts to provide quality psychotherapy to patients who are presenting in medical and surgical settings. Many of these patients need help for problems that are not medical but that are definitely contributing to medical and surgical costs: depression, stress, lifestyle problems (smoking, obesity, sedentary living), treatment noncompliance, and chronic disease management. When patients do not receive behavioral interventions for these problems, they return for medical care over and over again, driving up costs.[8] Most psychologists are unaware that 20% of all insured patients incur 80% of medical expenses. Many of these patients have behavioral health pathways that lead to this high utilization. Substituting good psychotherapy for some of this expensive medical and surgical treatment can result in lower costs, a phenomenon termed medical cost offset by the federal government. Cummings has shown that targeted, tailored group interventions for high utilizers saved 40% in medical costs and at the same time reduced the cost of providing behavioral health services by half, all within 18 months.

In addition, we can develop such adaptations as an e-health program (see Seligman's website),[9] as well as effective bibliotherapy; shorter-term therapies; alternatives to the 50-minute hour, especially time-limited/targeted group therapy; disease management; coaching, and so forth. Again, the key is not just saying, "You need to pay us more" or "You are paying us less so we will get angry, whine, and eventually sue you." A better approach would be to take responsibility: "You have a legitimate crisis in rising healthcare costs, and we are here to help you. Here is the evidence. Try us and we'll show you that if you spend more money with us, overall costs will decline."

Our research should not just focus on clinical outcomes, but also on financial ones. In short, we have to understand the economic problem and come up with solutions that make economic sense. A caveat is that most healthcare marketers have caught on to this problem and have turned it into a pitch: "I can save you money." Buyers have become skeptical and demand proof of the return on investment (ROI): "If I invest a dollar with you, do I save two or three dollars or what? And in what time period [usually a year is the time frame]? How strong is the evidence for this?" Our task is to develop sound responses to these questions if we are to be economically healthy.

## Endnotes

1. The manner in which innovation and progress displace out-moded industries and endeavors, often with painful initial consequences, is described by three-time Pulitzer Prize winner Thomas L. Friedman, a master of lucid dissections of abstruse economic phenomena (see T. L. Friedman (2005), *The World Is Flat*, New York: Farrar, Strauss and Giroux). Also helpful is Thomas Sowell of Stanford University and the Hoover Insti-tute (see T. Sowell (2003), *Applied Economics*, New York: Basic Books).

2. The prediction made at the 2002 Competencies Conference in Phoenix, Arizona—that psychology would become the most credentialed and lowest-paid doctoral profession in health—was published as N. A. Cummings (2003, Spring), "Just One More Time: Competencies as a Refrain," *Register Report*, *29*, 24–25.

3. Alain C. Enthoven, who is now professor emeritus of health eco-nomics at Stanford University, discusses the Jackson Hole model and the concept of managed competition (see A. C. Enthoven (2002), *Health Plan: The Practical Solution to the Soaring Cost of Medical Care*, Stanford, CA: Stanford University Press). Enthoven was for many years an advisor to the Kaiser Perma-nente Health System in its early stages, and was briefly on the board of directors of American Biodyne.

4. As previously noted, the saga of the Dirty Dozen is chronicled in R. H. Wright & N. A. Cummings (2001), *The Practice of Psy-chology: The Battle for Professionalism*, Phoenix, AZ: Zeig, Tucker & Theisen.

5. For those interested in more information about the Hawaii Project, see N. A. Cummings, H. Dorken, M. S. Pallak, & C. J. Henke (1993), "The Impact of Psychological Interventions on Health Care Costs and Utilization," The Hawaii Medicaid Project, HCFA Contract Report 11-C-983344/9. There is also a summary in N. A. Cummings, J. L. Cummings, & J. N. Johnson (1995), *Behavioral Health in Primary Care: A Guide for Clinical Integration*, Madison, CT: Psychosocial Press (International Universities Press).

6. The locust warning article is N. A. Cummings (1986), "The Dismantling of Our Health System: Strategies for the Survival of Psychological Practice," *American Psychologist, 41*, 426–431. The following year a number of notables joined in the edited book, L. J. Duhl & N. A. Cummings (Eds.) (1987), *The Future of Mental Health Services: Coping with Crisis*, New York: Springer. Among the renowned list of chapter contributors was the late Charles Kiesler, former executive officer of the American Psychological Association, who during his administration embraced change. He wrote penetratingly of the nature of guilds (such as the APA) and why they so often fail to cope appropriately with impending change.

7. See David Dranove (2000), *The Economic Evolution of American Health Care: From Marcus Welby to Managed Care*, Princeton, NJ: Princeton University Press.

8. The authors have pioneered the integration of behavioral health with primary care and have authored a number of books. See W. T. O'Donohue, M. R. Byrd, N. A. Cummings, & D. A. Henderson (2005), *Behavioral Integrative Care: Treatments That Work in the Primary Care Setting*, New York: Brunner-Routledge (Taylor & Francis). See also W. T. O'Donohue, N. A. Cummings, M. A. Cucciare, C. R. Ruyon, & J. L. Cummings (2006), *Integrated Behavioral Health Care: A Guide to Effective Intervention*, Amherst, NY: Humanity Books (Prometheus Books). The pioneering work in this regard is by N. A. Cummings, J. L. Cummings, & J. N. Johnson (Eds.) (1997), *Behavioral Health in Primary Care: A Guide to Effective Integration*, Madison, CT: Psychosocial Press (International Universities Press).

9. For a flourishing example of e-health in psychology see Dr. Martin E. P. Seligman's website, which has a $9.95 monthly subscription fee: www.authentichappiness.com is reputed to have 10,000 subscribers. Dr. Seligman is the founder of Positive Psychology and a former president of the American Psychological Association.

# 4 We Are Not a Healthcare Profession

The history of psychotherapy vis-à-vis medicine since World War II can be viewed as a landscape decorated with a wide variety of colorful paradoxes, some credible, others more amusing, but all adding up to the current tragic economic status for psychotherapy as the unappreciated stepchild of the healthcare system. In the 60 years I have been a psychotherapist, the worst accusation that could be leveled at a colleague, or in critiquing a therapeutic approach, was for someone to exclaim disdainfully, "That's the medical model!" Recoiling, the accused would backpedal to reestablish acceptable credentials that reflected the psychosocial, behavioral, or humanistic models, declaring loudly that psychology is not healthcare. In spite of its early roots in medicine, psychoanalysis likewise placed itself above the healthcare system.

However, in the 1970s, psychiatry read the handwriting on the economic wall and not only began to distance itself from psychoanalysis and psychotherapy generally, but also proclaimed it was "remedicalizing," ostensibly heralding its reaffirmation as a medical profession. At the time psychology was beginning to boom while psychiatry was in economic decline, with medical graduates shunning psychiatric residencies. Psychiatry correctly predicted that its economic future lay in being part of medicine, and it took drastic action to become part and parcel of their physician colleagues. As of this writing the annual healthcare budget has topped $1.6 trillion, all going to medicine and surgery, except for the paltry $75 billion (or $85 billion, depending on who is reporting) spent treating emotional and mental conditions. The perception of where the mother lode lay did not escape psychiatry, jolted by repeatedly voiced pronouncements that it was a dying profession. Ostensibly to save itself, psychiatry jettisoned its preeminent hold on psychotherapy, willing it to psychology and social work.

Psychiatry, now essentially a prescribing profession that prides itself on being an integral part of healthcare, is booming again, while psychology is in serious economic decline, akin to the trouble psychiatry was in 30 years ago. The difference is that where medical graduates avoided entering psychiatry until it was once again on its feet, students who go into psychology seem oblivious that at the end of years of graduate study there is only an economic storm, with no rainbow in sight. I talk regularly with graduate students who, by the time they are on the job market, will have amassed student loans somewhere between $90,000 (if they attended a regular academic program) and $150,000 (if they attended a tuition-based professional school). Though they are generally concerned, they believe they will walk into a busy solo practice. They have not confronted the fact that they are more likely to settle for a $40,000 annual income that is further depreciated by annual payments on their student loans, which amounts to $7,000 to $14,000 in interest alone. Is the profession inadvertently letting economic illiterates self-select its future members?

## Some Paradoxes

The list of paradoxes currently plaguing psychotherapy is long and perplexing. Only a few of the more blatant ones are enumerated here:

- We are not a healthcare profession, but we should be reimbursed by health insurance for our (non-healthcare) services.

- We treat "clients," not "patients" (this switch occurred in the 1970s), but we should be paid by healthcare systems, both government and private, that are set up to take care of patients.

- Physicians, nurses, dentists, podiatrists, optometrists, osteopaths, naturopaths, chiropractors, pharmacists, and veterinarians have patients, while lawyers and psychologists have clients.

- We deliver mental health services, but we are not a healthcare profession.

- Medicine is guilty of mind-body dualism, but we will not integrate into primary care so that we can finally declare that Rene Descartes is dead.
- We do have an oxymoronic group of colleagues that call themselves health psychologists that help physicians with diseases and do not really do psychotherapy.
- Real psychotherapy involves self-actualization, with such things as marital counseling, mindfulness, and rebirthing far more fun than such mundane interventions as helping diabetics comply with their medical regimens or helping somatizers resolve the causes of their high medical utilization.

These paradoxes have produced some nonsensical beliefs by the psychologists who are willing to go to the extreme to prove we are not a health profession and that we do not treat disease.

- Schizophrenia is not a brain condition, but the result of poor life choices (William Glasser); schizophreno-genic parents, especially mothers (Gregory Bateson, Leo Kanner); or wide-scale poverty and oppression (George Albee).
- Alcoholism is not a disease. There are no tissue or neurological changes or predispositions, and a chronic inebriate can be rendered a social drinker by cognitive therapy (Linda Sobell).
- There is no medication that is helpful in mental and emotional conditions since there is no disease pathology

involved (George Albee, Fred Baughman, William Glasser).

Despite their denial of the existence of disease and insistence that even the most serious mental illnesses are responsive to traditional therapy, very few psychotherapists treat schizophrenia and severe addictions. Rather, psychotherapists continue overwhelmingly to treat what Paul Ellwood, MD, 40 years ago called the "worried well" of the health system. This is why insurers' requirement of medical necessity for psychotherapy insurers strikes terror in the hearts of psychotherapists, who insist the health system pay for treatment that does not address illness in patients who are not sick. The preferred justification for psychotherapy is some variant of self-actualization, a term that masquerades under many names, but which in my 60 years as a psychotherapist no one has satisfactorily defined. In the meantime, schizophrenics and other psychotics are neglected because treating them is too much work and very little fun.

In 1943 my first psychotherapy mentor was the remarkable Frieda Fromm-Reichman, who attended regressed schizophrenics in an era before psychotropic medications.[1] Mental hospitals were noisy, chaotic snake pits where restraint was necessary to prevent the patient from inflicting violence to oneself or others. However, this restraint was very often the vehicle for abuse of patients and even outright sadism. Patients who smeared themselves with their own feces were a common sight that caused most doctors to recoil. But not Dr. Fromm-Reichman. She walked through the hospital wearing a white smock. One pocket contained sets of surgical gloves, while the other was stocked with candy bars. When she saw a patient smearing feces, she put on surgical gloves and began "helping" the patient with his unsavory pastime. After a while she would stop, discard the soiled gloves, and offer the patient a candy bar, saying, "Please try this candy bar. You might like it better than feces. I'll be by tomorrow, and if you are not playing with your feces, I'll know you prefer candy bars, and I'll give you another one." I never once saw the intervention fail. The next day the patient would be clean and awaiting this pleasant doctor and her candy bar.

A few years later when I was employed part-time at Patton State Hospital (California), again before the era of psychotropic medications, I used the intervention successfully many times. But first I had to get over my revulsion, not an easy task. I did it by making Dr. Fromm-Reichman my hero and my role model. She was a genuine, incredibly compassionate psychotherapist, but she was far from a squishy do-gooder. Rather, she was firmly grounded in treatment. She explained to me that the schizophrenic mind will not connect with the therapist until the therapist enters his distorted and delusional world by adopting the patient's distortions and delusions. Once the therapist has been admitted to that world, the patient trusts and listens to the therapist. She extended this concept as the basis of all healing: Until the patient and doctor are in the same space, healing cannot take place. There is only noncompliance.

I continued to marvel at the incisiveness of her approach as I employed her interventions. But soon I was to experience the antithesis of compassion. It was 1949, the year before the renowned psychosurgeon Walter Freeman boasted in *Psychosurgery* journal that he had performed his 5000th lobotomy. It was customary for state hospitals and other mental institutions to save their severely disturbed patients for Dr. Freeman's arrival every six months, the time it took for him to complete the circuit of all participating hospitals. Patton State Hospital had its usual array of patients to be lobotomized, all sedated and lined up in the hall awaiting their turn.

I was assigned by my psychology supervisor to watch. I stood next to the psychosurgeon as he successively did five- or six-minute transorbital lobotomies, a procedure in which a simple ice pick was inserted into the brain, first above the eyeball, then through the optical passage and into the prefrontal lobe.[2] He opened a cardboard box full of dime store ice picks that in 1949 cost about 15 to 20 cents each. He did not bother to sterilize them, but he did discard the ice pick after every patient. I had read books on the intricate, precise procedures in brain surgery and was amazed at the nonsurgical, if not barbarous, nature of the procedure. By the time I overcame my initial shock, Dr. Freeman, who had already performed several lobotomies, handed me an ice pick and asked, "Do you want to do the next one?" Aghast, I blurted, "I am a psychologist, not a physician or surgeon." He replied casually, "That's okay, I'll help you. It's not that complicated."

Lobotomy had its heyday for a decade or more, during which a storm of protest mounted. To thwart initial objections of cruelty, psychosurgeons insisted that lobotomy was a legitimate surgical procedure in which it was necessary to "damage the brain to save the mind." As legions of lobotomized patients in various degrees of vegetative states were produced, the practice disappeared. But guess what? In 2006 it made a comeback and started gaining momentum, all because psychiatrists, who no longer do psychotherapy, find that often their psychotropic medications fail, even with the practice of overmedication dubbed polypharmacy. Where are the psychotherapists who should be responding with the legacy of the stalwarts like Frieda Fromm-Reichman? It seems they are too busy doing marital counseling and mindfulness with the worried well. William Schofield, PhD, first pointed this out in the 1960s when he described psychotherapy as "paid friendship."[3]

Psychotherapists' neglect of the seriously and chronically mentally ill has been widely discussed, but usually not within psychological circles. Credit is due the relatively few colleagues who work with psychotics, but the criticism tends to be valid: Psychologists treat whom psychologists like to treat. This aversion to addressing the seriously mentally ill, coupled with psychology's insistence that it is not a health profession—and the added absurd assertion of many psychologists that such physiologically fraught conditions as schizophrenia and alcoholism do not exist—has garnered the understandable hostility of Alcoholics Anonymous, always on the frontlines of the dipsomania battle, and the National Association for the Mentally Ill (NAMI), an organization devoted to expanding access and services for the chronically mentally ill.[4] Thus, NAMI is forced to choose medication over behavioral interventions for the chronically mentally ill because the needed interventions are not usually available. This is not because psychotherapy cannot be effective, as has been demonstrated by systems such as American Biodyne. The psychological technology is there; the psychological interest is absent.

## Clinical Romanticism

Clinical romanticism is the name given to self-actualization and humanistic therapies by many of its proponents, like Kirk Schneider.[5] The name firmly emphasizes that these approaches are not healthcare and avoids deprecating references to touchy-feely therapy. But "clinical romanticism" seems to border on the oxymoronic. Its adherents are among the most vocal opponents of the healthcare model, evidence-based therapies,[6] and psychotherapy protocols.

Clinical romanticism experienced a Camelot decade in the 1970s, when the human potential movement swept the nation. Society was directing attention inward, not outward. It was popular to have a guru and a mantra and to make pilgrimages to Esalen or one of the many other self-actualization spas.

After occupying center stage for a number of years, the human potential movement imploded in its own narcissism. A golden opportunity was lost since during its ascendancy clinical romanticism maintained its laid-back attitude and failed to identify an appropriate place in the economy of psychotherapy. Before its eclipse, a great deal was learned, inasmuch as the human potential movement lifted us beyond rigid psychodynamics and sterile behaviorism to more aggressive interventions that are just now being honed into effective and efficient treatments. On the negative side, it left many quarters with a rather less than respectful attitude toward the importance of a scientific base to psychotherapy. Even Dr. Schneider now concedes the death of clinical romanticism. However, its stiff opposition to the inclusion of psychotherapy as part of healthcare has permeated and still rules most of psychotherapy.

## Stealth Romanticism Permeates: Who Needs Science?

It was a remarkable collection of pronouncements by some of the nation's most prominent psychotherapists before an assembly of 7,000 psychotherapists. At what has been termed the Lourdes of Psychotherapy, the disdain for scientific validity was startling.[7] The high priests of this conclave included all the stellar names, such as Bruno Bettelheim, Rollo May, Jay Haley, Salvador Minuchin, and other nationally prominent psychotherapists, 26 in all. To get a flavor of what went on, consider the dialogue between Carl Whitaker, a psychiatrist who readily admitted he hallucinated frequently and suffered murderous and incestuous feelings, and R. D. (Ronny) Laing, a Scotsman whom many would consider to have at least a thought disorder, if not outright schizophrenia. These are mentioned not to deny the fact that many schizophrenics have the ability to function productively, but to reflect on the peculiar nature of some of the information imparted to the audience. All this was proudly preserved and reissued in 2005 in an official document of the Milton H. Erickson Foundation that sponsored the so-called Lourdes conference.

**Question from the audience:** What do we know now about being with other people, about working in therapy, that we didn't know 50 or 100 years ago, at the time of the foundations of psychotherapy?

**Laing:** I can't think of any fundamental insight into the nature of human beings and relationships between human beings that people have come up with in the last 100 years that weren't imbedded in the records of literature, poetry, and drama. I don't think we've gone beyond Sophocles, Aeschylus, Euripides, Shakespeare, Tolstoy.... I can't think of anything that I've learned from professional [psychological] writing that I haven't found in those writers.

**Question:** Then why are we here at this conference?

**Whitaker:** We pay the rent for those who live in sandcastles.

**Laing:** There has developed a profession, as we know, which has been partly generated by client demand and partly by marketing professionals…. People want experts to tell them how to live, how to sneeze, and how to wipe your ass, and how to masturbate, and how not to masturbate, and how to make love, how to get divorced, how to get married, how to be happy, how to bring up your children. And there's a professional response to that sort of thing.

So much for the science and practice of healthcare. Even more startling is the apparent cynicism. Readers may be further surprised to learn that this large audience of psychotherapists applauded these utterances while putting down the very few skeptics who had the courage to speak up. The transcript of this conference is replete with examples devoid of any respect for advancing the field scientifically. No wonder Albert Ellis, one of the Lourdes participants, stated in one of his many publications, "The Judeo-Christian Bible is a self-help book that has probably enabled more people to make more extensive and intensive personality and behavioral changes than all the professional therapists combined."[8] So should the public save its money and shy away from psychotherapy? How would we pay the rent for those who live in sandcastles?

Just one more example must suffice. In a lengthy interview with an intelligent but chronically schizophrenic woman, printed apparently verbatim as a model treatment session, Laing confronts the patient's questioning of her own conspiracy delusion and sets out to prove to her that a conspiracy does indeed exist.

Soon the patient is acting less crazy than the therapist in response to a technique I have witnessed many times in my career: The therapist acts crazy in order to curtail the patient's craziness. But with Laing it becomes apparent that he really believes, on some level, in what he calls the conspiracy of the Universal Mind. The change in the patient seems remarkable at first, but, like all other schizophrenics treated with this intervention, she promptly resumes being crazy and the ostensible miracle cure evaporates. In this particular conference session, after many comments conveying something akin to adulation by members of the audience, one brave skeptic arose.

**Question:** I was wondering what you thought really went on therapeutically in that interview?

**Laing:** What do you think went on therapeutically?

**Question:** I'm mystified, to tell you the truth. So maybe you could explain it to me.

**Laing:** If you're mystified, I can't explain it to you.

**Question:** Did anything go on there?

[Dr. Laing ignored the question and the audience soon broke into loud applause, obviously approving the refusal to answer and effectively silencing the skeptic, who gave up, perhaps remaining as bewildered as I am after reading and rereading the episode.]

Keeping in mind that the Lourdes of Psychotherapy conveys the thinking of some of psychotherapy's most venerated icons, one cannot help but paraphrase a statement by the great physicist

Wolfgang Pauli: Some things don't even rise to the level of being wrong.[9]

To their credit, such stalwarts as Aaron Beck, Arnold Lazarus, and a number of others presenting at the Lourdes conference never succumbed to the siren song of romanticism over scientific verification. However, its influence is insidious and is enjoying a 21st-century resurgence. Disguised as old wine in new bottles, a veteran behaviorist none other than the much respected Steve Hayes is bringing back many of the wild techniques of Fritz Perl's gestalt therapy and calling it acceptance and commitment therapy (ACT). ACT was heralded by *Time* magazine, which seems to lack a historical perspective on how techniques seem to be resurrected, renamed, and then recycled as the next great phase in psychotherapy. At the same time cognitive behaviorism, which is looked upon to be the more scientific successor to previous therapies, has been renamed mindfulness and is turning to Buddhism rather than to needed scientific advances. For example, the highly respected cognitive therapist Marsha Linehan, in what appears to be the latest version of psychological romanticism, is being widely heralded by her followers, who, quoting her, insist that "1000 years of Buddhism can't be wrong." Will the new century witness another Lourdes rather than a long overdue commitment to scientific healthcare research and best practices?

## Public Expectations

The American public is understandably ambivalent about the proper role of psychology in our society. When referred by a physician for a service that is covered by health insurance, the patient certainly has a right to expect that the psychotherapist is part of the health system. Therefore, it is confusing when psychologists insist that they are not in the medical model, that psychotherapy is an art, and that inner understanding—not the patient's wish to overcome symptoms and pain—is the goal. After viewing or listening to the many pop psychology shows on television or radio (e.g., Dr. Phil or Dr. Laura), patients are led to believe that psychological interventions are instantaneously successful, the so-called 10-minute pop cure. They are also confused by the frequent media reports of prominent psychologists strongly questioning the effectiveness of much psychotherapy. Add to this disappointing personal experiences or those of friends, and it is no wonder that more and more Americans, abetted by their physicians, are choosing medication over psychotherapy.

Ultimately, the public will judge psychology on its contribution—or lack thereof—to societal improvement. Societal upheaval and individual dysfunction seem to be steadily worsening, and psychology cannot proffer any comprehensive, understandable solutions that can be readily implemented. Psychology's lasting contributions are pitifully small compared to the advances in medicine that have resulted in an astounding increase in longevity and the quality of life. The recent rise in the effectiveness of treatment has made cancer survivors common-place, and fewer people are dying of heart attacks. The much maligned Big Pharma has developed remarkable vaccines, such as that for cervical cancer, and is on the verge of developing a bird flu vaccine with expectations it will be ready before there is a pandemic. Medical technology affords imaging and delicate intrusions not even dreamed of a few years ago. Neuroscience is linking more brain hormones and areas, pinpointing their complex connectivity with behaviors and even attitudes.

The only breakthrough in mental health has been in the newer psychotropic medications, and in spite of their limitations and overhype, they are characterized by far fewer side effects and wider acceptance by patients. Psychology has woefully lagged behind in the healthcare revolution, all the while still debating whether it is a health profession at all and whether it would benefit by the three criteria of best practices that are guiding the rest of healthcare: the best in research, coupled with the finest in practitioner expertise and training, and response to the needs of society.

### Are We Moving?

With the emphasis on integrated behavioral/primary care by APA president Ron Levant, there seems to be some movement in the direction of psychology becoming an integral part of healthcare.[10] As the battle between practitioners and researchers over evidence-based treatment grows more contentious, there are signs of rapprochement in the emergence of views that take into account both facets of the argument, as illustrated by a recent volume by Carole Goodheart and her associates, which addresses the topic.

The resistance to abandoning psychosocial, romantic, cognitive-is-not-medicine, self-actualization roots will not make the movement easy, however, and the espousal of mindfulness and the resurrection of gestalt techniques under the ACT rubric in behaviorist and cognitive behavioral circles previously regarded as scientific does not auger well. A century ago the need for common ground was enunciated by England's Michael Balint, MD: "Physicians need to become more like psychologists, and psychologists more like physicians." Balint helped shape the psychological aspects of Great Britain's National Health Insurance system a half century ago. This author participated in bringing Michael and Alice Balint to the Kaiser Permanente Health Plan in San Francisco in the late 1950s for a series of sessions involving the medical, psychiatric, and psychological staffs, which exerted a major influence on the success of the nation's first HMO in involving psychology in primary care. So-called Balint groups are well known among family medical practitioners, but, according to Jeffrey Sternlieb, it was not until 2006 that the first such group took place within psychology.[11]

## Unblundering

There are several realizations that can help us end the fallacious argument that the psychology profession should not fall under the healthcare umbrella.

1. If it is our goal to help people, the medical setting is an important venue in which to achieve this aim. We must face the empirical fact that the medical setting is where most people seek help. The primary care medical clinic has been termed the de facto mental health system because 80 to 85% of treatment for depression, anxiety, and other mental health disorders is being done by primary care physicians. In respecting this consumer preference, it behooves us to be "where the action is"— in this case, the primary care setting. We should also understand that this patient preference makes sense in a number of important ways:

   - There is much less stigma associated with primary care settings.
   - The primary care physician is a trusted source.
   - Medical clinics are more ubiquitous and thus allow improved access. For example, in rural settings there is often access to primary care but not to specialized mental health clinics.
   - Medicine, although rendering important health services, lacks sufficient expertise in mental health services.

- Many problems have both a somatic and psychological element, and if both were presented in the same setting, more optimum treatment could occur.

2. We must realize that there are actually many meanings of the term *medical model*. We can reject most of these and still function usefully in medical settings. Here are some meanings that are worth rejecting:

- *All problems are due to an organic pathology.* The evidence is missing for this claim. We do not know the pathophysiology of many of the high-frequency problems we deal with, such as the many forms of depression and anxiety. In addition, other psychological problems simply are not the kind that stem from organic abnormalities, for example, marital problems, bereavement, and even anxiety.

- *The best treatments are organic ones, such as medications or surgery.* Meta-analyses of the literature do not bear this out. Many entities are realizing this and are making moves such as black-boxing certain antidepressants for children, and even mandating behavioral interventions with agitated elderly before chemical or physical restraints can be used. Our presence in the medical setting would expand the range of effective treatments.

- *Psychiatry should have more power than other mental health professions.* This is often the case and has to be dealt with gingerly. Psychiatrists and other physicians certainly have effective treatments, but so do we. That is not the distinguishing factor. It is true that in medical settings the MD is usually first in line for administrative authority, but this is not always the case, and neither profession is explicitly trained in management. It behooves us to develop administrative skills so we can be strong contenders for decision-making positions in these settings. Cummings and O'Donohue have developed a curriculum called the MBHA: Master's of Behavioral Health Administration, to help mental health professionals learn the skill set that is necessary to effectively lead and administer.[12]

3. We must resolve any psychological attitudes that foster hostility or other emotional reactions to medicine. We might feel inferior to higher prestige or richer physicians and thus reject medical practice out of envy. We might harbor anger at the way they may have treated us or our loved ones. These situations all can be resolved in positive ways: Healthy competition and defining win-win situations are better than hostile rejection. Many physicians— especially family doctors, primary care physicians, and those who have practiced for a time—see enormous advantage to having their practices augmented by relevant psychological expertise. They see noncompliance

with medical regimens, unhealthy lifestyles that do not respond to medical intervention, and stress and depression. They often prefer treating physical problems, and would welcome our help in ways that would not demean us. They do not want another pill dispenser, but rather a professional with a skill set they do not have. We can supply this if we overcome our outmoded hang-ups.

4. We must realize that health insurance policies are written to pay for treatments that are "medically necessary." This is an important phrase, not leveled only at psychotherapy since it excludes such medical procedures as breast augmentation, liposuction, dermabrasion, contact lenses, and Viagra, to name only a few. Although people may want them, they are not necessary for basic health. It is not our intention to debate here what should or should not fall on either side of medical necessity. Rather, our goal is to express that third-party payments utilize this concept and, until it changes, we had better orient ourselves to it. The health system is not geared, for example, to pay for psychotherapy aimed at "self-actualization," whatever that might mean.

David Barlow recently proposed an interesting distinction. Mental health professionals could offer two types of services: *psychological treatments* that would be evidence based, clearly health related, and reimbursable, and another set of services called *psychotherapy*, for which people would pay out of pocket.[13] Psychotherapy could focus on a number of issues, sometimes connoted by such colorful phrases as "finding your inner child," and could even involve such non-evidence-based procedures as rebirthing and self-actualization. Clinical romanticism will still have a place in the free market, but it cannot be reimbursed by third-party payers in the health system that is paying for medical necessity.

5. We clearly need to explain the value of mental health care to a confused public. We have to be honest about what we do not know and the limits of our abilities. We must also be clear about what we can do well. Physical medicine has a big ally in the pharmaceutical industry, which spends hundreds of millions of marketing dollars to influence physicians. Our limited budget makes it a bit like David and Goliath, and we have to face that this is a key problem. A startling statistic is that there is a downward trend in total expenditures for psychotherapy and a shift toward medication. Our major competition is not each other or another profession; it is pills! Marketing by the drug companies is conditioning people to expect a quick cure. But scenarios involving impressive limitations to drugs are starting to accrue, along with those showing the superiority of behavioral interventions for many problems. This information is now finding its way into medical journals, not just the psychology journals that

the health profession never reads.[14] The APA needs to vigorously publicize these mounting findings.

Many individuals search the Web for medical information. The authors have helped a leading provider of
TriCare (formerly Champus) healthcare services, Tri-
West, to develop a website with clinical tools for members and their families, as well as for their medical and
behavioral health providers. These tools held practice
guidelines with frank appraisals of the relative merits
of medical versus behavioral interventions. The reader
is encouraged to spend a little time exploring this effective innovation that receives as many as 20,000 hits per
month (see notes).

## Endnotes

1. Frieda Fromm-Reichman, MD, was one of the pillars of the
   Washington-Baltimore school of psychoanalysis, often referred to
   as the neo-Freudian movement, that was headquartered at Chest-
   nut Lodge. One of her mentors was Harry Stack Sullivan, MD,
   deemed the father of neo-Freudian psychoanalysis.
2. The reader who wishes to study the once discredited and now
   revived practice of lobotomy (psychosurgery) is referred to Elliot
   S. Valenstein (1986), *Great and Desperate Cures: The Rise and
   Decline of Psychosurgery and Other Radical Treatments for Mental
   Illness*, New York: Basic Books. Also of interest is W. M. Gaylin,
   J. S. Meister, & R. C. Neville (Eds.) (1975), *Operating on the
   Mind: The Psychosurgery Conflict*, New York: Basic Books.
3. William Schofield, PhD, wrote extensively in the 1960s of psychotherapists' propensity to treat whom they like to treat, thus
   avoiding treating those who need it the most. His landmark
   book, *Psychotherapy: The Purchase of Friendship*, caused outrage
   in the profession. Undaunted, Schofield published a series of

articles in the *American Psychologist* on the role of psychology in the delivery of healthcare. He taught for many years the importance of psychology's participation in healthcare delivery in the Department of Psychiatry, University of Minnesota School of Medicine.

4. The view of the National Alliance for the Mentally Ill (NAMI) is made explicit by its president, Suzanne Vogel-Scibilla (2006, summer), "From the President," *NAMI Advocate*, p. 29.

5. Kirk Schneider, PhD, formerly a leading faculty member of the Humanistic School of Psychology (later renamed Saybrook), reflects the preference of many of his colleagues for the term *clinical romanticism*, in spite of its somewhat oxymoronic connotation. In an entire issue of the *Journal of Humanistic Psychology*, 8, 1998, he laments the death of clinical romanticism, blaming it on the psychotherapy field's participation in insurance reimbursement. In the same issue Cummings points out the death of clinical romanticism was due to natural causes, such as the failure of psychotherapists to figure out how to make a living from it.

6. For a nonpolemic view of EBTs, see C. D. Goodheart, A. E. Kazdan, & R. J. Sternberg (Eds.) (2006), *Evidence-Based Practice: Where Practice and Research Meet*, Washington, DC: APA Books.

7. C. Amentia (2005), *The Lourdes of Psychotherapy* (pp. 49–50), Phoenix, AZ: Milton H. Erickson Foundation Press; Laing & Christy, pp. 141–153; "Skeptic," p. 154.

8. Albert Ellis (1993), "The Advantages and Disadvantages of Self-Help Therapy Materials," *Professional Psychology: Research and Practice*, 24, 335–339.

9. The great physicist Wolfgang Pauli as quoted by Michael D. Lemonick in his article on string theory (see *Time*, August 21, 2006, p. 55).

10. The authors have pioneered integrated behavioral/primary care and have authored a number of books on the subject. A recent one is W. T. O'Donohue, M. R. Byrd, N. A. Cummings, & D. A. Henderson (2005), *Behavioral Integrative Care: Treatments That Work in the Primary Care Setting*, New York: Brunner-Routledge (Taylor & Francis).

11. For Balint groups see J. Sternlieb (2006), "Balint—An Underutilized Tool," *Independent Practitioner, 26.* See also M. Balint (1957), *The Doctor, His Patient, and the Illness,* New York: International Universities Press.

12. For information on the Master's program in Behavioral Health Administration (MBHA), see the Milton H. Erickson Foundation website through its director, jkzphd@aol.com, or the Nicholas & Dorothy Cummings Foundation at www.thecummingsfoundation.org.

13. For the difference between psychological treatments and psychotherapy, see D. H. Barlow (2004), "Psychological Treatments," *American Psychologist, 59,* 869–878.

14. The growing body of research on the effectiveness of behavioral interventions (especially of cognitive behavior therapy) over medications for many conditions that is finding its way into medical journals was summarized in *Forbes* magazine. See R. Langreth (2007), "Patient, Fix Thyself," *Forbes,* April 9, pp. 80–86.

# 5 At War With Ourselves:
## *Failure of the Profession to Own Its Training*


Every profession has a major, if not decisive, influence on its training. This is accomplished by professional schools responding to regional accreditation in academic matters, and to an approvals process conducted by its professional society. Such professional approval is above and beyond the determination of academic excellence that is the sole prerogative of the regional accrediting body in higher education. The latter restricts its accreditation to academic matters, and defers to the professional society the responsibility to determine its standards of training and practice.

This arrangement is extant for the following health professions: dentistry, medicine, nursing, optometry, osteopathic medicine, pharmacy, podiatric medicine, social work, and veterinary medicine. It is also true for a number of nonhealth professions, such as law and engineering. All of these fields have professional schools accredited by the regional education bodies and approved by the relevant professional society. For example, medicine accomplishes this through medical schools, overwhelmingly but not always within a university, that receive their approval from the American Medical Association (AMA), which sets the standards of both training and practice. The same is true for nursing schools, which seek approval from the American Nursing Association (ANA). This holds true for every health profession except one. Curiously, and blunderingly, the profession (practice) of psychology is absent from this list.

How did this anomaly come about? Before Nicholas Cummings founded the first professional school of psychology in 1969—the California School of Professional Psychology (CSPP), with four freestanding campuses—and Gordon Derner three years later established the first university-based professional school of psychology on the campus of Adelphi University, graduate education and training in clinical psychology were solely conducted by psychology departments in traditional university systems. This has changed only somewhat. The several dozen professional schools that emerged on and off campus following CSPP and Adelphi sabotaged their own self-determination for political expediency. Graduate training in clinical psychology has become more professional, but it still does not come near the professional autonomy of all other health professions. It is of interest that social work, which now performs most of the psychotherapy in America, formed its first professional school in New York in 1894, 75 years before CSPP.

## Historical Perspective

The American Psychological Association was formed nearly four decades after the American Psychiatric Association when G. Stanley Hall convened a meeting of seven attendees in his home in 1892. The main order of business at that meeting was to determine what constituted a psychologist. All present were scientists or educators from various departments, inasmuch as psychology departments did not yet exist. Designating Professor Hall as its first president, the APA soon expanded to a few dozen members and began conducting annual meetings on university campuses, especially those that had established psychology departments. This tradition continued until just after World War II when the APA began to grow exponentially.

The original interests of this new group were pedagogical, thanks to G. Stanley Hall, and philosophical, influenced by William James, who was a physician but chaired the department of philosophy at Harvard. He founded the first psychology department, also at Harvard, earning him the appellation Father of Psychology. However, he appointed Meunsterberg as its chair while he remained chair of philosophy. James never practiced his profession of medicine and never held a professorship in the new discipline of psychology.

Soon laboratories emerged, with sensation, perception, and memory as dominant areas of study. Eventually German psychophysics permeated the field, Watson introduced behaviorism, and the psychology departments became nuclei of research and experimentation in an expanding field. Healthcare, regarded as the province of psychiatry, was absent as a subject, although some professors dabbled in such oddities as psychoanalysis, hypnosis, hysteria, astasia abasia, and automatic writing. Psychology was obsessed with learning theory, and was overwhelmingly dominated for 20 years by Clark Hull, a giant name that current graduate students have never heard of. Literature rarely quotes any of his myriad publications, although he was regarded as the last word in psychological thought during the era of the 1930s and 1940s. This was when academic psychology was dominated by a pervasive interest in learning theory, with most of the so-called discoveries deriving from rats and pigeons, not humans.

It was during this era that Kenneth Spence, another giant of the time, complained that a student of his obtained a master's degree by replicating one of his experiments, but with children, not rats. He could not understand why her master's thesis was frequently quoted, whereas his experiment, which was far more controlled and precise, was never cited. When I dared suggest that perhaps the readers are more interested in children than rats, he looked at me fiercely and replied with the question, "What does that have to do with it?"

Even though its advocates remained academic and did not provide any direct services, clinical psychology began to chafe from neglect by the rest of the discipline. Preferring to call itself applied psychology to avoid any healthcare connotation that the word *clinical* might imply, these psychologists broke away briefly from the APA and formed their own organization, only to return a few years later. This was the status of what we now call clinical psychology up until World War II.

## Influx of the New Breed of Clinicians

When I returned after my military service to the University of California, Berkeley, one of the banner psychology programs in the nation, I was surrounded by a number of brilliant professors, but my desire to be trained to offer direct services met serious disappointment. Edward Tolman, a behaviorist who anticipated cognition and was a thorn in the side of Clark Hull, readily expressed a total disinterest in clinical psychology. Those who called themselves clinical psychologists (e.g., R. Nevitt Sanford, Elsa Frankel Brunswick, Donald McKinnon) were delightful teachers, but none had ever treated patients. Clinical psychology was all theoretical; Henry Z. Murray's book *Explorations in Personality* was clinical state of the art, as was Abraham Maslow's hierarchy of needs. The findings of the cultural anthropologists, and particularly Margaret Mead's *Coming of Age in Samoa*, promised to provide important, if not definitive, clinical insights even for Americans. Psychoanalysis was on the ascendancy, but that was off campus. In our academic atmosphere, psychoanalysis was the object of derision, clinical services were scoffed upon, and any graduate student who openly expressed an interest in someday having a private psychotherapy practice would be eased out of the program. We lived a double life: one with our fellow students in which we expressed enthusiasm for a future in direct services, and one with our teachers with whom we were disdainful of such.

Who were we, this new breed of psychology graduate student? Most were World War II veterans, many of whom had come into contact with some aspect of military psychology and had been favorably impressed. They had just fought through a prolonged and bloody war and wanted to get on with their lives. They had lost several productive years in the military and were looking to go from point A to point B without further delay. They had no patience with liberal arts or professorial ramblings, and were iconoclastic in their rejection of their mentors' lifestyles, all the while absorbing their knowledge like sponges. And they intended to apply what they learned to direct services rather than pursue an academic lifestyle.

At the University of California, Berkeley, I experienced the shock of my life: Psychology did not seem to have anything to do with people. Psychotherapy training was nonexistent, as was the very word itself. We got all of our training in psychotherapy off campus, surreptitiously and by paying out of pocket. We hired psychiatrists to conduct seminars in the evening in their homes or offices. Had our graduate faculty learned of this, we would have been drummed out of the program. We did learn testing in graduate school—the ubiquitous battery of Wechsler, Rorschach, Thematic Apperception Test, Bender Gestalt, and the Machover Draw-a-Person—and soon our psychiatrist teachers had us administering this then-mandatory test battery in exchange for their psychotherapy teaching and supervising. The mutual trust that developed soon had us doing psychotherapy under psychiatric supervision with the overflow our teachers experienced during these prosperous postwar years. There were just too many patients seeking psychotherapy and not enough psychotherapists.

## A House Divided

With this degree of disdain for professional practice, why did psychology departments bother with us? The answer is simple: money. The federal government, first through the Veterans Administration and later the National Institute of Mental Health, gave liberal funding to graduate psychology departments that offered doctoral clinical training.[1] These funds were purloined by these same programs to beef up their laboratories and research programs, while strangling clinical needs. Even after the APA established an approvals program, site teams would fail any program that did not have sufficient scientific resources; however, they did not enforce the need for adequate clinical resources. It was 25 years later, through a fluke, that the first doctoral clinical psychology program was denied approval for lacking *clinical* resources.[2]

In those postwar years a deep schism was created between the newly minted clinical psychologists and academia, a divide that has persisted for 60 years and surfaces every time professional psychologists want to advance practice. The number of concerted efforts by academia to stop certain vital advances in practice, often working through the APA, which academia controlled, and even appearing before state legislatures to voice opposition, are many. This is a short list:

- Academicians actively opposed statutory recognition (both licensure and certification) of psychology practice in the state legislatures and managed to delay enactments for nearly 25 years from the first state in which it was instituted (Connecticut, 1954) to the last (Missouri, 1979).

- As the price for withdrawing their opposition, academics demanded and got exemptions from state laws. Fortunately, these exemptions have long ago been rescinded.

- Although a group of practitioner advocates known as the Dirty Dozen set it up with health secretary Joseph Califano to have psychologists accepted as providers in the newly enacted Medicare (1965), the APA dropped the ball and psychology was shut out for 25 years.

- The battle to obtain third-party reimbursement in the private sector for psychological services was fiercely opposed by academia.

- The scientific/academic community in psychology intensely opposed for years expanding the scope of practice to include prescription authority, called RxP, and many, if not most, still do.

- The schism runs both ways, and now that RxP has been enacted in two states and academia is establishing master's programs in psychopharmacology, practitioners do not want the very people who vigorously opposed RxP to determine its training.

- Ignoring the need for evidence-based practice in all health professions, practitioners are resisting evidence-based treatments as another incursion on practice by academics.

- When practitioners gained control of the APA, academicians felt so uncomfortable that they bolted and formed a new organization named the American Psychological Society (APS). As if to emphasize the schism, APS has been renamed the Association for Psychological Science.

- In response to the APA's effort to be ecumenical and its ostensibly selling out RxP training to the universities, practitioners formed in 2006 the National Alliance of Professional Psychology Providers (NAPPP)—no matter that the requirements for qualifying for prescription authority in Louisiana, the second state to obtain RxP, require the training to be university based.

## Finally, Professional Schools, but the Schism Persists

Recalling that professional self-determination in education, training, and scope of practice rests on the existence of professional schools responding to requirements set by the profession itself,

Cummings in 1969 established the four campuses of the California School of Professional Psychology (CSPP) as a model to be emulated. CSPP was so successful in capturing the imagination of the profession and attracting students from a nationwide pool that a number of professional schools were rapidly established, both on campus and freestanding.

CSPP initiated a series of radical changes to traditional academia: (1) Every faculty member was part-time, teaching only courses that reflected his or her expertise in whatever it was he or she made a living. Stated another way, they taught what they did, ending the old saw that "if you can't do, teach." For example, only a practicing psychotherapist could teach psychotherapy, only an employed statistician could teach statistics, and so on. (2) Academic rank was abolished, with everyone holding the title of instructor. (3) Tenure was also abolished in favor of three-year contracts, renewable on the basis of performance. CSPP had no difficulty recruiting faculty, since qualified applicants far exceeded the need. Additionally, part-time faculty cost less, which enabled a freestanding, tuition-based school to succeed economically while keeping tuition competitive with state universities. Though these innovations were shocking at first to the Western Association of Schools and Colleges (WASC), Cummings was successful in obtaining regional accreditation for all four campuses.[3]

As for APA approval, Cummings had other ideas. In his seventh and final year as president of CSPP he established the

National Council of Schools of Professional Psychology (NCSPP) and convened a meeting of the 28 already established professional schools. Before that he had obtained the green light from the Council on Professional Accreditation (COPA), an overarching body in Washington, DC, that accredits the accrediting organizations. NCSPP was to be the accrediting body for the professional schools of psychology. This would fulfill the second basic characteristic of all healthcare fields: professional schools whose curriculum is guided by the professional society. The APA was too severely fractured and balkanized to take on the task. The NCSPP approved the bylaws and chose Gordon Derner, PhD, the founder of the professional school on the Adelphi University campus, as its first president. However, Derner exited to run for APA president in 1977 (paradoxically, the office to which Cummings was elected that year), and NCSPP voted that the professional schools apply for APA approval.

The damage to the professional school movement was enormous. In complying with the APA requirements for approval, they became another set of me-too programs. Faculty became full-time, tenure was instituted, as was also academic rank. With this came an economic squeeze that has made tuition at these tuition-based schools noncompetitive with state universities. The financial arrangement that Cummings established enabling CSPP to provide tuition-free scholarships for 20% of the student body, giving the school the extraordinary ability to recruit underprivileged minorities, was abolished. This unprecedented financial structure enabled CSPP to graduate more Latino PhDs in its first three years than all APA-approved schools combined had heretofore granted. Additionally, the number of African American graduates was greater than in any other APA-approved doctoral program.

The APA approvals process has homogenized doctoral programs with the unfortunate difference that freestanding tuition-based schools are forced to accept a large number of students, many of whom would not make the cut otherwise, in order to pay the bills. Paradoxically, some of the best and some of the worst clinical graduates come from these schools, while the majority is just mediocre. The tenured, full-time faculty positions and faculty rank wrecked the fragile economic viability of professional schools, mandating large student bodies and stifling the innovation that was characteristic of doer-teachers.

### The Travail at Vail

In 1948, my first year in private practice, I attempted to testify on behalf of a patient who was a severely battered wife. As a psychologist I had no licensure or societal recognition as a psychotherapist, and the husband's attorney challenged my eligibility to offer expert testimony. The judge, who was bending over backward to qualify me, asked what competencies determine one to be qualified as a psychologist. Embarrassed, I admitted there were none yet established by the APA or the departments of psychology, and I was disqualified as an expert. A couple of weeks later I received a notice in the mail about a conference that was to convene the following year in Boulder, Colorado, to determine all of this. I was ecstatic. The Boulder conference came and went, and the Boulder model was enunciated: The science of psychology has not sufficiently progressed to justify the existence of the profession of psychology; therefore, training for professionals must be in science first, and practice secondarily. Known as the scientist-professional model, this has been the basis for training in university graduate departments of psychology. No set of competencies was enunciated, and well over 50 years and 60 competency conferences later, we still do not have defined competencies in psychology.

The establishment of CSPP and the rapid proliferation of professional schools prompted NIMH to sponsor the Vail conference, which was to promulgate the successor to the Boulder model. The mood in 1972 at Vail was that the science of psychology had progressed sufficiently to permit the existence of the profession of psychology, and I set out to propose the practitioner-scientist model, defined as intensive professional training resting on a solid foundation of science. It was shocking that I was the only one in favor of this. The group stampeded into the professional model, with no mention of science. Not surprisingly, the conference could not come to anything resembling a set of competencies.

## The Rift Is Alive, Well, and Growing

The Vail professional model has never been officially adopted by the APA or the NCSPP, but the consequences have been unfortunate. Whereas the Boulder model perpetuates the rift between science and profession to the neglect of practice, the Vail model perpetuates the rift to the exclusion of science. Most university-based programs adhere to the scientist-professional model and graduate second-rate practitioners. Fortunately, many of these go into academia, but unfortunately, as teachers they perpetuate deficiencies in practice without producing great scientists. In a similar manner, the professional model extant in most professional schools produces nimble, effective practitioners, but absent the commitment to science, much of what we see in psychotherapy today resembles pop psychology—the manufacture of dubious diagnoses to which we apply existing or modified treatments, or worse.

Psychology very much remains a house divided, with the consequent continued crippling of psychotherapy because:

- Competencies for education and training still have not been enunciated.
- Quality assurance, prevalent in all healthcare, has not been addressed.
- The role of evidence-based treatment is embroiled in controversy.
- The issue of best practices has not even begun to be addressed.

- When confronted with the inadequacies in psycho-therapy training and experience, many, if not most, university-based programs readily admit they are training academic clinicians and not practitioners.

- When further confronted that their graduates nonetheless get licensed and go into practice in spite of these deficiencies, the answer is usually, "That is not our problem."

### Unblundering

An important part of the profession's current problem is that we have not defined what our core competencies are. Constant debate and "letting a thousand flowers bloom" is what drives science to discovery; however, a practice must have a set of lynchpins that we might term *competencies, guidelines,* and even *protocols.* We seem to expect others to pay for our services (and pay well), but as a profession we have so many major internal squabbles that it is unclear to others (as well as to many on the inside) what exactly we are able to do for this money. We also expect students to devote years of their lives, forgo income, and pay high tuition to learn this "body of controversy." We need to put in place processes to reach some consensus so that all involved are clear about what our knowledge base and skill sets are.

This is not to say we should hide our warts. It is important to have fair assessments about what we can do and to be cognizant of our limitations. But we should not appear to be what the famous philosopher of science Thomas Kuhn called pre-paradigmatic, showing little or no agreement on fundamentals.[4] Part of the advantage of defining our core is that we can also then define what the cutting edge is and concentrate our research on this.

What is our expertise for which we can earn our keep? Let us quickly review some of these controversies to see why we may be confused about our skill set, and hence our professional economic worth. While we are not saying that any of these claims are true, the literature reveals that each claim has considerable support and impressive advocates.

## Major Controversies in the Field of Psychology

Consider the following:

1. Paraprofessionals can do therapy just as well as trained psychotherapists. (This research was big in the 1960s but has since dissipated.)

2. Master's-level therapists produce equivalent outcomes to therapists with doctorates.

3. It is unclear what clinical psychologists do that is unique compared to social workers, psychiatric nurses, marriage and family therapists, psychotherapists, and so forth. Some of these professionals are a lot cheaper, so why not hire them?

4. The specific techniques are not important to psychotherapy, which concentrates on the nonspecifics. Being

warm, caring, validating, empathic, and so on is what is really important in therapy, rather than specific therapy techniques.

5. Many therapy effects are quite small.

6. Many problems are "orphaned" and do not have any reasonably controlled outcome research attesting to the effectiveness of the intervention involved.

7. Many problems do not have any outcome research showing that psychotherapy can beat no treatment or a placebo.

8. Many psychotherapies do not have long-term effects. The immediate or small effects dissipate over time.

9. There is really no difference in outcomes among therapies. Any can be practiced with any problem.

10. Many psychotherapies may be culturally insensitive. At least their appropriateness for many cultures has not been shown.

11. Many practitioners "make up" therapies or use very strange therapies such as rebirthing, Rolfing, or EST (made famous by the late Werner Erhardt).

12. Our diagnostic system (DSM) is seriously flawed.

13. Many individual diagnoses are controversial; particularly problematic are aspects of their validity and inter-rater reliability.

14. Many of our psychological assessments have poor, little, or no psychometric data.

15. We really do not know how to perform many of the assessment tasks that are asked of us, for example, predicting dangerousness, performing custody evaluations.

16. All mental disorders are ultimately biological and thus are better handled by a physician.

17. Medications are more effective than psychotherapy for many problems.

18. Medication is a better first-line treatment for many problems than psychotherapy.

19. Psychotherapy is very stigmatizing.

20. There are a lot of barriers to receiving quality psychotherapy for many individuals.

21. Psychotherapy can have iatrogenic ill consequences.

Given that these sorts of claims have a fairly prominent place in the literature, can anyone wonder why clinical psychology as a profession is not highly paid and is in trouble? Again, it is not unusual that there is a camp that disagrees with many of the above assertions. However, one must recognize that successful professions such as engineering are not debating such fundamentals. How different the profession of engineering would be if in the literature one could find serious claims such as the following:

1. Ohms law does not apply to many electrical systems.

2. The periodic table of elements is incomplete and invalid.

3. Multiple engineers come up with multiple values when calculating stresses on a bridge.

4. Most of the measuring devices engineers use contain too much error to make accurate predictions.

5. Talking to an engineer may have negative iatrogenic effects and be stigmatizing (okay, this one might be partially true).

6. A first-year undergraduate in engineering, or a nongraduate engineer (frequently termed stationary engineer), can do as good a job as an experienced licensed engineer.

7. There are various schools of engineering, and if you question different engineers from these various schools you will get radically different answers.

8. There are many other professions that apparently do the same sort of job as engineers. Many of these charge less and require fewer years of education.

If such hypothetical suppositions were true, who among us would cross the next bridge on the highway or dare to climb aboard an airplane? If you imagine these items to be true of engineering, the status of the profession might resemble that of psychology.

## Where We Must Go

We do not want to hush up legitimate controversies. But our field has far more controversy than consensus, even on fundamental issues. We must do good intellectual work and identify priorities so that we can reach a consensus about these issues and our skill sets. Otherwise we look like a bunch of squabbling amateurs instead of qualified professionals.

Lilienfeld and O'Donohue have attempted to define the core knowledge set of clinical psychology. They identified 17 "great ideas" that can serve as the core of clinical psychology. The following chapter titles in their recent book state these core concepts:[5]

1. Science is an essential safeguard against human error.
2. The clinician as subject: Practitioners are prone to the same judgment errors as everyone else.
3. Decision research can increase the accuracy of clinical judgment and thereby improve patient care.
4. Psychometrics: Better measurement makes better clinicians.
5. Classification provides an essential basis for organizing mental disorders.
6. Psychotherapy outcome can be studied scientifically.
7. Clinical case studies are important in the science and practice of psychotherapy.
8. Treatment and assessment take place in an economic context, always.
9. Evolution-based learning mechanisms can contribute to both adaptive and problematic behavior.
10. Behavior genetic approaches are integral for understanding the etiology of psychopathology.

11. Evolutionary theory provides a framework for understanding abnormal behavior.

12. Personality traits are essential for a complete clinical science.

13. The cognitive neuroscience perspective allows us to understand abnormal behavior at multiple levels of complexity.

14. Early developmental processes inform the study of mental disorders.

15. Mental and physical health influence each other.

16. Some forms of psychotherapy are partially socially constructed.

17. Cultural factors influence the expression of psychopathology.

The book contains meaty discussions provided by scholars on these general ideas, which every good clinician should know. Such ideas can be viewed as a start toward defining what we hold in common and what is unique about our professional knowledge and skill set.

In addition, we need more work like that of the APA's Chambless committee, which identified what empirically supported assessments and therapies we have.[6] Leadership in our profession needs to think strategically regarding how these competencies are marketed and what gaps constitute priorities that need to be addressed.

Fisher and O'Donohue's book, *The Practitioner's Guide to Evidence-Based Psychotherapy*,[7] reveals the good news, along with the Chambless Report, that we do have unique core competencies. There is evidence that certain therapies work and that these are indeed better than doing nothing. We must provide training in these skills and establish quality improvement practices to make sure therapists continue to provide an ever-increasingly effective product.

### Endnotes

1. The federal government provided funds to train psychiatry, psychology, and social work personnel to staff the federal and state mental health facilities that were burgeoning after World War II. By providing its funds, the Veterans Administration anticipated that most graduates would fill the many positions that were going begging in the VA. The National Institute of Mental Health was not established until 1950, four years after the first VA funds. The first director of NIMH was Admiral Felix, a psychiatrist who, together with Jean MacFarlane, a psychologist working with the VA, pushed the APA to create an approvals process for doctoral clinical psychology programs that would ensure the federal government that it was getting its money's worth.

2. For 25 years the APA site committees demanded adequate scientific resources, frequently overlooking inadequate clinical resources. It was not until the mid-1970s that the first program was failed for having inadequate clinical facilities. The program was that at Arizona State University, and the person who failed it was Herbert Dorken, PhD. The APA's Education and Training Board (E&T, as it was called in that era) cherry-picked academic clinicians for its site teams who would demand scientific excellence and overlook clinical insufficiencies. Dorken was a stealth appointee. E&T did not anticipate Dr. Dorken, not a practitioner, would behave other than expected. However, having served in his career as deputy director of mental hygiene in two states

and one Canadian province, Dorken was well aware that clinical training was woefully inadequate in APA-approved doctoral programs.

3. For a comprehensive exposition of the professional school movement, see Chapter 2 of R. H. Wright & N. A. Cummings (Eds.) (2001), *The Practice of Psychology: The Battle for Professionalism*, Phoenix, AZ: Zeig, Tucker & Thiesen. Further comprehensive readings are found in Chapters 3 and 5 of J. L. Thomas, J. L. Cummings, & W. T. O'Donohue (2002), *The Collected Papers of Nicholas A. Cummings: The Entrepreneur in Psychology* (Vol. 2), Phoenix, AZ: Zeig, Tucker & Thiesen.

4. Thomas Kuhn's important contributions to the philosophy of science are found in T. S. Kuhn (1962), *The Structure of Scientific Revolutions* (1st ed.), Chicago: University of Chicago Press.

5. Proffering these 17 ideas as core competencies is the following book: S. O. Lilienfeld & W. T. O'Donohue (Eds.) (2006), *The Great Ideas of Clinical Science: 17 Principles That Every Mental Health Provider Should Understand*, New York: Brunner-Routledge.

6. The so-called Chambless Report, named after the chair of the APA special committee, is available from the American Psychological Association (1996), *Template for Developing Guidelines: Interventions for Mental Disorders and Psychosocial Aspects of Physical Disorders*, Policy Document, Washington, DC.

7. See J. E. Fisher & W. T. O'Donohue (Eds.) (2006), *Practitioner's Guide to Evidence-Based Psychotherapy*, New York: Springer.

# 6 Our Antibusiness Bias:

## *An Inadvertent Vow of Poverty*

The ratio of budgeted dollars per practitioner between general healthcare and mental healthcare is so startling that one can only wonder how its implications continue to escape the psychotherapist. Only failure to appreciate the meaning of this chasm can account for the steady flow of applicants into the psychological professions, the rationalization of university programs to continue training these students, and the otherwise inexplicable inability to understand that there is an enormous glut of psychotherapists, perhaps the greatest of any profession in history.

Let us do the simple math: The total general healthcare budget for 2006 was $1.6 trillion (with a *t*), while the total mental health budget for the same year was merely $75 billion. There are 750,000 licensed physicians in the United States and an almost equal number (700,000) of licensed or certified mental health practitioners. The latter figure includes not only doctoral psychologists, but also social workers, master's-level psychologists, counselors, marriage and family therapists, addictions counselors, and psychiatric nurse practitioners, as well as psychiatrists. Given that the budgets for both physical and mental healthcare include all expenditures (hospitalization, technology, medications, insurance, ancillary personnel, etc.) and that these are greater for general healthcare than for mental healthcare (which also includes hospitalization, medications, custodial care for mental illness, ancillary personnel, etc.), the disparity in resources is still overwhelmingly striking:

Medicine/surgery per capita dollars: $2,134,000 per practitioner.

Mental health per capita dollars: $107,000 per practitioner.[1]

The flow is 20 times greater in medicine/surgery than in mental health. Does this glut help explain why psychotherapy practice is economically depressed? After subtracting all other mental health costs, how much does $107,000 a year leave for a practitioner's income on average? And why does this economic reality continue to escape our perception?

## We Are Selecting Students With an Antibusiness Bias

Potential applicants, especially males who discern that psychology is in decline, will gravitate to more promising fields of study. Traditionally, the man has been the primary breadwinner in our society, and although this is changing, cultural lag predisposes male college students to go into the more lucrative endeavors such as technology and business. But applications for graduate study in psychology are as strong as ever, in direct contrast to what occurred when psychiatry was in dire straits in the 1980s before remedicalization took hold. Medical school graduates lost interest in becoming psychiatrists, and vacancies in psychiatric residencies could be only partially filled by foreign medical graduates. Even today the numbers entering psychiatry are relatively low, mostly because bright medical graduates do not relish the idea of spending their careers doing boring 15-minute medication evaluations. This despite the fact that psychiatry, being the prescribing mental health profession, is enjoying a new high in individual incomes, sustained by a continuing shortage of practitioners.

In contrast, psychology is attracting applicants who manifest a distinctly antibusiness bias that blinds them to economic facts. I do not believe it is merely because the profession is attracting mostly women. There is no profession more dominated by females than nursing; yet nurses, and especially nurse practitioners, are at the forefront of business innovation. Additionally, the men currently attracted to psychology manifest the same attitudes toward business as do women applicants. To be sure, these attitudes are more than shared by their faculty members, who doubtlessly reinforce the preexisting notions in their students. The difference is that the faculty is secure in its ivy-covered tenure, while the hapless graduate who goes into the world is blindsided by the reality of paying back enormous student loans on a depressed income.

In talking with graduate students, I am struck by their uniformly negative attitudes toward anyone who has succeeded economically. The honesty of millionaires is suspect unless they made their money as entertainment celebrities, rap stars, or athletes. Among faculty members, the prevailing attitude is to suspect anyone who makes $20,000 more per year than one does. If that faculty member has an upwardly mobile income, the bar of suspicion is conveniently raised to accommodate it. Larry Ellison, the billionaire founder of Oracle, is the poster boy for all billionaires. His unquenchable self-indulgence and ultra-conspicuous consumption, sometimes somewhat rivaled by Steve Jobs, the founder of Apple, justifies the label of greed for all the wealthy. In contrast, Bill Gates, the richest man in America and the world's foremost philanthropist, is not mentioned. The Bill and Melinda Gates Foundation does more for Africa than almost all other charities combined. The Merck misstep with Vioxx is touted as typical of corporate greed, and although it has received considerable attention, it goes without recognition that this same Big Pharma sustained billions in losses developing a vaccine for river blindness, knowing full well there was no market and it would be a gift to Africa. Merck spent additional hundreds of millions distributing and administering this vaccine, thus virtually wiping out a disease that left millions in Africa suffering early blindness.

Sometimes the bias surpasses the absurd. A prominent psychologist expressed opposition to including business courses in a doctoral psychology curriculum, even though such courses are routine in medical schools and most other healthcare training programs. He regarded such courses as antithetical to the compassion that was required of altruistic clinicians, even though their intent was to empower psychologists to innovate effective, efficient health delivery systems that might benefit millions of patients. However, when he subsequently experienced the rewards resulting from his being touted in *Time* magazine as "the next wave in psychotherapy," he effusively declared, "There are millions of dollars in pop psychology."

Individual and corporate economic abuse exists, but there are countless examples of good that go unnoticed. Such attitudinal selectivity might be a curiosity were it not for the consequences that seem to remand psychologists to an inadvertent vow of poverty. It is called economic illiteracy.

## Misguided Compassion and Economic Illiteracy

It has become increasingly apparent why the students we have been accepting into mental health training have failed to discern they were going into a declining profession. I wish a kinder phrase was applicable, but it is becoming inescapable that they are economic illiterates. Which came first—antibusiness bias or economic illiteracy—is a chicken-or-the-egg question. The fact is they work in unison to deprive the student of important real-world knowledge, a deficit that is enhanced by a theoretically oriented, cloistered faculty that is equally clueless.

In a recent doctoral psychology class at a major university the professor asked what the difference is between stocks and bonds. Not one student had even an inkling. In a graduate colloquium at a prominent university I became aware that my audience thought compound interest was a higher, or even double-digit, rate of simple interest. I delved further. Asked if consolidating credit card debt into a home mortgage was a reduction in debt, all but one, an older student who had been out in the real world, said yes. They argued they were going from 12% interest on their credit cards to 8½% on their mortgage, and did not think that paying this lesser interest for 30 years would ultimately cost them far more, many years after the products they purchased were consumed and forgotten. This type of gullibility is good for the mortgage industry that calls it "borrowing long to pay short." It is also good for psychology programs that want to fill their graduate rosters with unaware applicants, thus guaranteeing faculty positions.

A recent *Los Angeles Times* article that indicated physicians were beginning to charge $25 for refilling a prescription over the phone was circulated on psychology list servers and sparked outrage among faculty and psychology graduate students as an example of medical greed. When pointed out that a physician's practice must generate at least $300 an hour just to cover rent, high-tech equipment, ancillary personnel, clerks to fill out the burdensome paperwork imposed by government and managed care, ever-increasing malpractice insurance, and other items of overhead, these same students seemed ignorant as to the impact or exact meaning of overhead. The paperwork, insurance liability, and time to verify and call in the prescription could easily amount to $25 of overhead expense, a factor that made no sense to these students. No wonder there is a rude awakening among our graduates who go into private practice, accept a $45 to $50 per session fee from a managed care network, and have no idea that it is costing the psychologist more than half that fee in overhead. Factor in the payments on student loans and the newly minted practitioner suddenly realizes he or she is working for nothing.

When I talk to graduate students I continue to be amazed at how many became interested in futures as psychotherapists as a result of their own therapy experience. Add the high number of these graduate students who manifest an unresolved transference toward their former therapists by wanting to be and do exactly as they did, and the problem is compounded. Too often therapists respond disproportionately to what can only be called favorite patients, giving them far more than may be needed to let them develop on their own. This very frequently includes insight into the therapist, fostering adoration and emulation. I see this constellation too often in our current crop of trainees. Consider the following not atypical exchange between a professor and his graduate student.[2] Although this patient is considerably more aggressive and candid, most graduate students who disagree with their professors are careful to hide their belief that they learned more from their therapist than they will ever learn from their supervisors.

**Professor:** Before you see this difficult patient, I would like you to read this book.

**Student:** I don't want to read this book because then I will not be spontaneous with the patient.

**Professor:** It is important for you to know the appropriate therapeutic technique with what can be a very difficult psychological problem.

**Student:** No, what is important is that I be spontaneous. My therapist helped me because she was always spontaneous. She taught me that a therapist must be authentic. If I read this book, I will use someone else's words and not be authentic.

**Professor:** I insist you read this book before you see this patient.

**Student:** I refuse. I would rather not see this patient than to not be authentic.

Economic illiteracy, maintained by antibusiness bias, closes one's mind to the knowledge needed to face reality. Couple this with our misplaced compassion, and the personality of our psychology recruits is far from that of most healthcare practitioners, all of whom routinely receive sound business and marketing training in their graduate programs and are further trained to be tough-minded about the need to master therapeutic skills. We manifest personalities that are far closer to those of nuns than doctors. Having worked extensively with nuns, I have the highest respect for the calling. However, I do not want a nun to fly the airliner I am on, perform neurosurgery, or take over the practice of psychotherapy. The comparison is gender nonspecific, as the current male recruits into psychology closely resemble their female counterparts on these dimensions.

## What Is Our Product?

The practice of psychotherapy has all the characteristics of a business. A service is provided for which a fee is collected; a license is required to conduct these transactions, which take place on specially designated business premises; internal and external bodies, from state boards to ethics committees, monitor the activity; taxes are paid, records are kept; dissatisfied clients can sue, and the provider of the service intends to make a profit beyond overhead and other expenses from which his or her livelihood is derived. Every service is either tied to a product or the service itself is an implied product. It is not difficult to discern the products of medical practice: medications, inoculations, various medical procedures, including surgery, prevention through healthy counseling, and on and on. The existence of products is obvious.

Another way of measuring the value of a product is its long-term effects. In medicine there have been significant declines in the death rates of both heart attack and cancer patients, as only two examples. Another way of measuring the value of a service and product is cost effectiveness—that is, is the outcome received greater than the cost to achieve it? A recent study, the most sweeping and extensive to assess the value of healthcare, was conducted by researchers at Harvard and the University of Michigan, and is published in one of the nation's most prestigious medical journals, the *New England Journal of Medicine.* The researchers calculated that Americans spent an average of $19,500 on medical care for each extra year of life expectancy gained over the last four decades of the 20th century. According to the summary, the researchers started by calculating average changes in both medical spending and life expectancy for various groups in each decade. Then they divided changes in spending by changes in life expectancy, yielding the cost per year of life gained. As might be expected, values deteriorated seriously for older people, with higher costs coming from care that does not extend life very much. For the rest of the population, the cost for value received in the form of life expectancy is a bargain.

Can mental healthcare point to such gains? The national rate of suicide has increased rather than decreased, as have the rates of violence, social disorganization, and personal alienation, as well as other indicators of increased mental distress. In the last four decades of the 20th century, as medicine achieved stellar increases in life expectancy, what does mental health have to show for its expenditures? Before one can assess value, however, what is psychotherapy's product upon which expectations might be based? Defining our product is not as easy as defining the extensive products of medicine.

It is roughly 100 years since psychotherapy became an established practice. Have there been incisive breakthroughs in technique that can be discerned in the measurable national reduction of psychopathology and mental/emotional distress? Is psychotherapy, as William Schofield called it, still "the purchase of paid friendship"? It may be useful to briefly examine what the hot buzz is in psychotherapy circles today.

## MINDFULNESS

Unquestionably the most discussed techniques in psychotherapy circles today are those based upon, or outgrowths of, Buddhism, renamed "mindfulness" and heralded as the "practice of compassionate presence." Continuing education offerings exhort practitioners to apply specific mindfulness interventions, as many as seven, to their personal lives and their professional careers, enabling their clients as well as themselves to "move through the day with calmness and clarity."[3] These techniques undoubtedly may be helpful. But why has the practice of psychotherapy, after 100 years, not advanced beyond what Buddhism contributed 2,000 years ago? Medical historians marvel at the wisdom of Hippocrates, Galen, and especially Aesculapius, who advanced the healing arts as early as 293 B.C. But what if medicine were to announce that in the past more than two millennia we have not advanced beyond the Aesculapian Greeks?

## MEDITATION

Perhaps one of the most researched techniques in psychology is the ancient art of meditation. It has become ubiquitous in relaxation and stress management protocols and is even finding its way into disease management.[4] I have no doubt as to its usefulness, and I also believe in the therapeutic value of mineral baths, which were discussed by Hippocrates circa 400 B.C. along with the therapeutics of fresh air and sunshine. What would the world think, however, if medicine were to suddenly announce that not only are mineral baths therapeutic but among the best healing agents in medicine's armamentarium?

## ACCEPTANCE AND COMMITMENT THERAPY

Heralded in a lengthy article by *Time* magazine as the next wave in psychotherapy—a prognostication that is proving accurate by the streams of psychotherapists who are rushing to espouse its tenets—is acceptance and commitment therapy, known and pronounced succinctly as ACT.[5] Its primary premise is that happiness may be an unnatural state, and that emotional pain and unhappiness may be more natural. ACT interventions help the patient deal with this ostensible reality, an outcome that is neither hopeful to the patient nor flattering to the profession if this is the best it has to offer.

ACT's message is somewhat reminiscent of Morton's 18th-century discovery of ether. He proposed it as an anesthetic in surgery, a procedure that up until then frequently resulted in death from cardiovascular shock that accompanied the unbearable pain. The head of the Royal College of Surgeons opposed its use as an anesthetic, stating, "Pain is the wise provision of nature and ought not to be tampered with." The founder of ACT, Steve Hayes, a prominent radical behaviorist, is rapidly acquiring adherents and is sought after all over the world as a speaker and workshop leader. The espousal of unhappiness as a natural state painfully demonstrates how little psychotherapy has advanced as a treatment for individual and societal distress.

## Psychology's Own House in Which to Practice

For many years as head of clinical training at Case Western Reserve University and later at the University of Vermont, George Albee chided psychologists that they had no right to complain about second-class treatment as long as they practiced in the house of medicine. Psychotherapists feel awkward working in medical settings. They do not know the language or the way the medical system functions; they are intimidated by physicians' self-assurance, and they may respond inappropriately with either obsequiousness or belligerency. Albee insisted that psychologists must build their own house in which to practice, an objective that, with a few small exceptions here and there, has been elusive. When the human potential movement swept the country in the 1960s and 1970s, one wag pointed to Esalen and the other flourishing touchy-feely centers and joked to Dr. Albee in an open meeting that psychology had finally built its own house.

Fortunately, the rapid demise of these aberrations proved him to be actually funny instead of accurate.

In the early 1980s this author did, indeed, build psychology's own house in which to practice and he offered it as a gift to the profession; American Biodyne was a national company with 10,000 providers and 14.5 million covered lives that was totally run by psychologists. Not only were all decision makers psychologists, but medical directors reported to clinical directors, who were mostly psychologists and occasionally social workers. The profession, however, rejected the Biodyne model, reacting reflexively to its antibusiness bias. Bryant Welch and Rogers Wright, leaders in the APA's Practice Directorate, trumpeted what was to become the unofficial but actively militant position of the APA by calling it antithetical to good psychotherapy and therefore probably unethical.

While psychology was busy rejecting the gift, the implications of psychology running its own behavioral health plan did not escape psychiatry. There were a number of challenges by branches of the American Psychiatric Association in Tucson, Arizona, Rockport, Illinois, Orlando, Florida, and Cincinnati, Ohio, all of which came to naught because of the then-new federal court decisions that medicine was subject to the antimonopolistic and restraint-of-trade laws. However, there were a number of bitter exchanges, all reflecting psychiatry's concern that psychology was about to create its own house in which to practice, thus threatening the preeminence of psychiatry.

One such confrontation took place in Honolulu in 1982 when the Hawaii Psychiatric Society "summoned" Cummings to appear before it and explain what he was doing. It must be stated that the HPS president, Dr. Patel, was a gentleman throughout, but his constituency's behavior was nothing short of unruly. Cummings, Hawaii Biodyne state director Walter Fo, and a psychology intern that accompanied them were kept waiting for two hours before they were ushered into a decidedly hostile environment. The body language was assaulting, posturing was slovenly, empty beer cans that were strewn across the floor were kicked about in noisy fashion, and Cummings had been introduced and was speaking for less than two minutes when an empty beer can was hurled in his direction. Within another five minutes Cummings was loudly accused of coming there to "peddle snake oil," while the meeting degenerated into name calling and a demand that Biodyne cease and desist. Only HPS president Patel and Cummings remained unperturbed. Dr. Fo was quite shaken, and our intern exclaimed as the stars in her eyes faded, "Gee, I thought I was going to see an august assembly of doctors." All of this was set aside as American Biodyne spread from a successful venture in Hawaii to equally successful operations in Arizona, Indiana, Florida, Texas, Illinois, Ohio, and within seven years to all 50 states.

Training for Innovation

Whenever the U.S. Department of Labor rates our economy, at the top of the list is healthcare, accompanied by the statement that it is booming and will continue to boom. There are shortages of healthcare personnel in every sector, led by pharmacy and nursing, except in mental health, where there is a glut of psychotherapists. It may surprise readers that there are exceptions and that personnel shortages exist even in mental health. However, they are largely new, emerging endeavors beyond the control of psychology or psychiatry. Ponder these few examples in which shortages are acute:[6]

*Animal-assisted therapist*: Apply various techniques derived from the study of animals to improve mental, physical, and social issues through animal-human companionship. Requires a bachelor's degree in psychology, social work, physical therapy, nursing, or education, followed by certification in animal-assisted therapy (AAT).

*Art therapist*: Treat physical, mental, and emotional disabilities through art expression. Requires a master's degree in art therapy, plus 1,000 hours of direct client contact after graduation. Certification is by the American Art Therapy Association.

*Genetic counselor*: Assist families who have members with birth defects, especially those who are mentally, neurologically, or behaviorally challenged. Required is a bachelor's degree in biology, psychology, genetics, or nursing, with a master's degree in genetic counseling. The certification can be by either the American Board of Genetic Counseling or the American Board of Medical Genetics.

Why is health delivery innovation so prevalent in nursing, dentistry, medicine, and a number of other healthcare professions, while it is startlingly absent among psychology? Is it because all healthcare professions except psychology and social work now receive business and finance training in graduate schools or in postgraduate seminars, while this is discouraged and even prevented by our antibusiness bias? Of all the healthcare professions, psychology remains in the greatest need of leadership in innovating new and more efficient/effective delivery systems that will finally lift it out of the horse-and-buggy era of the 50-minute hour, which is being financially strangled by third-party payers.

## Unblundering

The process of business innovation called *entrepreneurship* (different from entrepreneurial) evokes even more negativity in psychology circles than does the word *business*. An entrepreneur is one who organizes, manages, and assumes the risk of an innovative business enterprise. Note that the key words are *risk* and *innovative*, the very attributes that are so absent in psychology's leadership yet so woefully needed in this era of healthcare industrialization. These words are especially alien to the tenured faculties that are failing to prepare our students for the real world. So pervasive is the negativity to the word *entrepreneur* that the following myths about entrepreneurship evoke an overwhelmingly universal belief they are true:

- Entrepreneurs are born, not made. *Fact*: Most entrepreneurs learn from each other or emerge from the growing number of entrepreneurship programs in prestigious business schools that differentiate the endeavor from the usual management training.

- Entrepreneurs start young. *Fact*: The average age of starting is 35 to 40.

- The overriding goal of an entrepreneur is to become a millionaire. *Fact*: Most successful entrepreneurs sacrifice for years because they are driven by what they believe in.

- Entrepreneurs are unscrupulous characters. *Fact*: Most successful entrepreneurs are so square they may be called rhomboids, my polite word for nerd. Unscrupulous behavior is more common in the general population.

- Entrepreneurs take chances. *Fact*: Entrepreneurs are not gamblers and are never day traders. Their high-risk behavior comes from the "fire in the belly" (as David Packard, the founder of Hewlett Packard, named it) that tells them they are right when everyone else says their idea will never work.

- Getting an MBA is the way to go. *Fact*: Ninety-nine percent of entrepreneurs do not have such a degree because the daily management of a business is far different than innovating something that was never there before. Innovation requires thinking out of the box, which is antithetical to the status quo and many tenets of established business management techniques.

Entrepreneurs find needs and opportunities and fill these voids. There is good news here. There are tremendous needs and opportunities in behavioral health. We are not competing against established companies with strong, highly satisfying products like Toyota and Starbucks. Our competition is small-time cottage industries or outright charlatans who sell products and services because there is such a void.

Some of these opportunities have been filled in a more entre-preneurial way than is typical for mental health professionals. David Burns, author of the self-help book *Feeling Good*, must have reasoned that some people would be interested in a quality self-help book for their depression. He took a therapy with a significant amount of evidence, Beck's cognitive therapy, and did a very nice job of describing it and making it accessible to the general public (for about $10). He and others have conducted outcome research on this book and have found positive results. And he has sold more than 4 million copies!

Former APA president Marty Seligman has constructed a website (authentichappiness.com) through which one can gain access to his positive psychology for depression. Again, he is filling a need for stepped care treatments for depression and for those who may not want or cannot afford conventional face-to-face therapy. One recent report indicated that he had about 10,000 monthly subscribers at $10/month. Again, he conducts outcome research that he makes visible to potential customers.

These are just two examples. One problem with our field is that we do not have an entrepreneurial tradition, and thus there is little mentoring or modeling available to us. We might need to look at the few mentors we do have available and see how we can learn from them. We also may need to look at entrepreneurial mentoring available from other industry sectors and see how these can be applied to behavioral health.

In response to the critical absence of entrepreneurship within the psychological professions, the authors and their colleagues created a special master's curriculum that can be taught as part of the doctoral requirements in clinical psychology. The master's of behavioral health administration (MBHA) was designed to help psychologists achieve the skills to compete with their physician (including psychiatrist) counterparts who hold the MMM degree (master's of medical management). The MBHA is now offered through the Forrest Institute of Professional Psychology.

The creators took it one step further. Realizing that obtaining the MBHA through expensive college tuition would be a hardship for many, they created an online certification program that allows inexpensive continuing education credits. It also allows busy professionals to obtain these credits in a way that fits their schedules. To ensure that such a certificate would have the credibility of an educational degree, the creators canvassed the CEOs, COOs, and medical directors of the largest behavioral healthcare organizations in the United States. The response was universally positive. Those surveyed stated that not only was there a need for such trained personnel, but they would rather have executives trained by successful entrepreneurs than by ivory-tower theoreticians who have no hands-on experience.

Emboldened by such positive responses from the industry, the Cummings Foundation for Behavioral Health taped and transposed to DVDs the first five courses, each 30 hours: (1) mental health entrepreneurship, (2) mental health management, (3) healthcare economics, (4) medical psychology, and (5a and 5b) the Biodyne model of mental healthcare delivery. All were taught by leading experts in these subjects, and all are geared toward responding to the absence of entrepreneurship in mental health. These courses are being offered in conjunction with the Milton H. Erickson Foundation, which has been conducting CE courses for decades and has mounted the successful Evolution of Psychotherapy conferences. The *Monitor on Psychology*, which goes to the 100,000 members of APA and is read by many of our graduate students, published a very positive article about the MBHA.[7] Ads were placed in the *Erickson Newsletter* with a circulation of more than 80,000, as well as in the *National Psychologist*.

Results could not be more disappointing. Forrest Institute of Professional Psychology received five inquiries, none very serious, about the MBHA. The ads did not generate a single response. There may be tangential reasons why the ads may not have been effective, but the ultimate conclusion is that the antibusiness bias among practitioners is pervasive, and the prospect of studying entrepreneurship may be so frightening that we will continue to lag behind all the mental health professions that are booming around us.

## CONCLUSION

Because psychology has failed to heed the warnings and harbingers that healthcare, and especially mental healthcare, was industrializing, and because nearly seven decades after the Boulder conference we still have not defined a set of competencies for psychology, we do not have a set of marketable products to offer the public. In spite of a plethora of research ostensibly yielding evidence of efficacy or refinements of techniques, we are recycling the same old approaches and even rediscovering and championing ancient methods. The latter half of the 20th century that produced so many medical breakthroughs resulting in a remarkable increase in life expectancy has not done the same for psychology, which has not offered any solutions to ameliorate the growing individual and social disorganization.

Our antibusiness bias is so pervasive that we cannot even begin to contemplate the entrepreneurship necessary to incubate desperately needed innovation. Our counterparts in healthcare are prospering with entrepreneurship, whether it be cosmetic surgery or dentistry, the explosion of Botox and collagen treatments, or nurse practitioners running emergent cares in shopping malls. However, all these embellishments are dwarfed by unprecedented advances in lifesaving medicine and surgery that are prolonging life, and by remarkable new medications and vaccines, the overblown press about Big Pharma notwithstanding. While this is happening all around us, mental health practitioners are unable to extrapolate this progress to psychotherapy. Our antibusiness bias has truly become our inadvertent vow of poverty.

We need to realize that the only way a business survives and prospers in a free market is to persuade individuals that they should make a voluntary exchange of their hard-earned money for the product or service the business is selling. Businesses that endure must satisfy (or exceed) expectations of their purchasers. Thus, businesses are not "bad" when they imply a satisfied voluntary exchange. As a profession we must understand this and defeat our antibusiness attitudes. Part of the value of successful business is that it creates jobs. Our antibusiness attitudes have resulted in very poor job creation by psychologists.

To flourish, a business must find an opportunity and actualize it. In the behavioral health business we must understand what our customers want. They want many outcomes that are theoretically in our domain: to lose weight, stop smoking, feel happier, decrease anxiety, manage a chronic illness better. However, our product development efforts have not incorporated their perspectives very well. Instead, we have developed therapies and products that we like to deliver. We need to determine what gaps exist between what our customers want and what is currently available, then design and produce services and products that fill these voids. We also need to understand the nobility in doing this—satisfying legitimate needs (often in our business involving pain) with a strong value proposition and all the while creating jobs that help not only the behavioral health professional but society as a whole.

## Endnotes

1. The joint Harvard and Michigan University study that measured the value of per capita healthcare expenditures with increases in life expectancy is reported in the August 31, 2007, issue of the *New England Journal of Medicine* and was summarized in *USA Today*, p. 4D, on the same date.

2. This spontaneous, authentic interchange between the professor and his student occurred with Dr. William T. O'Donohue, co-author of this volume.

3. Typical of continuing education offerings on mindfulness is that offered by PESI, a large nationally continuing education firm. The description quoted in the text can by accessed through its website www.pesi.com.

4. The often exaggerated claims of meditation, which are somewhat ameliorated by the extensive research, are represented by one of its long-standing proponents, Andrew Shugyo Bonnici, PhD. Dr. Bonnici is a member of the APA who calls himself a doctor of applied meditation psychology and can be reached by e-mail: Dr@ZenDoctor.Com.

5. Readers wishing to read more on acceptance and commitment therapy (ACT) are referred to Steven C. Hayes (2005), *Get Out of Your Mind and Into Your Life*, available in paperback through Amazon.com as the book that prompted an extensive article in *Time* magazine.

6. The opportunities in unusual mental healthcare jobs were compiled by Candace Corner for Career Builders and was posted as *Hot Jobs for 2007* on August 22, 2006, on CareerBuilder.com.

7. Advertisements for the Practicing in the 21st Century Series appeared in the April 2006 issue of the *Milton H. Erickson Foundation Newsletter* and July 2006 issue of *The National Psychologist*. The *Monitor on Psychology* article on the MBHA (master's of behavioral health administration) is as follows: Laurie Meyers (2006), "Mastering Behavioral Health: A New Online Master's Degree Can Enhance Practitioners' Business Skills," *Monitor on Psychology*, March, p. 32.

# 7  Our Public Relations:
## *Disaster or Just a Fiasco?*

In 1999 psychology was blindsided by a public relations disaster of incredible magnitude: The American Psychological Association became the only scientific and professional society in America to be censured by the U.S. House of Representatives. As if this were not bad enough, the ineptitude of the APA in its appearance before the House pushed the vote to censure to a unanimous one, turning what PR experts would deem the penultimate disaster into its ultimate.[1] Not a single congressional member known to be friendly to psychology voted against the censure motion. At the time there were two psychologist representatives in the Congress, and they both abstained rather than vote against the measure. Although there was a storm within APA governance at the time, most members of the association have never heard of the incident. The only reason for reviewing this unfortunate page in our history is because it explains much of the difficulty psychology is having in restoring its credibility.

One of psychology's prime journals had just published a paper reporting a meta-analysis, as well as a study of interviews of college students who had been sexually molested as children. The study challenged the notion that these experiences had been deleterious and suggested that pedophilia may not always have psychopathological consequences. The questionable methodology and its sweeping generalization ignited a storm of controversy within the APA, with many psychologists objecting to its publication. However, the journal editor made the decision to proceed in the interest of the freedom of scientific inquiry. This controversy, which grew even louder after publication, came to the attention of "Dr. Laura" Schlesinger, who cleverly used her talk show pulpit to turn the APA internal debate into a national firestorm. She was joined by powerful conservatives in the Congress, led by then Majority Whip Tom Delay, which culminated in the APA being asked to explain to the Congress whether it was dismissing the significance of pedophilia.

The CEO of the APA testified before the House of Representatives with a carefully crafted statement, mostly written by the APA's information officer. Here is where the disconnect occurred. Living in its own bubble, the APA assumed that the internal battle waged around academic freedom could be extrapolated to the American people. Consequently, in the time allotted, the testimony made academic freedom the major concern and relegated pedophilia to a secondary level. Unquestionably, the American people stand behind academic and scientific freedom, proven through their consistent votes and by numerous court decisions. They even tolerate such extremism as that of Ward Churchill, who declared in the classroom that the 9/11 victims were no better than Nazis and deserved to die. But they do not put academic freedom before protecting our children, especially in an era in which child predators appear to abound. Had the testimony made pedophilia the primary concern, with academic freedom secondary, I am convinced the vote to censure would not have been unanimous. I talked with several members of Congress, who stated that the APA testimony was so inept that to vote against the censure motion would be tantamount to endorsing pedophilia.

### Unto the Next Generation

A stain mars the beauty of a fabric long after the spillage that caused it is forgotten. Likewise, the fallout from this disaster continues in the form of diminished APA credibility for psychology long after the House censure. In the 1960s, 1970s, and even 1980s, psychology was constantly and favorably in the news. In those years hardly a month went by in which I was not interviewed on the radio, television, or by the press. The demand seemed insatiable, and I often found it an annoying duty. I once asked the interviewer who was videotaping me for a national broadcast series why the demand on psychology seemed so insatiable. Her reply, "Psychology is good copy," the journalistic term for high subject matter interest among the public. Have you noticed that *real* psychology is no longer good copy? Only in pop psychology is the interest greater than ever as audience voyeurism is titillated by Dr. Laura, and especially Dr. Phil, who seems to have achieved rock star status.

How far we have fallen is illustrated by the extensive and overly generalized press release the University of California at Berkeley put out in 2003 championing findings by four prominent psychologists, whose test revealed that the personality of Ronald Reagan was almost identical to those of Hitler, Stalin, and Mao. I have long ago learned not to be surprised when my intelligent colleagues are not outraged, and I mused that if a test in biology could not differentiate between jackals and humans, it would be tossed out with disdain and the researchers would be drummed out of the science. But I was curious why the media did not make more of this. I called the *New York Times*, the *Wall Street Journal*, and the *Los Angeles Times*, and got a ho-hum response. The report was dismissed as another peculiarity of an esoteric profession. "Besides," one editor told me, "psychology is not that important to the public anymore."

As if to prolong the deleterious fallout from the congressional censure, the APA has embarked on a series of public relations fiascos, some minor and others major. A minor PR fiasco would be the 2005 official declaration of the APA condemning the mascot names of athletic teams. This brought a series of guffaws from the public and distress among psychologists, who asked why in an era when psychology is in decline the APA Council of

Representatives was spending its time with something that was far from a burning issue. More serious was the 2004 official declaration in favor of gay marriage, which implied there was psychological evidence to back up this stance. The evidence given, that loving relationships are mentally healthy and that gay marriage is a loving relationship and thus psychologically healthy, is so flimsy that it could be used to promote polygamy and even justify marriage to one's own mother. This official APA resolution had strong, unintended consequences as it became part of the armamentarium of the proponents of a ban on same-sex marriage.

### One Good PR Disaster Deserves Another

A different kind of PR disaster, but nonetheless as far reaching, occurred when the APA, in conjunction with the American Psychiatric Association, sought to demonstrate that managed care was unnecessary. They suggested that all that was needed to achieve medical cost offset savings was an unfettered benefit structure with all restrictions to access and session limits removed. Congress was persuaded to attempt this, and CHAMPUS (now TriCare) in Fort Bragg was chosen as the site. The APA insisted on moving ahead with this project in spite of all indications to the contrary and warnings that there would be serious unintended consequences.

The results were even more disastrous for traditional mental health care than had been predicted. Within three years an

$8 million program mushroomed 1,000% to $80 million with no demonstrable improvement in services, as admitted by the researchers themselves. Dr. Bickman, the principal investigator, stated in his report that "more is not always better." The entire matter was dialogued in 1996 in a special issue of the *American Psychologist*, never to be referred to again by the APA.[2] However, actuarial and operations officers of the managed behavioral healthcare companies are well aware of the study and can quote it chapter and verse when psychologists attempt to assert that they can curtail costs without the draconian interference of managed behavioral healthcare.[3]

To this date most psychologists are unaware of the Fort Bragg Study disaster. It is not taught in our clinical training programs, and what should have been a valuable learning experience remains unlearned. Consequently, the mental health profession continues to be clueless about how to design and implement a behavioral care delivery system that would obviate the need for the current evolution of managed care, which is essentially nothing more than a funding conduit with no direct delivery of therapeutic services.

## A Campaign Made in Heaven

Mental health leaders are ignoring a public relations campaign made in heaven, even as a PR blitz is successfully promoting psychiatric drugs as *the* solution to emotional and psychological problems. We are not without a potential rejoinder. There is a plethora of research indicating the treatment superiority of a combination of medications and psychotherapy. Other research reveals that behavioral interventions are superior to medications alone or even to medications in combination with psychotherapy. All of this is nicely embalmed in our many scientific and professional journals, unbeknown to the public or to primary care physicians, who are increasingly prescribing the touted drugs in the belief that they are providing the best for their patients.

As a few examples of the importance of behavioral interventions, consider the evidence that medicated bipolar disorder or schizophrenia without psychotherapy increases the risk of relapse since the patient will frequently go off meds. Schizophrenics do so most often because they dislike the side effects of the psychotropic drugs, while bipolar patients give into the welcome underlying feeling that weeks of "low" are abating and a "high" is developing. They look forward to the relief, if not joy, of this underlying hypomanic state and interrupt their meds, fully intending to resume them in time to prevent a relapse. Even a slight high more often transcends good intentions; the manic state sets in as the patient pops too many pills in desperation and is hospitalized with toxicity resulting from overmedication.

Consider also that antidepressants, given by well-intentioned PCPs, interfere with mourning, nature's own healing process, and thereby prolong the grief accompanying bereavement for unnecessary years. On the other hand, bereavement counseling enhances and accelerates healing and even prevents the sharp rise in somatization that afflicts so many older persons who have lost relatives and friends. Some depressions respond to a combination of medication plus psychotherapy, while reactive depression is best treated with behavioral interventions alone. There are even guidelines from the Food and Drug Administration (FDA). One such guideline that is consistently violated by prescribing physicians states that medications for insomnia are ineffective and should be a last resort, while psychotherapy and other behavioral interventions are recommended because they are far and away superior.

The pharmaceutical industry spends billions of dollars annually in a successful campaign to convince both the American public and their physicians that they need "pills, not skills." The research showing that psychotropic medications are not nearly as effective as the public has been led to believe is somehow not disseminated, and the often egregious "drug cocktail" is seldom discussed. The latter involves the practice of prescribing an increasing number of drugs for patients who have not responded as expected to the meds they first were given. Often the meds added are of the same class of drugs as those that have not worked. Eventually the patient is so overmedicated that the troublesome behavior is overwhelmed, a zombie-like demeanor emerges, and medication success is declared.

All these findings regarding the limitations of medications and the efficacy of behavioral interventions provide a golden PR opportunity for mental health leadership to educate the

American public about the advantages and limitations of both medication and psychotherapy, and the appropriate use of each. Such a campaign would seize the burgeoning concern of a hyper-aware public and acquaint them with the research that demonstrates the prevalent instances in which behavioral interventions are more cost effective and more therapeutically effective than drugs. This would require only a minuscule fraction of what Big Pharma spends since such a campaign would have "legs"—the publicity industry's term for information that is so compelling it propels itself in the media. There is also another factor in psychology's favor. Although it has done a spectacular job of turning pharmaceutical sales into a torrent, there is an undercurrent of suspicion and distrust of Big Pharma in our country. The media thrives on such controversy and would make the most of it, thus disseminating the information widely. If psychotherapy is to survive, and the day is not too far hence when it may be too late, such an attractively factual PR campaign is imperative. It will do abundantly more for psychology than continuing abortive campaigns for parity legislation.

## Why Physical Healthcare Is Revered Over Mental Health

Medicine is beset by a number of serious failings, yet it remains revered. This reverence allows us to overlook the 90,000 Americans who die every year because of medical errors, and ignore malpractice judgments that result in skyrocketing health costs and a shortage of physicians in high-tort areas. In plaintiff-plagued

Nevada, as just one example, a pregnant woman in Reno must travel to California to receive prenatal care. There is an overreliance on medications such as Phen-fen and Vioxx that have proved harmful and even fatal. There is widespread dissatisfaction not only with lack of access, but also with the "seven-minute" session once patients get to the physician.

Although the physician cannot be blamed for a number of situations—such as the 46 million uninsured, the rapidly increasing premiums and out-of-pocket expenses passed on by the employer to the employee, the continuous ratcheting down of fees paid by Medicare and Medicaid so that more and more physicians are opting out—such factors do rub off. In spite of all this, the physical healthcare system, in contrast to the mental healthcare system, enjoys a PR bonanza. The gains in life expectancy have been striking. When this author was born in 1924, life expectancy in the United States was 57 years. In 1950 it had risen to 68, and to 74.4 by 1990. By 2010 it could well be in the 80s. We have already experienced the large population growth among centenarians. Death from heart disease has been halved, most cancer patients survive, and even patients infected with HIV/AIDS are living into their senior years. Economists have been prompted to declare that the rising cost of healthcare has resulted in corresponding increases in longevity, health, and well-being. Thus, medicine's many failings are trumped by its contributions to the physical well-being of the American public.

In contrast, depression in the United States is said to be epidemic, suicide rates continue to rise, social disorganization and individual dysfunction are rampant, divorce afflicts more than half of all marriages, the family continues to disintegrate as gang membership takes up the slack for teens, increasing hordes of children grow up in single-parent families, and many children are abused and neglected. Physical health may be a considerable distance from nirvana, but its gains are spectacular when compared to the monumental failures in our mental health system.

Recently *NewsMax* listed the 10 top medical breakthroughs of the past few years.[4] One may disagree with some of the choices to the neglect of others, or the sequence of importance, but no one can disagree that any advances in mental health (other than in the new psychotropic medications) are paltry in comparison. So far behind is mental health that nothing we have accomplished even approaches inclusion in the following list:

1. *Cervical cancer vaccine*: Gardasil, developed by much-maligned Merck, is so effective that it will likely wipe out the effects of human papilloma virus, and essentially eliminate the cervical cancer that often results.

2. *Genome mapping*: Unlocking the mysteries of DNA prompted a scientific revolution that is boosting research in the treatments of cystic fibrosis, Alzheimer's, and cancer, with much more to come. These are only the beginning.

3. *Rotavirus vaccine*: There is finally a vaccine for the virus that is the third largest killer of children (just behind AIDS and malaria), claiming 3.1 million children's lives worldwide in 2005.

4. *Clot-busting TPA*: If tissue pasminogen activator (TPA) is administered within three hours of a stroke, most victims will escape permanent disability or death.

5. *Botox*: Originally used in cosmetic medicine, botox has proven remarkably effective in treating the severe pain of migraine, and shows promise in the treatment of a number of neuromuscular disorders.

6. *LASIK surgery*: Originally developed by IBM to create computer chips, LASIK is now used to reshape the cornea to improve vision, a procedure that has changed the lives of millions.

7. *Viagra*: The brunt of many a joke, Viagra, developed by Pfizer, is used to treat erectile dysfunction and has become one of the most widely prescribed drugs in the world.

8. *Peptic ulcer cure*: Two Australian scientists, Barry Marshall and Robin Warren, won the 2005 Nobel Prize for finding the bacterial basis of peptic ulcers, the world's second most prevalent disease, and one that is often life threatening. This discovery ended the prevailing psychological myth that peptic ulcers are caused by stress

in hard-driving business executives and other successful Type A persons.

9. *Artificial heart*: In 2004 the FDA approved the first implantable artificial heart, made by AbioCor. This is only the beginning of the future for artificial devices.

10. *Computer-driven technology*: A less painful alternative to endoscopies involves swallowing a capsule that contains a camera, radio, and light. Physicians can now use digital technology to view the colon as well as the heart, and literally observe the heart in action.

## What Does the Public Want From Psychology?

Anything psychology can point to pales in significance with the preceding list of medical accomplishments. Moreover, psychology is often viewed by the public as contributing to, rather than ameliorating, the burgeoning social disorganization. Its politically correct pronouncements and esoteric interests are not understood by the public as concerns mount for solutions to some of our society's greatest challenges. At the 2006 APA convention in New Orleans I presented a series of important social-psychological issues, a solution to any one of which would command the gratitude of a nation and renew respect for psychology.[5] These issues range from problems of children from single-parent households, to problems among sexually active teenage girls, to the causes of depression, divorce, and parenting troubles. (See Blunder 8 for a wider discussion of these issues.)

In 1997 the APA information officer, Dr. Rhea Farberman, discussed the results of a study that concluded that the public does not differentiate among psychologists, social workers, and other nonpsychiatrist mental health providers, lumping us all under the label of "therapist."[6] Some years earlier we uncovered this fact at American Biodyne: Our psychologists and social workers were lumped into the rubric "therapist," and our patients addressed social workers they were seeing as "doctor." This in spite of title and profession being prominently displayed on all office doors and walls and clearly listed in our brochures and literature. Our social workers were required, in the interest of transparency, to correct a patient who addressed them as "doctor." This latter made the difference: Patients became aware that the therapists were either psychologists or social workers, not just collectively therapists. In her own published article, Dr. Farberman proposed that the APA embark on a public education campaign to acquaint the public with the unique training and services of psychologists. Unfortunately, a well-meaning but less-than-vigorous campaign produced no demonstrable results.

Once psychology frees itself from trivial and largely inconsequential research that fills tens of thousands of pages in our too-many journals, we may fall short of the required number of publications necessary to qualify our university professors for tenure and promotion. However, we can then begin to address and eventually resolve for a desperate society some of the above problems. The failure of our schools should demand top priority.

This would easily make the list of top 10 healthcare break-throughs, more than rivaling those in the *NewsMax* list.

Yes, the challenges involved in any one of the issues that are in the purview of psychology are formidable, and this is only a partial array of what society expects us to address. We are facing many years of extensive research before answers might be forthcoming. But meanwhile we are reaping the wild wind of societal disdain because we are not even contemplating how to address the behavior problems facing us, fearing we might violate the sanctions of political correctness. Even a serious beginning would be noticed by a grateful society.

## Unblundering

My coauthor tells of a patient he was seeing who needed a very technically advanced macular surgery to keep from going blind. At the time, less than half a dozen ocular surgeons in the United States were qualified to perform this delicate procedure, and the patient was referred by her ophthalmologist to one that practiced on the West Coast. After a presurgical consultation she refused to go back to see this highly skilled specialist because he had John Birch Society political literature in his waiting room. No amount of logic would persuade her to return; she preferred to risk blindness instead. The perception was based on his politics, and reasoning with her that this had nothing to do with his skill as a surgeon was of no avail. She steadfastly insisted she could not trust a right-wing extremist.

This may be an isolated case, but its message is not unique: People do not trust a healthcare professional who is an avowed partisan, especially if he or she is in a different part of the political spectrum than the potential patient. It also applies to lawyers, accountants, and other advisers, but to a lesser extent than healthcare professionals. We expect our doctors to be "perfect," as judged and measured by our own yardstick. This is one reason why professionalism mandates that political identification and other signs of partisanship be absent from a doctor's office. A well-qualified physician would not dream of imposing personal politics on a patient. Then why, when the American Medical Association is far too savvy, does the mental health profession insist on an in-your-face political image?

## Shedding Our Adolescent Exuberance

To rectify this situation, we first need to realize the significant cost to our profession of public overinvolvement with political causes. It behooves us to be clear about whether the benefits of indulging the political leanings of the profession are worth the price we pay. There was a time when as fervent adolescents and young adults with nothing to lose we would appear at any rally at a moment's notice, taking pride that we were doing something important and being a part of the future. We suggest that it is time for us to outgrow such self-indulgent posturing. We now have much to lose.

As a profession, we have publicly supported political hot-button positions such as the Equal Rights Amendment (relatively old news), abortion, affirmative action, gay marriage, getting rid of the death penalty, retirement of American Indian mascots, gay adoption, employment rights of gay teachers, critique of the military's "don't ask, don't tell" policy, legal benefits for same-sex couples, and antisodomy laws, among others. If the data were overwhelming for these positions—which clearly they are not—it would be reasonable for us to describe these data, including their limitations, which is the way scientists operate. However, the mental health profession is not doing this. This is partially because these political positions are not entirely determined by scientific data but also by values. Psychologists need to be mindful of alienating the public by embracing a certain set of values, particularly when both sides of the questions have reasonable arguments. Unfortunately, however, psychologists are not just letting the overwhelming data of science "speak," but instead are also allowing political biases to creep into pronouncements from our professional organization. Because of our nonscientific, nonbiased attitude, we injure any trust the public has for our professionalism.

## THE NEED TO RECONNECT WITH THE PUBLIC AND REGAIN ITS TRUST

The consistently "leftist" positions that APA has taken on many political issues alienate the large majority of Americans who identify themselves as moderate or conservative. A recent AP-Ipsos poll found that only 6% of Americans described themselves as "very liberal," 15% as "somewhat liberal," 34% as "moderate,"

27% as "somewhat conservative," and 14% as "conservative." The positions described by policy resolutions from the mental health field are slanted toward those describing themselves as "very liberal." Thus, these positions place the APA out of sync with the majority of the American public.[7]

Moreover, because the "science" that our spokespersons cite to support these political stances is often weak, indirect, and generally partisan, it causes mistrust regarding the candidness of psychology. If scientists are supposed to be skeptical, cautious, and critical, why are psychologists seemingly unequivocal in their support of these positions? Part of the fuel for the controversy over the recent child sexual abuse meta-analysis debacle may be the suspicion that the purported finding of no demonstrable harm may be used in the "progressive" movement to legalize adult-child sexual conduct. Some psychologists (John Money, Theo Sandfort) have made this argument. They suggest that society has a prejudice against what they call "intergenerational sex," ascribing harm to these interactions when, in fact, benefit, no harm, they allege, results. They view themselves as "liberators" trying to push back prejudice against these sexual interactions. We view their arguments as flawed, their data incomplete, and their agenda reprehensible. We have explicated our arguments elsewhere.[8]

The public can reasonably feel that too much is accepted and rationalized in psychology's house. It has lost some standards of decency and restraint. In short, much of the public believes psychologists are more sympathetic toward child predators than interested in protecting children. This may be erroneous and unfortunate, but we perhaps have brought this misperception upon ourselves. We need to come to terms with this and take no stances that are unsupported by evidence. Whatever our personal beliefs, we must be judicious, prudent, and nonbiased in our speech and actions. Society expects a certain standard of understanding and even-handedness from psychologists, and we must maintain this level of professionalism if we are to garner the trust of the public we are committed to serve.

## A LESSON FROM THE AMERICAN MEDICAL ASSOCIATION

We suggest a clearer demarcation between professional and scientific psychology, on the one hand, and political activity, on the other. The AMA and physicians have done a better job of this than we have. The AMA has taken no position on abortion, Zionism, and gay marriage. Instead, physicians with liberal leanings have organized a group called Physicians for Social Responsibility, and it is this organization, not their major professional and scientific organization, that serves as an outlet for their political activism. We suggest that the APA leave pseudoscientific political activities to others, who can form and participate in a political organization such as Psychologists for Social Responsibility. We have been more resourceful in doing this with our support of guild issues by forming a semiautonomous practice organization.

## Public Support Through Quality Practice Standards

A final way in which we can improve our public relations is to adopt and practice quality standards for the practice of psychology. We have too many charlatans and kooks in our house. And they are protected by our silence. We know they are there, and we allow them to practice and potentially harm clients. We know therapists are practicing rebirthing. We know that there are psychologists who help their clients recover after what they diagnose as trauma induced by alien abduction. We know that individuals who are struggling with depression and may even be suicidal are having their dreams interpreted according to Jungian archetypes. We know that there are therapists who just make up the therapy they deliver in their offices. We know there are psychologists who look at children's drawings and diagnose sexual abuse.

We are well aware of what is going on in our field and we do nothing—until we hear it has gone too far and a child has suffocated while being rebirthed. The list of malpractice—or to put it in the best terms, shoddy practice—is formidable. We need to get our house in order and enforce reasonable quality and evidential standards for the practice of psychology. Instead of the current "anything goes," we must look to a standard of "only quality goes." Until we do this, we do not deserve to be trusted and our bad public relations is an appropriate warning to the public.[9]

We need to divert attention away from the latest issues grab-
bing the political headlines. What resolution can be passed on
global warming? Instead, our mission should be to define quality standards more clearly. These should be noted in our ethical
code. Infractions should be detected and adjudicated. We need
to serve the public, not by gracing them with what we regard
as our superior political values and positions, but rather by our
thoroughgoing commitment as a profession to ensure that the
public receives only quality services at a fair price.

## Endnotes

1. The unanimous censure of the APA by the U.S. House of Rep-
   resentatives and the deleterious effect of political correctness on
   the credibility of American psychology is discussed in R. H.
   Wright & N. A. Cummings (Eds.) (2005), *Destructive Trends in
   Mental Health: The Well-Intentioned Path to Harm*, New York:
   Routledge (Taylor & Francis Group).
2. The original report of the Fort Bragg Study is L. Bickman (1996),
   "A Consortium of Care: More Is Not Always Better," *American
   Psychologist, 51,* 689–701. The reader might wish to read this
   entire special issue, which includes several commentaries by APA
   leaders, including that of past president Dr. Patrick DeLeon.
3. The rise in healthcare costs, which is impinging directly on the
   consumer's pocketbook, was reported in *Time* magazine in its
   November 2008 issue, pp. 53–54 (Kathleen Kingsbury, "Pressure on Your Health Benefits"). Several articles by economists
   have been published, perhaps the most impressive being by the
   Federal Reserve Bank of San Francisco in its *FRBSF Economic
   Newsletter*, Number 2001-36 (December 14, 2001).
4. "Top 10 Medical Breakthroughs" appeared in the November
   2006 issue of *NewsMax* magazine. Written by Brenda McHugh,
   it is found on pp. 80–81.

5. The full manuscript of Dr. Cummings' address to the August 2006 APA meeting in New Orleans is available on the website www.NAPPP.org. It is titled "APA and Psychology Need Reform" and was part of the symposium "Psychology Needs Reform: Past Presidents Debate the 10 Amendments."

6. The results of the study reported by Dr. Farberman, as well as her recommendations for a PR campaign, are found in R. K. Farberman (1997), "Public Attitudes About Psychologists and Mental Health Care: Research Guide to the American Psychological Association Public Education Campaign," *Professional Psychology: Research and Practice, 28,* 128–136.

7. The APA's public interest–related resolutions can be found at http://www.apa.org/pi/resolutions.html. On the AP-Ipsos poll of March 2007, see, for example, http://www.outsidethebeltway.com/archives/2007/03/twice_as_many_americans_conservative_over_liberal.

8. See O'Donohue's arguments against adult-child sexual contact in W. O'Donohue (1992), "Definitional and Ethical Issues in Child Sexual Abuse," in W. O'Donohue & J. Geer (Eds.), *The Sexual Abuse of Children: Theory and Research,* Hoboken, NJ: Erlbaum.

9. For more on quality improvement in mental health, see W. O'Donohue & J. E. Fisher, "The Role of Practice Guidelines in Systematic Quality Improvement," in J. Fisher & W. O'Donohue (Eds.), *Practitioner's Guide to Evidence-Based Psychotherapy,* New York: Springer.

# 8 Political Correctness:

## We No Longer Speak as a Science and Profession

> Sir, you are entitled to your own opinion, but you are not entitled to your own facts.
>
> **—Daniel Patrick Moynihan, late U.S. Senator (D-NY)**

No one precedes a statement by saying, "What I am about to say is politically correct, and therefore true." An even less likely statement is, "How dare you be politically incorrect and state such untruths!" We might be hard-pressed to define political correctness. Yet we all recognize it and think and behave accordingly lest we offend or be accused of being insensitive, lacking in compassion, or just plain stupid.

In critically examining political correctness, let us start by looking at it historically, beginning with the present and rewinding its progression. On November 17, 2006, the Associated Press released the startling news story "Scientists Propose Pollution to Cool the Planet." The upshot of the story was that as the sun continues to warm the earth too dangerously, the time may soon come to deliberately spew pollution into the atmosphere to provide shade and thus cool the planet. Paul Crutzen, the Dutch climatologist who was awarded the 1995 Nobel Prize in chemistry for uncovering the threat to the ozone layer, suggested balloons bearing heavy guns be used to carry sulfates high aloft and fire them into the stratosphere. Such explosions would provide a "shade" of pollution that would deflect the sun's rays. All this was taking place in a closed-door, high-level meeting at the National Aeronautics and Space Administration's Ames Research Center in Moffett Field in California.[1]

I read and reread the story, fascinated as one must be after spending the past 20 years being persuaded that global warming is the result of man-made pollutants. To be certain, scientists are divided, many attributing the warming of the planet to another of naturally recurring climate cycles. I recalled the cold cycle that occurred in the 1930s and then again 40 years later. So compelling was the latter that climatologists were predicting another ice age brought on by the abundant use of fossil fuels. Scientists urged the government to stockpile food because in 30 to 40 years the earth would be too cold to grow food.[2] Schemes were proposed to slow down the impending ice age, one of the most preposterous being to melt the ice caps by covering them with black soot. Then came a 180-degree turn, and now it is politically correct to predict that burning the same fossil fuels will bring about global warming and the extinction of millions of plant and animal species.

### Political Correctness Uses Intimidation, Speculation, and Junk Science

Most of my colleagues were not around or were too young to remember when the pollution-equals-ice age mentality ruled, and those who would not climb aboard the bandwagon were accused of being destroyers of the planet. Without as much as a whimper of embarrassment, as soon as the cold cycle ended and a warming cycle began the intimidators suddenly shifted from ice age to global warming. With the same vehemence the politically correct crowd continues to attack, but the skeptics are now on the opposite side of the thermometer. Such an unabashed turnabout is not unusual in political correctness, and PC adherents see no contradiction. Again, historical perspective makes it apparent that PC is impervious to critical self-examination.

A number of near universally accepted fallacies illustrate this. In 1968 Paul Ehrlich's *Population Bomb* frightened America into believing that the world would run out of food before the 21st century. In 1962 Rachel Carson's *Silent Spring* predicted the disappearance of all birds due to pesticides within 20 years.[3] These, along with the ice age myth of the 1970s, are conveniently overlooked.

### Political Correctness Is Red-Green Colorblindness

A critical self-examination reveals that all these stances, including the latest preposterous idea of deliberately exploding pollutants into the atmosphere, are nothing but speculation. Science often proceeds in its early stages through speculation, whether it is string theory or the big bang theory that astrophysicists have been debating for decades. It may be said that speculation is even necessary. The fault lies in ideologues that turn speculation into fact and resort to intimidating those who recognize their assertions as speculation.

One cannot help but be skeptical when following the 2005 severe hurricane season in the Gulf of Mexico climatologists confidently predicted a repeat and even worse hurricane season for 2006, and in advance blamed it all on global warming. To the contrary, there were no destructive hurricanes in the Gulf the next year, and the error was welcomed inasmuch as it spared a repeat of Katrina. However, expecting that Gulf oil production would once again be curtailed, speculators drove up the price of oil to all-time highs, hitting millions of Americans in the pocketbook as gasoline rose to $3.50 per gallon. Had speculation been called speculation instead of fact, we would have been spared an oil crisis along with no landfall hurricanes.

In January 2007, my wife and I spent several days in Antarctica. A highlight was the opportunity to interact with 16 of the scientists from the Palmer Station, a post so conscientiously maintaining the pristine environment of Antarctica that anything that goes in must also be taken out, including all waste, human or otherwise. After we discussed the difference between loneliness and isolation, the talk not surprisingly turned to global warming. The scientists acknowledged that the ice in Antarctica is melting but stated this has been going on for at least 10,000 years. Scientists agree that the earth is warming but disagree as to the cause. Is it another of earth's climate cycles that were occurring eons before humans began powering their SUVs and private jets with fossil fuels?

They showed a several-millennia-old map of the North American continent in which the Eastern seaboard was 150 miles wider (and at that time there were no polluting autos, factories, and incandescent light bulbs, the latter among the latest PC targets). As the ice caps melted and seawater increased, the continent narrowed. As the ice continues to melt, coastlines will surely continue to narrow accordingly. But the question remains whether natural climate cycles are so strong as to be impervious to human attempts to alter them. One of our fellow visitors interjected with some anger that this was not in keeping with "conventional wisdom." The response was quite direct: "We are scientists; we don't know about political correctness." Another scientist muttered in a stage whisper, "And if you doubt man-made global warming you might never get funded again." Then he uttered, "Oops," and covered his mouth as if to repudiate his own statement.

The lesson to be learned is that if climatologists cannot predict one year ahead, then making predictions about what will occur decades and even half a century ahead must be regarded as speculation. Typically, in accordance with political correctness, we are inundated with doomsday scenarios. Who are those who push these dire warnings as fact and inevitability? And who are they that they demand concurrence and are disdainfully hostile toward anyone disagreeing? Our historical perspective reveals that when the Soviet Union first faltered and then fell, the sympathizers, known in the vernacular as "reds," suddenly became what we now call "greens," bringing with them their well-known vehemence toward the United States and its economic powerhouse. Not able to differentiate red and green is the most common form of colorblindness in nature, and it is not surprising that it would be found in political extremism. The attacks on the American economy as politically imperialistic and destructive as sounded by the reds for decades could now be shifted to criticism of America as a polluter that is destroying the earth, albeit in a different way.

This is not to say that all environmentalists are extremists. To the contrary, most environmentalists are responsible and have done much to improve our air and water. Certainly much of the environment needs cleaning up or protection, and I pride myself in being among the environmentally aware. But, unfortunately, the very important matter of global warming has been politicized, and in the extreme it becomes an ideology that needs no proof. Unfortunately, it is often spread by those who use intimidation and accusations of ignorance to push forward their unsubstantiated views. The subject of global warming serves as the prototype for all political correctness since intimidation can also accompany cultural sensitivity and compassion. When these become mandatory and even dictatorial, they foster censorship and limitations on thought and expression. There can be no argument, no debate, no dissension. Thus, PC is the antithesis of science. How, then, did it permeate psychology?

## Political Correctness Invades Psychology: A Historical Perspective

So pervasively has political correctness permeated psychology that the president of the APA in his monthly column in *Monitor on Psychology* (October 2006) was driven to declare, "Psychological science is not politically correct."[4] Coming after two decades of politically correct proclamations by the APA, all without scientific or professional credibility and with no apologies, Dr. Gerald Koocher's assertion is reminiscent of President Richard Nixon's declaration at the height of the Watergate scandal that brought him down, "I am not a crook."

Before 1960 it was difficult, and often impossible, to get the APA to advocate for psychology. Congressional testimony was so rare as to be virtually nonexistent. As psychology began to gain ground as a practice it became necessary for advocacy to help the fledgling profession overcome myriad obstacles in acquiring licensure, third-party reimbursement, and government recognition of psychological services. The Dirty Dozen was actively fighting to move the APA toward professional advocacy, a fight that reached critical proportion with the Medicare fiasco of 1965.

In response, angered practicing psychologists across the land formed the Council for the Advancement of Psychological Practice and Science (CAPPS), which established itself as *the* voice of psychology in the White House and in the halls of Congress. The APA countered by establishing a special committee: the Committee on Relations between the APA and CAPPS, which was succeeded by the Association for the Advancement of Psychology (AAP), whose purpose was to advocate for professional practice in the political arena, which it continues to do so to this day.

With a board appointed by both APA and CAPPS, the AAP set out vigorously on its mission, creating an aura of successful advocacy that became the envy of social activists in the APA Council of Representatives. They began to demand advocacy for purely political stances that were emerging (e.g., civil rights, the Equal Rights Amendment, gay and lesbian rights, and even animal rights), even though they might lack scientific psychological evidence. Alarmed, in 1973 the APA council and board of directors reaffirmed and revised a prohibition against non-psychologically-based declarations, adopted as the Leona Tyler principle (named after the then-current president of the APA). Its simple rule: As citizens, psychologists have a right to advocate for any cause through the myriad political advocacy organizations, but when psychologists spoke as a profession through APA public stances and proclamations, it should be only from science and professional experience.[5]

Subsequent APA presidents judiciously abided by the Leona Tyler principle. As an activist, in my own presidency (1979) I appointed the first standing committee on ethnic minority affairs, the first task force on gay and lesbian issues, and I insisted that council cancel the Atlanta convention site because Georgia was not an ERA state. However, these were *internal* political stances, not public proclamations. Years before my presidency, I also introduced resolutions in council proclaiming that homosexuality was not a disease diagnosis and that being homosexual must not bar anyone from any employment. Impinging on society in general, these resolutions carried the proviso that the APA would sponsor research to substantiate the positions taken. Sadly, this research was never initiated, and years later I learned that the call for mandatory research was "sanitized" (i.e., removed) from the resolutions.

As president presiding over the Council of Representatives I ruled out of order any resolution that would result in a public proclamation that violated the Leona Tyler principle. My resolve early in my presidential year was to test the thrust for the APA to disaccredit already-approved faith-based doctoral clinical programs because they required a creedal oath. Such programs as Fuller, Rosemead, Brigham Young, Fordham, and Loyola were graduating credible, well-trained clinicians, and there was no evidence that the requirement of a creedal oath in any way negatively influenced their objectivity to practice.

national problems effectively.[6] He writes that the boomer generation comprising our political leadership might have to pass on or
retire from the scene before the United States can address our
problems with a fresh perspective.

Past perspectives and priorities have rendered psychology
impotent to move practice forward. While medicine, nursing,
dentistry, and apparently every health profession except psychiatry, psychology, and social work have realized that practice is a
business and have trained their students accordingly, psychology's antibusiness bias has stemmed the tide of progress. Unable,
or unwilling, to address our economic plight, we harp on our
greatest success, perhaps above all other health professions:
diversity. This is certainly an important accomplishment, but as
practices languish, is it supposed to make us feel good while we
become healthcare's most diverse but extinct profession? If our
patients were using success in one area to substitute for failure
in an unrelated area, every capable clinician would be able to
address it therapeutically without blinking an eye.

Our inability to think economically means that psychology
lacks the capacity to pursue innovative business solutions that
are becoming commonplace in all other sectors of healthcare
practice. When this deficit is pointed out, most psychologists
respond that lack of business acumen is a good thing. Such a
mind-set ensures that psychology will continue to decline as
healthcare in general booms.

## Psychology Has Replaced Science With Political Correctness

Writing in 2001 in the *American Scholar*, Michigan University psychology professor Joseph Adelson laments "...an important, though largely unnoticed, development within psychology: the capture of many of its institutions and much of its scholarship by the forces of political correctness." Referring to the Leona Tyler principle, he goes on to state, "Not long ago psychology had in place an immune system that could resist the more virulent intrusions of ideology.... It is now a mark of merit when psychologists exhibit their parti pris, even when they purport to speak not for themselves alone but for the discipline as a whole."[7] The quickest way to grasp the extent to which this has happened, continues Adelson, is to examine the *Monitor on Psychology*, an official organ of the APA. Every issue has stories touting psychology's "scientific" expertise to comment on political problems and disputes. So pervasive has this become that Adelson is writing a book on the politics of psychology, describing how selective are the facts of *Monitor*'s reportage. He cites a long list of issues toward which psychology could make an important contribution by focusing on psychological science and practice unfettered by political correctness.

That the APA is largely perceived as another political organization is unfortunate in itself, even if it were not for the accompanying erosion of its science and the inhibitions placed on the development of its practice. This has not gone unnoticed.

Most of the advances during the past two decades in the under-standing of aberrant human behavior have come from biology, genetics, and neuroscience, not from psychology. Examples of political correctness trumping both science and practice integrity are so numerous that only some of the most egregious can be recounted here.

## CAUSES OF MENTAL ILLNESS

Ever since George Albee's discredited view captivated the profession in the 1950s, the prime causes of mental illness have been encapsulated in slogans about poverty, racism, sexism, unemployment, corporate greed, and the more recent emphasis on the so-called national lust for violence. I publicly debated the late George Albee at a time when biochemical and genetic advances, as well as a greater understanding of brain defects, were pointing to a more enlightened view of mental illness. He challenged me to name just one mental illness that was biological, and I quickly mentioned bipolar disorder and childhood autism as merely two examples. He leaped upon the latter, insisting that childhood autism was due to "refrigerator moms," whose inadequacy as parents was a response to sexism.

The current stream of PC articles are far more sophisticated than Albee's well-meaning, but simplistic and erroneous message. The elimination of poverty would end much suffering in this world, but as the etiology of mental illness, poverty has been disproved time and again. Yet the *Monitor on Psychology*, in article after article, subtly or openly chants the platitudes regarding poverty, sexism, racism, violence, and corporate greed. In recent APA publications, for example, we are told that the higher rate of depression in women is the result of sexism and the plight of women in American society; yet this higher rate of depression in females is found in many countries and cultures.

## POLITICAL CORRECTNESS INHIBITS MUCH-NEEDED RESEARCH

In the past decades medicine has made monumental advances. People live longer, heart attacks have fallen dramatically in number, and more cancer patients are recovering. Even HIV/AIDS patients are living long enough to have problems related to old age. In the meantime, what far-reaching societal problems has psychology resolved? Many of the taboo areas for psychological research would address major social problems confronting our society, resulting in contributions rivaling those of medicine. So pressing are a number of these problems that other areas of science have moved forward to fill the gaps created by psychology's neglect.

- A large body of evidence outside psychology reveals that children of single parents are several times more likely to be in trouble with the law in adolescence or early adulthood. Why is psychology not studying this? Is it because it is politically incorrect to question challenges to traditional marriage? A woman has a right to be a single mom, but do we not have an obligation to help her make an informed decision?

- Teenage girls who are sexually active are three times more likely to be depressed and three times more likely to attempt suicide than girls who are not sexually active. Where is the psychological research on why this is so? Is it because it is politically correct to counsel teenage girls on latex but incorrect to encourage them to refrain from early sex, as Miriam Grossman has pointed out in her celebrated book, *Unprotected?*[8]

- Oxytocin, extensively studied by neuroscientists, is a peptide (amino acid) chain manufactured in the hypothalamus, stored in the posterior lobe of the pituitary, and released into the blood to trigger a fascinating group of related functions. In the brain, oxytocin receptors are found in the amygdale, the ventromedial hypothalamus, the septum, and the brain stem. Of importance to psychology, it is a "messenger" from the brain to relevant organs, such as to the uterus to induce labor and control post-delivery bleeding, and to the breasts to let down milk. It is instrumental in mother-child attachment, and is thought to play a role in bonding, such as in friendship and romantic attachment. We now know that it is released in sexual activity, and may account for why young women are more devastated by casual sex than men. Or to be overly trusting of undeserving and even violent males. The release of oxytocin can be conditioned, a discovery made by neuroscientists, not psychologists, who should be the experts. But now that it has been shown by nonpsychologists that oxytocin can be classically conditioned, and often with unintended consequences, such as causing the female to be more susceptible to depression in superficial relationships, does psychology shy away because it is politically incorrect to say women and men are different in this regard? Our physician counterparts do not hesitate to warn women who smoke that they have twice the risk of lung cancer than men. They do not hesitate to tell women they are several times more likely to suffer illness from excessive drinking than men. Are they more committed to science and patient protection over political correctness than we are?

- Recent studies, mostly in medical rather than psychological journals, reveal that men suffer far more depression than had been thought, perhaps as much as women. However, they suffer in silence and are much less likely to be diagnosed. When portraying the degree to which women suffer from depression, is mention of the incidence level in men avoided so as not to detract from the mantra that sexism toward women results in a gender disparity in frequency of depression? Also overlooked is the fact that the highest incidence of suicide in the United States is among men over 55, most of whom have seen a physician just preceding the undetected depression that resulted in suicide.[9] Finally, psychology research on depression overlooks all of the nonpsychology studies that demonstrate religious persons are happier than those who are nonreligious, Republicans are happier than Democrats, and both of the latter are happier than Independents. Does a structured value system contribute to happiness and mitigate depression? Where is the psychological research that has so often focused instead on victimhood?

- Our political correctness has crippled our ability to solve one of the greatest crises ever facing any Western civilization: Why can't our children learn? Taboo is the study of intelligence that might reveal innate individual differences and challenge our obsession with so-called self-esteem, thus preventing meaningful research that might address the so-far elusive reason why so many children cannot learn. We have substituted social passing for learning, creating a population of high school graduates who cannot perform on an eighth-grade level. Worse yet, many of our youth do not graduate from high school, even though all they have to do is show up. Anyone still insisting that the bell curve exists in *all* of nature, including humans, will be savaged, as was Arthur Jensen.[10] Psychology established itself in the 1930s and 1940s as the study of learning. For 20 years the now-forgotten names of Clark Hull, Edward Tolman, and

Kenneth Spence dominated the psychological literature of the period. Along with these theorists, Lewis Terman and David Wechsler loomed large as the study of intelligence and its impairments was a paramount field of inquiry. No one questioned the bell curve of intellectual endowment. These have all but disappeared as research into these areas threatens political correctness. Currently, such studies can literally get a psychologist drummed out of the corps.

- More than 40% of adults in the United States today are single. Half of married unions end in divorce. As Drs. Goldberg and Popenoe[11] separately ask, "Are people increasingly unable to form and maintain meaningful connections and relationships? Are people today unable to parent correctly? Has personality broken down so extremely that the interpersonal is moving beyond reach? Are we producing increasing numbers of dysfunctional children not because of a lack of knowledge as to how to do it, but because of who and what we (our personalities) are?"

- We have long known that narcissistically impaired persons are highly subject to depression, of which there is now an epidemic in the United States. Are we truly a narcissistic generation, overreacting to the vicissitudes and annoyances of daily living, rushing to the divorce courts if our marriages are not perfect, and establishing

the other hand, some research has shown promising, but limited, results. If the APA rushes to judgment in the matter of sexual reorientation therapy while remaining derelict in its silence toward proven harmful techniques, therapists will be intimidated and patients will lose their right to choose their own treatment objectives. The APA, not the consumer, will become the de facto determiner of therapeutic goals.

## POLITICAL CORRECTNESS DELIBERATELY SLANTS KNOWLEDGE

That a scientific body would deliberately slant facts and consciously mislead would have seemed improbable and even impossible before political correctness captured the APA. But this appears to have been the case according to a Yale University psychologist, who voluntarily communicated with me in apparent distress over what occurred in Connecticut. As a member of the board of directors of the Connecticut Psychological Association, she was asked to sign on to an amicus brief being filed by the APA.[14] The brief ostensibly was to educate the court about the literature regarding gay parenting. She writes:

- "It took a good deal of detective work—searching out many original sources—to be able to conclude with certainty that the brief was misleading in generalizing from children of lesbian parents to those of gay men. The brief seemed to have been crafted carefully to avoid revealing the true state of knowledge."

- After contacting the head of the APA Gay, Lesbian and Bisexual Concerns Office, she wrote, "…he eventually sent me a more recently written brief that he said had been changed to address the concern I was raising. The revision in the new brief was simply to change the title of the relevant section from *Gay and Lesbian Parents Are as Fit and Capable as Heterosexual Parents, and Their Children Are as Psychologically Healthy and Well Adjusted* to read *There Is No Scientific Basis for Concluding That Gay and Lesbian Parents Are Any Less Fit or Capable Than Heterosexual Parents, or That Their Children Are Any Less Psychologically Healthy and Well Adjusted.* The rest of the section was unchanged, with the exception of some added references, none of which indicated new data about children of gay parents. The fact that the APA office had revised the brief in this way struck me as quite offensive, since they now were making a factually correct statement, but one that seemed to be deliberately misleading."

Of course our colleague is referring to the age-old principle in science that absence of evidence is not evidence of absence.

## POLITICAL CORRECTNESS COULD DESTROY THE PROFESSION

There have been a number of incidents that have grossly embarrassed psychology, and rather than learn from the ensuing negative publicity, the APA continues to declare dubious public stances that at times have made us a laughingstock.

- The APA is the only scientific/professional society ever censured by the United States House of Representatives. Most APA members are unaware of the event, and those who do seem to blame "Dr. Laura" Schlesinger, who seized upon the publication by an APA journal of a meta-analysis and interview study of college students who had been sexually molested as children. The publication challenged the notion that these experiences had been deleterious, setting off a firestorm that culminated in the APA being summoned by a congressional committee to explain its views on the effects of pedophilia. The APA testimony before the U.S. House of Representatives focused on academic freedom, thus relegating pedophilia to a subordinate role. The public and the Congress are in favor of academic freedom, but not at the risk of harm to their children. So enormous was the disconnect between psychology's leadership and American society that it was shocked when the censure motion passed unanimously. Several psychology-friendly members of the House of Representatives told me, on assurance of anonymity, that the APA testimony was so bad that to have voted against the censure motion would have been tantamount to voting in favor of pedophilia. It should be noted that the testimony, delivered in person by the CEO of the APA, was prepared by his information officer. Although she no longer is in that position, she continues her disconnect with the American public as editor in chief of the *Monitor on Psychology*, overseeing its plethora of politically correct articles.

- The APA's official endorsement of gay marriage, citing the flimsiest of research evidence, may have contributed to the backlash against gay marriage. Does any serious scientist regard as evidence the following: Loving relationships are mentally healthy, gay marriage is a type of loving relationship, therefore gay marriage is mentally healthy. Good grief! This statement is so elastic it could be stretched to justify polygamy, marriage to your own mother, or even to your lovable pet dog.

- How far we have fallen is illustrated by the 2003 publication in a prestigious APA journal by four prominent psychologists who found that on their test the personality of Ronald Reagan was almost identical with those of Hitler, Stalin, and Mao.[15] I have long ago learned not to be surprised when my intelligent colleagues are not outraged, and I mused that if a test in biology could not differentiate between jackals and humans, it would be tossed out with disdain and the researchers would be drummed out of the science. A serious rebuttal pointing to researcher bias has received little attention from psychologists, even though it is well recognized that the

items chosen for a political "personality" questionnaire
are more likely to determine the outcome, just as the way
a poll question is asked has a greater influence than the
beliefs of the person polled. I was curious, however, why
the media did not make more of this. I called the *New
York Times*, the *Wall Street Journal*, and the *Los Angeles
Times*, and got a ho-hum response. The report was dismissed as another peculiarity of an esoteric profession.
"Besides," one editor told me, "psychology is not that
important to the public anymore."

- A new horizon in trivial pursuits was demonstrated in
  2005 when the APA Council of Representatives declared,
  while speaking as psychologists, that the current names
  of athletic mascots are harmful and demeaning. This
  would evoke a chuckle were it not for the fact that faced
  with monumental problems that threaten the very existence of the profession, the council devoted its valuable
  time to this matter. Perhaps the need to demonstrate
  something in spite of the bankruptcy of effective ideas
  prompted this waste of time.

## POLITICAL CORRECTNESS INTIMIDATES AND LIMITS STUDENTS' CRITICAL THINKING

If psychology is ever to get beyond issues of the 1960s and 1970s
it will be because the next generation has been able to transcend
where we are now. This hope is mitigated, however, by the fact
that political correctness is used by faculties to select students

who are in their own image, and to intimidate those accepted into their PC mold. Perhaps these students will be able to develop their own critical thinking and subversively keep it from becoming known to the faculty.

- In my frequent speeches that address psychology's need to develop business knowledge and acumen, I often receive an eager interest from graduate students and a cold shoulder from faculty members. Graduate students continuously ask where they might obtain training without their advisors knowing it, in much the same way my generation had to hide its interest in practice from a prohibiting faculty.

- When Rogers Wright and I were editing *Destructive Trends in Mental Health: The Well-Intentioned Path to Harm*, a number of potential contributors opted out, while others agreed to participate only if their names were kept secret. They cited fear of retaliation through denial of tenure, being passed over for promotion, loss of referrals in their practices, or just a general shunning by their colleagues. This was especially true of younger colleagues, who complained that intimidation was pervasive. As one who lived through the era of McCarthyism, as egregious as that was, it was not as bad as the unspoken intimidation that exists today. In the 1950s I knew the enemies that would restrict my freedom: the John Birch Society, the KKK, the American Nazi Party, Stalinists, the evangelist in the revival tent down the street. Now the intimidator is more likely to be my colleague in practice, my fellow faculty member, and my own APA.

- Reports abound of intimidation of students by faculties. Critical thinking differing from the familiar mantra that mental illness results from poverty-racism-sexism-violence-corporate greed is scorned. One psychologist, who after graduation established a large successful group practice, learned early in graduate school never to mention his interest in the business of psychology. Another, who had served as a marine before returning to school, was asked in class by the professor, "Do you kill babies?" Such extreme cases are more frequent than we might wish to admit, but open derision of students whose critical thinking is outside the accepted norm is commonplace. Hopefully, students will learn to hide what they are thinking and break the mold of the boomer mire. At the worst, they are being brainwashed and will simply continue it.

The progress of psychology in regard to diversity and social justice has been exemplary and one that other professions would do well to emulate. While the APA will and should continue to do more, these issues should not become a focal point simply because psychology lacks a solution to the rapid decline of its practice and the erosion of its reputation. Much of the problem stems from the current generation of psychologists, which remains mired in the priorities of the 1960s–1970s era, when it had its defining moment. It appears unable to move on to innovatively address ways to resolve society's serious problems. Much of the difficulty lies in the profession allowing science to yield to political correctness. Intimidation and perpetuation of the status quo stymies psychology's ability to transcend its self-imposed limitations and has resulted in a continuing loss of prestige. It remains to be seen if the next generation of psychologists that replaces the short-sighted boomer generation can break out of the failure mold. There is danger that those currently in control of psychology's institutions and scholarship will select students in their own image, or brainwash them through politically correct intimidation.

Our self-imposed PC limitations have been the undoing of the relatively young, but very vibrant, progressive, and innovative science and profession of psychology. We did not become the lowest-paid doctoral profession in healthcare by accident; we brought it on ourselves with our unreasonable antibusiness bias, which cripples practice and blinds us to solutions that are rapidly being espoused by all other health professions.

## Unblundering

Unblundering the tangled web of political correctness would not be a simple matter even if the profession were united in a determination to do so, which it is not. Reform must begin at the top. We must choose far-sighted leaders with keen insight, unbiased attitudes, fortitude, and the knowledge necessary for the monumental undertaking of bringing the mental health field into the 21st century.

## REFORMING AND SIMPLIFYING THE APA STRUCTURE

The APA has more than 100,000 members, associates, and affiliates, yet less than 200 elitists control its governance. They rotate year after year through its offices, boards, Council of Representatives, and its plethora of committees, in a kind of organizational musical chairs that ensures the perpetuation of political ideology and essentially disenfranchises the thousands of psychologists who might disagree. This same organizational structure handpicks the editors of its many journals, who then cherry-pick reviewers who will not pass for publication any scientific or professional paper that is not in synch with sanitized thought. Hundreds, if not thousands, of psychologists have chosen not to belong to the APA, have recently dropped out, or have defected to the Association for Psychological Science (APS) or to the new National Association of Professional Psychology Providers (NAPPP). Others who feel their needs are not being met hang in there to maintain their malpractice insurance or other benefits offered to APA members.

Our national organization is balkanized into 60 divisions and even more by its affiliated state associations, which represent special interests that vie for seats on the Council of Representatives. There is even more fractionation. Some of the divisions have sections, sometimes as many as six, which further hone the special interests and add to the already high dues' burden. The council chooses the members of the various boards, including the board of directors. The only office the membership at large votes for directly is the president. Since many members do not belong to divisions, they have little voice in the manner in which most of the APA policies are promulgated and how the public declarations that repeatedly violate the Leona Tyler principle are foisted on us.

A long-time APA watcher who has attended the council meetings for the past two decades sums the society's member activities thus: 20% of the council's time is spent on diversity, 60% on ensuring the perpetuation of the incumbents' participation in the various aspects of governance, and only 20% on issues of vital interest to the general membership. And why should it be different? Because they are not elected by the members at large, those in governance are only tangentially, or even unlikely to be, responsive to their interests.

At the 2006 APA convention in New Orleans[16] I (Cummings) participated in a forum entitled "The APA and Psychology Need Reform," which drew a lively, engaged audience. I noted in that forum that I had been urged to call for a new division that might somehow balance the APA's tilt to the left, but this seemed like another band-aid. At present, the warring academic and professional coalitions on the council are unable to prevail against each other without making alliances with the third, or public interest, coalition, from which most of the ideologies spring. In this way we sell out our science and profession to political ideology and political correctness. What we need is a gut-wrenching sweep of our troubled house.

We propose that we do away with the current divisional governance, wiping out the special-interest fiefdoms and returning the organization to the membership through a one-member, one-vote democratic election process that would include not only the president but also the board of directors and the Council of Representatives. Divisions and state associations could continue to exist and even advance candidates for election to the council and the board of directors, but not solely determine them.

We are aware that such a clean sweep of our fractionated special interests for the good of the science and profession is a drastic step and will be fought tooth and nail by the status quo. In 1945 the APA saved itself by forming a dozen divisions. In the 1970s it saved itself again by granting power to divisions to elect the council through an allocation system of votes that determined how many seats each division/state association would have. These reforms sufficed for years. However, we are now bogged down in fractionation, growing divisiveness, and member alienation, and we need a force independent of the current governance.

Since making this proposal for reform in New Orleans, the comments have appeared on a number of psychology list-servers and we have received scores of e-mails, including several from former APA presidents, endorsing such drastic overhaul of the APA. But there has not been even one word from anyone officially or in a leadership position within APA. Not surprising, those in power are not willing to relinquish it, and a democratic one-member, one-vote process can be a real threat to musical-chairs elite governance.

## THE MENTAL HEALTH FIELD NEEDS TO BYPASS POLITICAL CORRECTNESS IN THE INTEREST OF SCIENCE AND NEEDED RESEARCH

Organized psychology needs to stand firm for academic freedom and freedom of inquiry. When someone who addresses subjects that fall within our purview is being unfairly attacked by the self-appointed PC police, we need to defend him or her by articulating the violations of the principles of free critical debate. There was no formal support from organized psychology when now ex-president of Harvard Larry Summers (former Clinton cabinet member—not exactly a member of the right-wing conspiracy) made some remarks at a conference on diversifying the science and engineering workforce. His speech resulted in his being fired by Harvard, even though he made it plain that the differences he observed between men and women in the workplace were based on conjecture.[17]

### SCIENCE REQUIRES ONGOING DEBATE

Scientific progress moves at a deliberate pace from theory to research with its myriad replications, which lead finally to discovery—after which the process begins all over again as future discoveries are made. There are two forces that can disrupt this process: journalists who prematurely inform the public of the progress long before it is firmly established, and politicization, which has the effect of ending debate and stymieing future replications and alternative research needed to determine scientific fact.

Psychology has in place a mechanism to address the problem of overzealous journalists. Research publications are required to indicate the uncertainties in the findings and to call for continued refinement and replication. This is conveyed to reporters during interviews, and most responsible journalists state that it may be years before these findings are sufficiently established to impact on consumers. Unfortunately, too often journalists overly hype their articles, suggesting fact when actually scientific debate and research are continuing. Just one example of this was hormone replacement therapy (HRT), which was first highly touted, then regarded as dangerous, and, finally, its appropriate uses, limitations, and side effects established based on emerging facts. In the meantime, the public has been left with the understandable but erroneous feeling that science waffles and cannot make up its mind.

The second barrier to sound science is politicization of premature findings. Often promulgated by our well-meaning social scientists and their organizations, this is more egregious and requires the vigilance of the profession itself. Once a scientific finding or discovery is politicized, debate is discouraged, opposing scientists are often vilified, grants and other scientific funding flow only into the politically correct channels, and true scientific inquiry is derailed. Political correctness is the antithesis of science, and our social sciences, often falling prey to it, must vigilantly resist its intrusion. Politically correct proclamations, no matter how well-meaning, prematurely end debate and slam the door on skeptical research, which is the very essence of all science. These proclamations have become an unfortunate hallmark of mental health organizations, causing our science to be questioned and even discredited. If our profession is to be spared continued decline, it is imperative that political correctness is once and for all eradicated from the science and practice of psychology.

## NEUTRALITY IN PRACTICE: A CORNERSTONE OF PSYCHOTHERAPY

A psychotherapist's objective is to aid and guide the patient toward achieving his or her own successful, happy individualism. Meticulous care must be taken to avoid imposing the therapist's own preferences, beliefs, or biases. A surgeon who has political or religious pamphlets in the office risks rejection, no matter how competent he might be in his profession. Even more is at stake in psychotherapy. The transference in the treatment process often leads to the patient desiring to emulate the therapist. This is a positive force if the patient identifies with the therapist's fairness, compassion, dedication, and other such qualities. If, however, the therapist reveals political, religious, or other biases, the patient may seek to adopt these, thus aborting his or her own maturational achievement. Even worse, if the therapist's prestige is used to bend the patient toward the therapist's own beliefs, a great injustice may have been foisted on the patient.

I once overheard a conversation in a restaurant between two friends who were seeing the same psychologist, unbeknown to both of them until that evening. One, who was apparently a Catholic, insisted the psychologist was Catholic. The other insisted with equal vigor that he was Jewish. I knew this psychologist and was aware that he was neither, but it was a credit to his therapeutic neutrality that each patient firmly believed that he was part of her religion.

A violation of this principle of therapeutic neutrality is reflected in a therapist who believes homosexuality is morally wrong and endeavors to transform every gay patient into a straight one. The opposite is also a violation of therapeutic neutrality: a gay therapist who subscribes to the ideology that treating a gay patient who wants to go straight is unethical and nontherapeutic. Both positions reflect ideology and have no legitimate presence in the treatment room. Unfortunately, there are religious therapists who believe they are justified in treating the gay lifestyle as pathology, while the gay and lesbian lobby seems determined to make unethical the treatment of homosexuals who seek change. These are obvious violations of the therapeutic neutrality principle. However, there are many subtle intrusions of bias, known as countertransference. A male therapist in the throes of his own ugly divorce may be unconsciously overly critical of the wife in couple's therapy, or a childless female therapist may impart questionable child-rearing information to a mother. Whether overt or insidiously unconscious, the therapist must guard psychotherapeutic neutrality as sacred.

## STAYING ABOVE THE FRAY

None of this should imply that scientists are not passionate in presenting and defending their findings; the more plausible the theory, the more likely there will be ardent supporters. In the meantime, research continues, each finding is scrutinized and debated, and further replications are designed and implemented. This is how flaws in research design are discovered and facts ultimately derived. If one has attended a scientific debate, it is apparent that scientists and practitioners are enthusiastic about their own work and critical of contrary findings. But no one is calling anyone names, the debate remains scholarly, and scientists with opposing theoretical orientations are often close friends outside the laboratory. This congeniality seems to evaporate once politics or political correctness becomes part of the debate. When science is overcome by ideology, debate is suppressed and progress is deterred.

In the annals of scientific debate, the disagreement between Albert Einstein and his physicist colleagues is considered a classic of how science advances. In his era, Einstein was seen as a maverick, with most of his colleagues arguing opposite views of those he espoused in quantum theory, relativity, what would now be called intelligent design, and a number of other issues regarding the makeup of the universe.[18] The debate, often quite passionate, raged for decades, and Einstein emerged as one of the three giants of the 19th and 20th centuries, along with Charles Darwin and Sigmund Freud. During these debates some of his detractors would utter in affectionate frustration, "Einstein, Einstein, Einstein!" This atmosphere of scientific inquiry reflects debate at its best, free of political correctness, animosity, and ideology, bespeaking an era that could well be emulated in our current politicized climate.

We believe that psychology needs to take an active position against the poison of political correctness. We have a lot of tough problems to consider: gender differences, group differences, causes of crime, definition of a mental disorder and what constitutes healthy sexual behavior, and so forth. If we let political correctness stifle free inquiry, we will not be a rational, scientific profession but rather a cowardly, political one. We applaud the Russians' move away from politics determining science. Is academic America moving in the opposite direction? We have to make sure that we are not simply parroting the political views of those we empowered to lead us. We must do away with the PC police, even if they are our own colleagues.

## Endnotes

1. "Scientists Propose Pollution to Cool the Planet" was an Associated Press release on November 17, 2006, 12:00 A.M., and was carried nationally by every major newspaper. Typical is the news story by Shaun McKinnon in the November 17, 2006, *Arizona Republic*. The author goes on to cite new "evidence" involving several paradoxes; for example, attempts to curtail the blazes of

forest fires may actually prevent the release into the atmosphere of carbon dioxide and methane that might otherwise help cool the planet.

2. *Newsweek* magazine's extensive coverage summarized all of the then-current and seemingly compelling "evidence" that the earth was entering a new ice age in which it would be impossible to grow food. See *Newsweek* (1975), "The Cooling Earth," April 28, pp. 11–53.

3. The Paul Ehrlich and Rachel Carson books that for two decades acquired almost gospel status with political correctness are P.R. Ehrlich (1968), *The Population Bomb*, New York: Sierra Club–Ballantine, and R. Carson (1962), *Silent Spring*, New York: Houghton-Mifflin.

4. The APA "President's Column" quoted is G. P. Koocher (2006), "Psychological Science Is Not Politically Correct," *Monitor on Psychology, 37*, October, p. 5.

5. The reader may be interested in a sampling of the public policy declarations made over the years by the APA Council of Representatives; most of them absent any evidence from psychological science. Two of these resolutions were made by the senior author of this book, and one more was introduced at his behest. Also, the reader will note the broad range of issues with disparate importance:

1969 Abortion, especially in the first trimester, does not create psychological hazards for most women undergoing the procedure. (Author's note: This does not address the many women who later enter psychotherapy having had a change of heart, or who later found they could not have another child.)

1974 Resolution against corporal punishment, citing no psychological evidence.

1974 Resolution that homosexuality is not a mental illness (submitted by this author, with a proviso that relevant research sponsored by the APA would follow, but none did).

1975 Resolution that being gay does not bar one from any employment (submitted by this author with the proviso that subsequent research would follow, but none did).

1975  Resolution urging the adoption of the Equal Rights Amendment, citing no psychological evidence.

1977  Resolution terminating existing convention contract with Atlanta, New Orleans, and Las Vegas. This was an internal decision prompted by the senior author who was then APA president-elect designate. He indicated he would not preside over these conventions in non-ERA states when the women members stated they would not attend. The author cited the cancellation of previous conventions in Miami and Chicago when, respectively, African American members protested segregation and young members protested police brutality.

1984  Resolution against violence on TV, again citing no psychological evidence.

1985  Resolution for society's elimination of both amateur and professional boxing, challenged by the boxing and other sport associations with no evidence or response forthcoming from APA.

1986  Resolution against apartheid in South Africa. This was solely political.

1988  Resolution equating Zionism with racism. This was both solely political and gratuitous.

2004  Resolution supporting gay marriage as mentally healthy. No evidence or literature cited.

2005  Resolution calling for the banning of athletic team mascot names. No evidence or literature cited.

6. The mired in the 1960s–1970s concept is compared with the views of U.S. Senator Barack Obama (2006), *The Audacity of Hope: Thoughts on Reclaiming the American Dream*, New York: Crown.

7. Joseph Adelson is quoted from his article, J. Adelson (2001), "Politically Correct Psychology," *American Scholar*, *60*, 580–583.

8. Miriam Grossman's book was originally published under a nom de plume, Anonymous MD (2006), *Unprotected*, New York: Penguin. She feared retaliation and subsequent firing from her position at the student counseling center of the University of California at Los Angeles.

9. Regarding depression and the high suicide rate of men, see B. M. Kuehn (2007), "Men Face Barriers to Mental Health Care," *Journal of the American Medical Association, 296,* 807–815.

10. The savaging of Arthur Jensen, professor of psychology at the University of California, Berkeley, has been documented by Linda Gottfredson (2005), "Suppressing Intelligence Research: Hurting Those We Intend to Help" in R. H. Wright & N. A. Cummings, *Destructive Trends in Mental Health: The Well Intentioned Path to Harm* (pp. 155–186), New York: Routledge (Taylor & Francis).

11. Dr. Herb Goldberg's concerns are addressed in his unpublished manuscript, *Reframing the Identity of Psychologists,* which can be obtained by contacting Drherbgoldberg@aol.com. See also B. D. Whitehead & D. Popenoe (2005), *The State of Our Unions: The Social Health of Marriage in America,* retrieved April 28, 2006, from http://marriage.rutgers.edu/Publications/SOOU/TEXTSOOU2005.htm.

12. For the critique of motivational experts and self-help gurus, see Steve Salerno, *How the Self-Help Movement Has Made America Helpless.* The author is a journalist living in Pennsylvania.

13. At its February 14–15, 2007, meeting the APA board of directors authorized the five-member Task Force on Appropriate Therapeutic Responses to Sexual Orientation, with nominations to be submitted by March 19, 2007. Information may be obtained from the APA's Lesbian, Gay, and Bisexual Concerns Office, phone number 202-336-6041.

14. The name of the writer regarding the deliberately misleading amicus brief to the Connecticut court is withheld to protect her, inasmuch as there have been incidents of retaliation for speaking out. She wrote a letter to the editor of a relevant journal, which was not published. This author has permission from the writer to convey any reader's query directly to her for reply.

15. The equating of Ronald Reagan's personality with those of Hitler, Stalin, and Mao is found in J. T. Jost, J. Glaser, A. W. Kruglanski, & F. J. Sulloway (2003), "Political Conservatism as Motivated Social Cognition," *Psychological Bulletin, 129,* 329–375. The rebuttal is in J. Greenberg & E. Jonas (2003), "Psychological

Motives and Political Orientation—The Left, the Right, and the Rigid: Comments on Jost et al.," *Psychological Bulletin, 129,* 376–382.

16. N. A. Cummings (2006), "The APA and Psychology Needs Reform," presented as part of the panel "Psychology Needs Reform: Past Presidents Debate the 10 Amendments," with former presidents Frank Farley, Bonnie Strickland, and Nicholas Cummings, APA Convention, New Orleans, August 12, 2006.

17. A complete transcript of Dr. Summer's speech is available from Harvard and can be found at http://www.president.harvard.edu/speeches/2005/nber.html. The reader is encouraged to read it in its entirety to attempt to find offensive material, let alone offensive material sufficient to fire someone.

18. Walter Isaacson (2007), *Einstein, His Life and Universe,* New York: Simon and Schuster. See also Phillip Frank (1947), *Einstein, His Life and Times* (George Rosen, Trans.), New York: Da Capo Press (reprinted 2002).

# 9  Creating Patients Where
There Are None

Everyone is crazy but me and thee, and sometimes methinks thou art
a little queer.

—**Boswell's** *Life of Samuel Johnson*

In contrast to what his biographer said of the mentally tortured
Samuel Johnson, in this postmodern era it may be said that everyone is mentally ill but no one is crazy. It seems that all behavior
is currently covered by some diagnostic label, and no one is just
a plain, run-of-the-mill jerk. Reflecting on his extensive personal
psychotherapy, my good friend and now-retired highly successful colleague Len Blank[1] would delight in recalling, "After years
of analysis, in one group session with Fritz Perls I learned I was
just obnoxious."

Consider that the *Diagnostic and Statistical Manual* (DSM)[2]
has increased from a mere 50 pages to nearly 900, while the
number of psychiatric diagnostic labels has increased from about
100 to more than 800. When this author returned from World
War II and resumed his graduate education in psychology, there

were less than 200 psychologists and approximately 3,000 psychiatrists practicing in the entire United States. The membership of the APA was barely 5,000, but by the time I served as president (1979) it had exceeded 100,000. In 1997 then APA president Dorothy Cantor declared that the nation had 625,000 mental health professionals (psychiatrists, psychologists, social workers, counselors, marriage and family therapists (MFTs), and addictions counselors), only about 100,000 less than the number of physicians.[3] Some believe that as the number of mental health professionals increases, so does the number of diagnostic labels. This author pointed out several years ago that as the number of professionals increases, competition for a set number of patients becomes fierce, which is the subject of a forthcoming book by Carol Austad.

While this book was in preparation, the giant Ford Motor Company experienced severe competition from the Japanese automakers, principally from Toyota. Its car and truck sales fell drastically, resulting in factory lots and sales rooms overflowing from overproduction. Ford did what any company would do under such staggering competition: Production was cut back, plants were closed, workers were laid off, and incentives for early retirement of permanent employees were introduced. Economically chastened, the company set out to design autos and trucks that would have greater appeal to buyers. In short, it took severe, often painful steps to become more competitive.

Psychotherapy now finds itself in a competitive situation somewhat analogous to Ford's. There is an overproduction of psychotherapists and low demand for their services. The difference is that while Ford is one company that can take rapid corrective action, psychotherapy is many independent practitioners who look for direction from several somnambulistic organizations (e.g., APA, ACA, AMFTA, NASW). As indicated in previous chapters, in the last decade referrals for psychotherapy have drastically declined as a result of the biomedical revolution. Referrals to psychologists by primary care physicians have dropped by 65%, and the number of psychiatrically hospitalized patients who on discharge are referred for outpatient psychotherapy has dropped from 95% to 5%. We have markedly overproduced psychotherapists, at a time when an increasing number of practitioners compete for a shrinking pool of referrals.

If we were like Ford, we would immediately stop training more psychotherapists. But, alas, we have accelerated the minting of new psychologists, social workers, MFTs, and counselors. Only the ranks of psychiatry have shrunk. Psychology is of considerable interest to young college students, who remain unaware that the future holds declining incomes and staggering student loan payments. Men, being the traditional breadwinners, have tumbled to this fact more than women; thus, mental health is rapidly becoming a female profession. In the face of this fierce competition, graduate faculties are willing to continue to train psychotherapists as long as the students want it. Whether it is unprofessional for graduate programs not to warn prospective students of the economic conditions, and whether it is folly for the profession not to be innovating delivery systems that the public needs or wants, inevitably there will be a day of reckoning, just as in the case of Ford, which ignored years of dire harbingers.

## The Attempted Mental Health Solution

The initial purpose of the DSM was to provide a useful taxonomy that would bring some order into a field in which diagnostic labels more likely followed the precepts and nomenclatures of particular schools of psychotherapy. Diagnoses were often contradictory or in outright conflict with one another, and the same condition was often reflected in different terms. With all of its early limitations and shortcomings, the first DSM did accomplish its original purpose. Assured for the first time of some reasonableness in reimbursement for mental health services, third-party payers eagerly adopted it as their payment standard.

Seemingly overnight the DSM acquired a second status that seemed to overshadow the first: It became mental health's reimbursement bible. Practitioners learned that submitting the diagnostic labels of the DSM resulted in reimbursement from the health insurance companies. As the number of practitioners sharply increased while the number of patients remained the same or even declined, the heated competition inevitably tempted the authors of the succeeding DSMs to increase the patient population by redefining and expanding diagnoses. This was especially

tempting in the face of the field's inability to stem the minting of an increasing number of psychotherapists. Additionally,
when psychotherapists found themselves unable to compete with
the biomedical revolution, the solution seemed obvious. If such
thoughts never crossed our leaders' minds consciously, at least
they must have done so unconsciously, a process that we would
recognize in our patients (if not ourselves) as unconscious fiscal
convenience.

### Victimology: The Unintended Consequences of Axis II

Initially, the DSM was a rather simple and straightforward taxonomy, which is now embodied in Axis I. But with the addition
of Axis II things changed.[4] In Axis II, what had been termed
"character disorders" were renamed "personality disorders,"
a seemingly innocuous change were it not that it heralded the
trend to regard all negative social behaviors as a form of disorder.
This agreed with the postmodern dictum that there is no right or
wrong since all things are relative. It also helped usher in the era
of victimology: Everyone is a victim of his or her circumstances,
and ultimately no one is responsible for his or her behavior.

Defense attorneys were quick to take advantage of this sudden defense bonanza. They formed alliances with willing psychotherapists, and forensic psychology blossomed overnight.
This is not to demean the importance of the forensic specialty,
but to point out how this new field suddenly burgeoned. America
was shortly thereafter subjected to two criminal cases in which

psychologists' testimony was prominent: the "Twinkie defense" that acquitted the hate-murderer of gay San Francisco supervisor Harvey Milk, and the "his hate for women because of his inadequate mother defense" of infamous and charming serial murderer Ted Bundy. Examples of psychologists contradicting one another continued, and we witnessed a series of nighttime murders in which the defense was the dubious somnambulism (sleepwalking) syndrome. As the "diminished capacity" defenses grew in number, public skepticism increased and soon was reflected in juries that increasingly rejected it. Defense attorneys now seek more solid ground, such as the recent John Couey case. Accused of raping and murdering nine-year-old Jessica Lunsford and burying her alive, he pleaded "slow intellect," with no mention of his years of drug-addled behavior. These are only a few examples of how Axis II would expand the McNaughton rule (mental illness in which the individual does not know right from wrong) to the elastic diminished-capacity defense.

The Twinkie defense acquittal so enraged the American public that diminished capacity does not prevail very often, and this may have crippled legitimate defenses based on the McNaughton rule. But within psychology it fostered the runaway growth of victimology, which ignores the sequence that bad choices in life lead to bad consequences. One member of the American Psychiatric Association's committee that created the DSM III declared openly years ago that the most prevalent psychiatric condition is "criminosis," apparently no longer to be termed criminality. No one was bad or evil, not even the church deacon that eventually confessed to killing more than 50 women during his lifetime. Everyone suffers from a psychological cause, and no one is a jerk, a weirdo, a ne'er-do-well, or even (in spite of Len Blank's self-disclosure) obnoxious. Succinctly put, everyone is mentally ill, but no one is crazy.

Not only has psychotherapy suffered from growing distrust of psychologists in criminal cases, but confidence in the efficacy of psychotherapy has diminished. The treatment success rate of Axis II (personality or character disorders) is low at best. In the case of sociopaths the success rate is near zero, with religious conversion in prison having a more lasting effect. By lumping these conditions with neuroses, our overall success rate is lowered, making psychotherapy appear less efficacious than it would if we were to admit that we can effect only small changes in personality disorders.

## Expanding Real Diagnoses

### ATTENTION DEFICIT DISORDER

When the DSM IV expanded the definition of attention deficit/hyperactivity disorder (ADD/ADHD), it literally quadrupled the number of children who qualified to be so diagnosed. This inclusion of even the mildest cases also increased fourfold the number of children that would qualify for treatment reimbursement, an overnight economic boom. Further, it was applauded by schoolteachers struggling with overcrowded, unruly classes, and by parents who now could not be blamed for their child's inability to learn. It was also undoubtedly welcomed by the makers of Ritalin and Cylert, the two stimulant drugs most often prescribed for ADD/ADHD. Drug sales boomed, practitioners had millions of new cases, teachers could remand students to special classes, and parents were off the hook. Troublesome behavior was eliminated by rendering many children relatively inert. What a win-win situation!

This expansion of the diagnosis was based on a collection of symptoms and was more of a syndrome than a disorder. Furthermore, it ignored the requirement that preceded the diagnosis of minimal brain damage (MBD), which required the presence of certain neurological and other organic signs. Also ignored was a body of research evidence that suggested inadequate parenting could produce the same symptoms (hyperactivity, inability to learn, poor attention span, etc.) and other studies that demonstrated children do not learn when school discipline breaks down or when social promotion requiring little achievement prevails, rendering the students bored silly with a school setting that rewards one for mere attendance. The latter requirement is prompted less for concern for the learning of the students and more from the economic structure that funds schools on the basis of average daily attendance.

In 2001 my colleague and fellow past APA president Jack Wiggins and I mined the data warehouse of one of the largest (14.5 million covered lives in 39 states) psychology-driven behavioral care companies, retrospectively extracting data on all ADD cases of children and adolescents seen from July 1, 1988, to July 1, 1992. The total number of children and adolescents was 168,113 who, including sessions with the parents, received more than 2.5 million total treatment sessions. This is perhaps the largest cohort ever so intensively treated and studied.[5] It was noted that most of these children were from divorced or single-parent families, and the treatment plan that was developed included a male psychotherapist, along with the introduction of other male role models in the community (Sunday school teachers, Big Brothers, coaches, pediatricians, etc.). Participation of the parent in treatment was mandatory, and the average episode was 17.2 sessions—6.3 for the child/adolescent and 10.9 for the parent (in some cases the child/adolescent was being reared by the grandparent).

The results were startling. When referred for behavioral treatment, 61% of the males and 23% of the females were on medication, predominantly Ritalin and Cylert. By the conclusion of treatment only 11% of the boys and 2% of the girls remained on medication. It should be noted that the criterion for discontinuing medication was a stringent one: The complaining entity (teachers, juvenile authorities, parent) had to agree that the child/adolescent was doing so well that medication was unnecessary. It was believed by the psychotherapists that the outcome number of children/adolescents who remained on medication represented the set that never really needed to be medicated.

Just as very mild medical conditions do well and even better without medication, it may be that the mild cases usually swept up in the expanded net of ADD/ADHD might eventually find their place in life without being subjected to the zombie-like side effects of Ritalin or Cylert. It occurs to this writer, whose winter home is in Scottsdale, Arizona, a desert community where almost everyone has a backyard swimming pool, how many pool boys manifest (to this professional eye) mild ADD/ADHD that does not interfere with their work or their daily lives. And this does not even begin to address the number of spirited boys who are increasingly labeled because current society does not tolerate normal boyish behavior. I was such a boy and am convinced that were I to live in today's father-deprived culture, I would be among the first to be legally drugged as ADHD.

The growing intolerance of typical boyish behavior was underscored in March 2007 when two 13-year-old boys in Oregon, a state that seemingly strives to outdo political correctness, were charged with felony sexual abuse for slapping girls on the butt. It turned out they were engaging in behavior that was also common among 13-year-old boys of my era, and seemingly this group continues to be among the most annoying creatures on the planet. The game is one of immature aggression, not sex. The boy sneaks behind one of his good friends and hits him hard in the middle of the back with his fist. Since the boys do not want to hit girls (again, only friends) that hard, they substitute a slapping on the buttocks. Both male and female students involved in the Oregon incident testified this game may be annoying but not sexual. Nonetheless, the politically correct authorities in Oregon continued their pursuit of the boys on felony sexual abuse charges, accusations that are usually reserved for such prime offenses as rape.

## Depression, the Common Cold of Psychiatry

Rivaling the overdiagnosis of ADD/ADHD is the expansion of depression to encompass the usual vicissitudes of daily living, including the so-called Monday morning blues. In daily living depression is nearly ubiquitous and perhaps unavoidable, although people differ in degree of resiliency. It is not surprising that depression can accompany chronic physical illness, job loss, death of a loved one, divorce, and on and on. But when is depression of the magnitude that psychotherapeutic intervention is required? The DSM now includes a plethora of depressive diagnoses, all of which ostensibly require treatment (and reimbursement); not to leave any stoned unturned, there is even an official "depression not otherwise specified," or NOS.

One would believe that this enormous pool of potential patients would suffice, but there is considerable agitation to claim every normal mood alteration associated with daily living as a treatable depression. This is not only being pushed by many mental health professionals, but a number of celebrities, including Tipper Gore (wife of former vice president Al Gore). Certainly our health system all too frequently misses real depression that needs to be treated. However, to remand to treatment every mood swing would render depression as the common cold of psychiatry. Everyone with a common cold now demands antibiotics, even though such medication is not indicated for viral infections. Just as such misprescribed antibiotics are ultimately harmful because they increase the resistance of microbes and eventually lower the immune systems of humans, treating every mood swing as a disorder interferes with normal resilience to the vicissitudes of daily living. Perhaps the ultimate goal is that expressed by former APA president Max Siegel, who declared that everyone, including those who might not need it, could benefit from psychotherapy.[6]

## UNINTENDED CONSEQUENCES

If psychotherapists were expecting that these expansions in the DSM would provide a steady flow of referrals, they are understandably disappointed. Rather, these have benefited the dispensing of drugs. Ritalin and Cylert continue to be the treatments of choice for ADD/ADHD, and the overwhelming majority of depressions are prescribed the newer antidepressants. Where once primary care physicians were reluctant to prescribe psychotropic medication, the new drugs, particularly the SSRIs, are easy to dispense and manage, so 80 to 85% of all psychotropic medicines now are prescribed by primary care physicians, not psychiatrists. Physicians are thus increasing their billings and avoiding acrimony from patients who resent being sent to a "shrink."

## Known Treatments Applied to New Areas

The last 15 years have seen the application of effective interventions that have been refurbished for use in new settings. Some of these new applications have captured societal attention, especially where people have been convinced of their value. As research evidence develops, however, some of the most widely accepted new applications have been called into question.

### GRIEF COUNSELING

Developed over many years and especially applied to bereavement and other situations of severe loss, grief counseling has gone big time. There no longer can be a crisis, from Columbine to Katrina, in which grief counselors are not rushed in, usually on the heels of first responders. This is based on the notion that grief as a collective, if not universal, phenomenon can have lasting deleterious effects on the individual. The media coverage of volunteer mental health workers sweeping in to comfort all who may have been affected has impressed the American public, who became convinced this is a necessary and effective form of mass therapy. Recent research, however, casts doubt on this assertion. Grief counseling can be effective when the individual asks for it, but when foisted as a blanket intervention it can often retard the natural healing process, prolong the grief, or even increase it through mass suggestion and the encouragement of histrionics.[7]

## POST-TRAUMATIC STRESS SYNDROME

Post-traumatic stress syndrome (PTSD) was identified in the Vietnam War as a response to the trauma of combat. It replaced older labels of "battle fatigue" and "battle neuroses" used in World Wars I and II, respectively. The disorder has been refined during the Iraq War, and treatment for PTSD has become standard in all branches of the military, the Veterans Administration, and TriCare.

In the interim between the Vietnam and Iraq Wars, PTSD was extended from combat situations to include so-called traumatic experiences in civilian life. The intensity of combat is more or less ubiquitous, but in noncombat (civilian) situations the extent of the trauma can vary enormously. Consider the wide variability in seeing your mother killed before your eyes by an intruder versus almost being hit by a car while crossing a busy street, both actual claims filed in 2006. In 2007 accused terrorist Jose Padilla pleaded that he was unfit to stand trial because of three years of incarceration. Had the federal court not dismissed his claim, every convict would have been able to plead PTSD as the reason for any subsequent crime. The military is spearheading progress in the understanding of PTSD, especially in understanding it as the exhaustion of a person's normal resiliency by extreme stress, and is looking to identify and encourage patterns of resiliency.[8]

## Caricature Treatments

The preceding are examples of the overexpansion of real diagnoses, or the expansion of efficacious treatments to include questionable uses. In the quest to enlarge the shrinking pool of referrals, there is also the practice of creating treatments so outlandish that they appear to be caricatures. Some of these have been totally discredited, others are looked upon askance, while still others continue to have proponents in spite of their lack of efficaciousness. Here are a few.

### RECOVERED MEMORIES OF INCEST

As previously noted, not too long ago fathers were being incarcerated on flawed psychological testimony. This was before it was discovered that overzealous psychotherapists were implanting false memories of incest, an egregious incompetence for which the APA and other mental health professions have not apologized or condemned. Fortunately, the courts have put an end to this charlatanism.

### REBIRTHING (ATTACHMENT) THERAPY

The process of simulating the birth process for children who are unable to form attachments is psychotherapy at its most absurd. The danger of suffocation in tightly wrapping the child in blankets led to the death of a child in Denver, and the practice has been discontinued except for a few fringe therapists. However, attachment therapy in its far less extreme form continues to have its proponents, and the APA has sidestepped its responsibility to address the original and the modified approaches.

## EMDR Enters the Realm of PTSD

During and after World War II, it was believed that war neuroses were caused by unconscious guilt feelings for having lived when one's buddies died. This was based on now discredited psychoanalytic theory, and it was even applied by some therapists to the persistence of neurotic symptoms in holocaust survivors. The military made extensive use of sodium pentothal injections to recall and recreate the combat situations that launched the unconscious self-punishment, a treatment that was expanded to a variety of situations in civilian life. Nonmedical psychotherapists used hypnosis in an attempt to accomplish the same cathartic response, while most used directed psychotherapy to bring about the recall of the lost memory.

It has been some time since this psychoanalytic theory was discredited and more appropriate understanding of PTSD prevails. Pentothal therapy has all but disappeared, and cognitive interventions prevail in the treatment of extreme stress. This is why it is surprising to see the recent application of eye movement desensitization response (EMDR), itself a highly controversial approach, used as the vehicle for eliciting repressed guilt responses to combat. This is especially true of psychologists in New Mexico, who in 2007 received a grant to train other therapists in the method, which involves encouraging the patient to break through the repressed memory barrier while being put through eye movements.

## DISSOCIATIVE IDENTITY DISORDER

Originally called multiple personality disorder, dissociative identity disorder was discovered in the 19th century by the French neurologist Pierre Janet. It was rejected by Freud as a diagnosis since he preferred to see it as a symptom of hysteria rather than a separate diagnosis. The condition was rare until 1959 when Hollywood released the movie *The Three Faces of Eve.* Joanne Woodward, who starred as Eve, won the Academy Award and subsequently married superstar Paul Newman. Overnight she became an American icon, and the incidence of DID exploded, especially among two categories of patients: borderline personality disorders that can replicate any condition to draw attention, especially if the therapist encourages it, and patients being treated by psychotherapists who strongly believed in the existence of multiple personalities, in contrast to the majority of their colleagues. In the 1970s the TV movie *Sybil* further glamorized the condition. Patients now presenting with two or more personalities (called alters by proponents) were also emulating Sybil by reporting in large numbers that they had been subjected to child abuse, a complaint that was a rarity before the airing of Sybil.

Most authorities do not regard DID as a viable diagnosis.[9] As psychologists (and the public) became more aware of its controversial and problematic status, it lost favor and the number of its proponents declined. Of importance was the disclosure by therapists who treated the real Eve (Drs. Thigpen and Cleckley) that therapy for the condition steadily increased the number of alters to as many as 30 or 40, with one psychotherapist reporting that he had a patient who eventually manifested 300. Widely circulated among health insurance companies were instances of psychologists billing several times for the same patient, but separately under the name of each alter. A number of absurd stories were widely disseminated in the media, such as the woman who had consented to sex but afterwards charged the man with rape. She contended that during the sex act one of her personalities who had not consented awakened and was traumatized. In a number of celebrated cases, criminals pleaded that the crime was committed by one of their alters, not the person charged.

The experience of the last two decades continues to demonstrate that the proliferation of questionable diagnoses and the use of nonefficacious therapeutic interventions do not stem the steady decline of referrals, and may even raise skepticism about what we do.

## New Products That Consumers Want

The obvious solution, as it finally occurred to the Ford Motor Company, is the development of new products the public wants. With the exception of mental health, all of the health professions have been actively developing these new products, many winning such favor from consumers that they are willing to pay out of pocket when the service is not covered by health insurance.

## FROM COSMETIC MEDICINE TO MALL HEALTHCARE AND SURGICAL CENTERS

With so many physicians, surgeons, and dentists going into full- or part-time cosmetic practice, it is now estimated that as much as 25% of the nation's total doctor time is no longer available for traditional medicine and surgery. This has caused a new wave of physician shortages, especially in more upscale communities. Patients report it is difficult to find a dermatologist who has time for the removal of basal cell carcinomas or other skin treatments because botox has become so lucrative. Cosmetic dentistry has become the norm rather than the exception. Finding a podiatrist who will do biomechanics (such as orthotics) has become almost impossible. Statistics reveal that cosmetic surgery, botox injections, liposuction, and cosmetic dentistry are no longer limited to the wealthy. Patients in more modest circumstances are willing to forgo vacations, other niceties, and even necessities so the money can be spent on costly beauty-enhancing procedures.

Nurse practitioners have largely captured the emergent care market and are expanding into malls and large retailers such as Wal-Mart. The public likes these clinics because of their convenient location, the fact that they can walk in without an appointment, and because they receive more individual attention than busy physicians' practices permit.

Most routine surgeries not requiring overnight stays are performed outside the hospital in conveniently located surgical centers. These are more economical for the patient than hospital stays and less time consuming for busy surgeons. The centers have proven benefits and accordingly have burgeoned. Their continued safety record has permitted the inclusion of more kinds of procedures than originally conceived.[10]

Large corporations have determined that on-site medical clinics are cost effective. In 2006, one-third of the Fortune 1000 corporations already had such centers in operation, and it is anticipated that most of the remainder will follow. This is a new product that will benefit physicians, nurses, and other health personnel.

## Does Psychology Have New Products?

In all fairness, psychology does have new products. This does not refer to the growing number of boutique practices, important as they are, that focus on such subspecialties as women's issues, fertility treatment, and other esoteric areas, but to actual industries involving large numbers of psychologists requiring special training and even certification. There are two such outstanding new products:

*Forensic psychology*: Born in the latter part of the 20th century, forensic psychology grew in response to the judicial system's increased focus on diminished capacity and psychological causation and to psychiatry's having opted out of the field of psychotherapy, leaving a gap in testimony that was quickly filled by psychology. Using our measuring stick of society's willingness to pay out of pocket, forensic psychology more than qualifies as a success as lawyers and the courts eagerly engage and pay for these services.

*Neuropsychology*: Another product of the latter part of the 20th century, neuropsychology began with a few outstanding proponents and innovators such as Ralph Reitan. Despite its being relatively expensive, neuropsychological assessment has become standard in cases of brain injury, for both the health system and the courts.

The fields of forensic psychology and neuropsychology share four characteristics that qualify them as industries in which practitioners can thrive:

- These products are valued, and consumers have shown that they are willing to pay for them.
- They are not endangered by incursion from subdoctoral and less trained practitioners.
- They employ hundreds of practitioners who have been specially trained and qualified.
- They have freed themselves from the 50-minute hour that has clinical psychology in a rut.

Admittedly, pop psychology is booming, but we have not included it here as a product or industry. Dr. Laura has a large radio audience, and Dr. Phil has an even larger TV audience. He was even invited to the 2006 APA convention in New Orleans as a plenary speaker. Additionally, a number of psychologists have lesser local followings on radio and television, and there is even an APA Division of Media Psychology. Pop psychology is lucrative for the relatively few psychologists who possess theatrical skills. In short, pop psychology is more show business than it is science or practice.

## Dentistry, the Recovered Poster Profession

Dentistry offers a prime example of a recovered profession. When the dental profession fell into severe economic doldrums, the American Dental Association swung into action, teaching dentists how to move out of the slump. Now dentists are not only thriving, but many are making more money than physicians. How this was accomplished will be discussed in the following "Unblundering" section. The ADA is the poster organization for what the APA and other mental health associations should be doing in the face of psychotherapy's doldrums.

## Unblundering

The profession of dentistry was in dire straits after the United States decided several decades ago that cavities were a public health problem and fluoridated the water supply. This markedly reduced the number of cavities in the population, and curtailed the bread and butter of dentistry. The income of dentists dropped precipitously, many dentists retired early, and fewer young people entered dental school. However, a 2005 *Wall Street Journal* article tells a very interesting story about the dental field, particularly in relation to the income of psychologists during the last decade.[11]

While psychologists' incomes vary according to location, subdiscipline, experience, and education, look at the following facts:

- According to the *Monitor on Psychology*, in 2000 psychologists' annual incomes ranged from $60,000 to $80,000. The APA has not published any figures since then, perhaps because the annual incomes of psychologists have remained flat and have even declined when inflation is factored in.

- According to a national survey of occupations, the median income for psychologists in 2007 was $76,000 annually. In the seven-year period during which healthcare was booming, psychology remained financially static.[12]

### WHY DENTISTS ARE SMILING

Randy Bryson and his brother-in-law Larry Fazioli are both healthcare professionals in their 40s who practice in Pennsylvania. The similarity ends there. At Dr. Bryson's office near Philadelphia, a fountain burbles in the reception area and patients are offered cappuccino or paraffin-wax hand treatments while they wait. Dr. Bryson works four days a week, drives a Mercedes, and lives in a 4,000-square-foot house. Together, he and his wife, who works part-time in the same practice, take home more than $500,000 a year. At Dr. Fazioli's busy practice near Pittsburgh, patients crowd a utilitarian waiting room and his cramped office is piled high with records awaiting dictation. Dr. Fazioli says he works between 55 and 80 hours a week, and his annual income of less than $180,000 has been stagnant or down the past few years. He drives a Chevrolet. The key to their different lives: Dr. Bryson is a dentist, and Dr. Fazioli is a family practice physician.

Once the poor relations in the medical field, dentists in the past few years have started making more money than many types of physicians, including internal medicine doctors, pediatricians, psychiatrists, and those in family practice, according to survey data from the American Dental Association and American Medical Association. On average, general dentists in 2000, the most recent year for which comparative data are available, earned $166,460, compared with $164,100 for general internal medicine doctors, $145,700 for psychiatrists, $144,700 for family practice physicians, and $137,800 for pediatricians. All indications are that dentists have at least kept pace with physicians since then.

Those figures are a sharp contrast to 1988, when the average general dentist made $78,000, two-thirds the level of the average internal medicine doctor, and behind every other type of physician. From 1988 to 2000, dentists' incomes more than doubled, while the average physician's income grew 42% (slower than the rate of inflation).[13] Factor in hours worked—dentists tend to put in 40-hour weeks, the ADA says, while the AMA says physicians generally work 50 to 55 hours—and the discrepancy is even greater.

The article goes on to state that in competing for patient dollars, dentists have become more entrepreneurial. Many dental offices display ads for everything from $400 whitening treatments to $1,200-per-tooth veneer jobs. There are even $30,000-plus full "smile makeovers" offered by dentists specializing in high-end cosmetic procedures.

Psychologists currently seem to be making what dentists made in 1988. This despite the fact that it often takes about twice as long to become licensed as a psychologist as it does a dentist! And because of inflation, one would have had to make $130,000 in 2006 to have the equivalent buying power of $78,000 in 1988.

Each dentist did not change and develop product lines individually. Instead, they had tremendous leadership and help from their professional organization. First, the American Dental Association explicitly adopted the view that it was necessary to understand and disseminate business principles to its membership. Its website now contains business-oriented DVDs and pamphlets such as:

- *Develop a Dynamic Web Site for Your Practice.*
- *Smart Hiring: A Guide for the Dental Office.*
- *The Power of Internal Marketing: The Key to Dental Practice Success.* Take advantage of this powerful manual and gain the marketing savvy to effectively attract new patients, keep existing patients satisfied, and create positive word-of-mouth promotion that generates

patient referrals. Loaded with creative ideas and specific examples.

- *The Ultimate PR Kit for Dentists and Dental Practice.* Whether you are looking to develop promotional and PR campaigns for your own practice or to help shape public opinion about the profession of dentistry, discover the insights of this comprehensive kit and its "real" examples of press releases, speeches, and other promotional materials.

In addition, the American Dental Association helped to develop new product lines that consumers wanted. Instead of just extractions, fillings, and root canals (who really "wants" these?), they developed attractive products such as treatments for gum diseases, cleanings, sealants, whitening, veneers, bonding, and other cosmetic procedures. They also improved the experience of going to the dentist, particularly for children. There are now free high-quality video games, prizes for good oral health, and attractive, fun waiting rooms. In fact, my children's dentist rents out the Water Park in our town the day after it closes to the public, and all the children in the practice can play there for the day for free. In addition, any new referral results in an entry for a monthly drawing for an Ipod. Parents and children are happy with these innovations, and dentists' incomes have skyrocketed.

We believe that the American Psychological Association needs to take such entrepreneurial leadership. We have a lot of catching up to do!

## INTEGRATED HEALTHCARE

One major way in which we can catch up is to develop a product line in integrated healthcare. We serve a variety of consumers, but two of the most important are the patients sitting across from us in our offices and the insurers who pay our bills. We need to ask ourselves: What products do these customers want?

Patients certainly want highly effective psychotherapy for their mental health problems. We should ensure that we offer them a good value proposition—that is, for their considerable outlay of time, effort, and money (co-pays), we should make sure they overcome their problem in the most efficient manner. This forces us to pay attention to evidence-based treatment and quality improvement processes. It weans us as a profession away from our self-indulgent choosing of therapies based on their appeal to our emotional or intellectual needs. We believe that when prospective patients believe that therapy will work and be worthwhile, compared to simply waiting for possible spontaneous remission or trying a medication, business will improve. However, we have to face the fact that we clearly are not giving, and cannot currently honestly give, this value proposition to our potential consumers. This needs to be a strategic priority.

Additionally, we need to realize that behavioral health goes beyond the usual mental disorders in our realm of expertise. There is a huge and generally untapped demand for these services. By behavioral health we mean problems such as:

- Obesity (both childhood and adult)

- Smoking
- Lack of routine exercise
- Stress
- Lack of treatment compliance (especially related to chronic diseases such as diabetes)
- Relationship problems (e.g., poor social support)

These behavioral health problems contribute to poorer quality of life, medical afflictions, and medical expenditures. The obesity industry (from books to clinics to bariatric surgery) is tremendous. So is the exercise industry (from health clubs to trainers to equipment). However, psychologists—with their skills related to individual assessment, motivational interviewing, relapse prevention, and process and outcome evaluation—play a very small role in these multi-billion-dollar industries. Patients want effective, high-value products, and they are willing to spend what is necessary for products that work. These are tough problems, but we believe psychologists have many of the skills needed to make progress on them. If they combine their skills with business acumen (product development, marketing, quality improvement, financial analysis), psychologists could have a large role in the future of the behavioral health industries.

It is estimated that chronic diseases such as diabetes, asthma, COPD, arthritis and other pain, heart disease, and Alzheimer's disease account for nearly 40% of total healthcare expenditures. This represents more than $600 billion of total expenditures. Yet all agree that the contemporary healthcare system is structured to take care of acute medical problems, not chronic conditions. There is a huge opportunity here.

Cummings, nearly two decades ago, showed in a randomly controlled trial how identifying high medical utilizers with chronic conditions and placing them in group psychotherapy resulted in a 40% decrease in medical utilization.[14] Patients were given education on the self-management of their diseases, help with treatment compliance, social support, stress management, help with any depressive symptoms, relapse prevention, and impetus to start a medically appropriate exercise program. These programs were developed by psychologists, who also mainly ran these groups.

## INSURERS, EMPLOYERS, AND MANAGED CARE

Savings of 40% on medical costs are music to the ears of those involved with the financial side of healthcare: government, employers who ultimately pay the bills, insurers, and managed care, who are the fiscal intermediaries. Psychologists too often dismiss their financial interests as greed, but think again. As do all individuals, psychologists have problems when bills increase and always want better value for their money. Everyone looks for value for their dollar, and may shift buying habits to accomplish this. Having psychologists become involved with behavioral problems in a way that can ultimately decrease medical costs is exactly the kind of product insurers and managed care want.

Consumers also like these kinds of interventions. In recent studies conducted by Cummings and O'Donohue, consumer satisfaction was in the range of 4.6–4.9 on a 5.0 scale. Part of the reason why consumers prefer these services is that they are demand side oriented instead of supply side. Traditional managed care tried to curtail the *supply* of healthcare services by limiting them, resulting in financial savings but angering the public. Integrated care seeks to decrease the *demand* by providing services that help patients become healthier and more effectively self-manage their medical problems.

However, payers realize that accomplishing this takes a special kind of psychologist, and most psychotherapists are trained to meet behavioral health demands. Traditional core skills are still necessary to address the usual mental health problems; however, psychologists need skills beyond their traditional core competencies. First, attending to behavioral health demands necessitates that psychologists leave their private practice offices to go where the "action" is, such as medical clinics, emergency rooms, and, particularly, primary care settings. Among the new skills needed by behavioral health psychologists are:

1. Working as part of a medical team
2. Consultation liaison skills with the physician leading the team
3. Brief but valid assessments resulting in action plans
4. Medical literacy (Type II diabetes is *not* a disease that is just twice as bad as Type I diabetes)
5. Group intervention skills

6. Chronic disease management skills (education, self-management)

7. Treatment compliance skills

8. Lifestyle change skills

9. Motivational interviewing

10. Brief-focused medically relevant treatment skills

These are all valuable skills that could result in a win-win-win situation for consumers, payers, and psychologists.

Unlike the assistance and leadership the ADA provided to dentists, the APA is doing little to help actualize the potential for psychology in the behavioral health field. Psychologists should expect, and have a right to demand, crucial guidance from our leaders, our professional organizations. But even with such guidance, we must as a group become committed to the need to change with the times to ensure the future of our stagnating profession.

## Endnotes

1. Dr. Leonard Blank in 2005 published his autobiography (*Chinese Paper*, New York: Author), which is fascinating inasmuch as his brilliant career intertwined with some of the most illustrious psychologists of the 20th century.

2. The reference for the current DSM IV is American Psychiatric Association, *Diagnostic and Statistical Manual IV*, Washington, DC.

3. For the explosive growth of the *Diagnostic and Statistical Manual*, see W. C. Follette & A. C. Houts (1996), "Models of Scientific Progress and the Role of Theory in Taxonomy Development: A Case Study of the DSM," *Journal of Consulting and Clinical Psychology, 64*, 1120–1132. Dorothy Cantor (1997) announced

the staggering growth in mental health professionals in her article "A Bill of Rights for Patients: 625,000 Practitioners Can't Be Wrong," *Independent Practitioner, 17*, 5–7. For the relation between number of practitioners and growth of diagnostic labels, see also Carol Austad (2008), *Psychotherapy and Counseling: Theory, Practice and Research.* New York: McGraw-Hill.

4. The nonpsychologist reader may be interested in the new additions. Axis II pertains to personality disorders as well as developmental disorders. Axis III refers to any medical comorbidities that accompany the psychiatric diagnosis. Axis IV pertains to psychosocial stressors (e.g., divorce, loss of job, unruly children). Finally, Axis V is the Global Assessment of Functioning (GAF) on a 0 to 100 scale. A score below 40 might indicate the need for hospitalization, a score of 40 to 85 usually indicates a need for psychotherapy, and a score above 85 may not need treatment at all.

5. The Cummings and Wiggins study of ADD/ADHD is as follows: N. A. Cummings & J. G. Wiggins (2001), "A Collaborative Primary Care/Behavioral Health Model for the Use of Psychotropic Medication With Children and Adolescents," *Issues in Interdisciplinary Care, 3*, 121–128. Current society's lack of tolerance for normal but robust boyish behavior is addressed by C. F. Sommers (2000), *The War Against Boys*, New York: Simon and Schuster. See also W. Pollock (2000), *Real Boys' Voices*, New York: Random House.

6. The late Max Siegel served as APA president in 1983. In commenting on a New York serial killer, Son of Sam, who was dominating press coverage at the time, Dr. Siegel gratuitously asserted that everyone could profit from psychotherapy, whether they needed it or not. This remark, which Siegel subsequently repeated in public several times, received considerable attention in the news media, both pro and con.

7. Reports of the negative effects of crisis counseling and the mass application of PTSD to civilian situations are increasing. See R. McNally (2003), as extensively quoted in S. Begley, "Is Trauma Debriefing Worse Than Letting Victims Heal Naturally?" *Wall Street Journal*, September 12, p. B1. See also J. Lebow (2003),

"War of the Worlds: Researchers and Practitioners Collide on EMDR and CISD," *Psychotherapy Networker*, September/October, pp. 79–83.

8. Information on the advances in understanding PTSD is available in B. P. Dohrenwend, J. B. Blake, N. A. Turse, B. G. Adams, K. C. Koenan, & R. Marshall (2006), "The Psychological Risks of Vietnam for U.S. Veterans: A Revisit With New Data and Methods," *Science, 313*, August 18.

9. Discussion of the controversy over dissociative identity disorder can be found in S. O. Lilienfeld & S. J. Lynn (2002), "Dissociative Identity Disorder: Multiple Personalities, Multiple Controversies" (pp. 109–142), in S. O. Lilienfeld, S. J. Lynn, & J. M. Lohr (Eds.), *Science and Pseudoscience in Clinical Psychology*, New York: Guilford. Also A. M. Ludwig, J. M. Brandsma, C. B. Wilbur, F. Bendefeldt, & D. H. Jameson (1972), "The Objective Study of Multiple Personality; Or, Are Four Heads Better Than One?" *Archives of General Psychiatry, 26*, 298–310. See also S. S. Marmer (1998), "Should Dissociative Identity Disorder Be Considered a Bona Fide Diagnosis?" *Clinical Psychiatry News*, December. The original report of Eve on which the movie was based is still available: C. H. Thigpen & H. M. Cleckley (1957), *The Three Faces of Eve*, New York: McGraw-Hill.

10. For an overview of the new walk-in clinics and surgical centers, see L. Landro (2006), "The Informed Patient," *Wall Street Journal*, July 26, p. D1.

11. For more information on the *Wall Street Journal* article on the dramatic rise in dentists' incomes, see http://wsjclassroomedition.com/archive/05apr/care_dentist.html and read the comparison between dentists and physicians in incomes and working conditions.

12. For the APA article published in the *Monitor on Psychology* regarding psychologists' incomes in 2000, see http://www.apa.org?monitor/mar00/facts.html. The national survey of 2007 psychologists' salaries is found in http://swz.salary.com/salarywizard/layouthhtlms/swazl_compresult_national_HC07000044.html.

13. See http://www.westegg.com/inflation/infl.cgi for an inflation calculator.

14. The seven-year prospective and randomized study conducted by Cummings and his colleagues as referred to in the "Unblundering" section is extensively discussed in N. A. Cummings, J. L. Cummings, & J. N. Johnson (Eds.) (1997), *Behavioral Health in Primary Care: A Guide for Clinical Integration*, Madison, CT: Psychosocial Press (International Universities Press). The quality/satisfaction studies of Cummings and O'Donohue are reported in N. A. Cummings, W. T. O'Donohue, & K. E. Ferguson (Eds.) (2003), *Behavioral Health as Primary Care: Beyond Efficacy to Effectiveness* (Vol. 6), Cummings Foundation for Behavioral Health: Healthcare Utilization and Cost Series, Reno, NV: Context Press.

# 10 Diversity Fiddles While
# Practice Burns

Change is the law of life. And those who look only to the past and
present are certain to miss the future.[1]

—**John F. Kennedy, 35th president of the United States**

Psychology is to be lauded for having become the exemplar in
diversity among all the health professions. This did not happen
automatically; it required a great deal of commitment, resources,
persistence, and decades of dedication on the part of the APA
and all of psychology. The fact is that the momentum began
to show promise only three decades ago. As APA president, I
appointed in 1979 the APA's first Committee on Ethnic Minority Affairs, as well as the first Task Force on Lesbian and Gay
Issues. Seared into my memory is Dr. Ray Martinez's speech at
the Vail conference in the early 1970s.[2] He excoriated psychology for the paltry number of Latino psychologists, admonishing,
"You have to do better." I took his message seriously, and when
I was president of the four campuses of the California School
of Professional Psychology (CSPP) we graduated more Latino

doctorates in the next four years than had been minted previously by all the APA-approved doctoral clinical programs combined. CSPP had already become the gold standard in training African American psychologists, and we hastened to attain the same accomplishment with Latinos, and shortly thereafter with openly gay graduate school applicants.

We should all be proud of psychology's leadership in diversity, even though we all agree that even more can be done. However, I am saddened by our tendency to showcase our diversity in order to divert attention from our lagging behind in so many critical areas. Our success in one area has become a substitute for failure in another.

## Psychology Is Not as Diverse as It Purports to Be

Although psychology celebrates diversity, which has become one of its core values, Richard Redding[3] has pointed out that the profession lacks sociopolitical diversity. Putting partisanship aside, this has resulted in a culture in which needed debate may not occur, even though certain areas may be opposed to existing beliefs. Differing points of view are never investigated or researched, and there is insidious restriction on what may be said or asked. While encouraging sensitivity to cultural biases, we have failed to recognize our own one-sidedness. One is reminded of the conventional wisdom at the time of the maiden voyage of the *Titanic*—that it was unsinkable. A ship's captain was chosen who believed the steamship company's slogan, and he in turn insisted on such confidence in his officers. One wonders whether this single mindedness translated on the bridge into reduced vigilance to the dangers of icebergs, contributing to one of the world's greatest sea disasters.

The inevitable outcome of such lack of sociopolitical diversity is political correctness, one-sidedness that effectively discourages any contrarian thinking. The characteristics of political correctness have been discussed, but it is important to examine how PC has impacted on diversity in psychology.

## Victimology Cripples Critical Examination

James D. Watson,[4] a Nobel Prize winner for his scientific work with DNA, cautions: "If you can't be criticized, that's very dangerous. You lose the concept of a free society." He was responding to the notion that certain groups are to be protected from criticism and thus may be deprived of critical self-examination. As might be expected, Professor Watson has garnered considerable criticism of his own for his boldness.

Psychology has rendered certain oppressed groups to be sacrosanct and above criticism. To do otherwise is called racism, homophobia, insensitivity, lack of compassion, bias, and oppression. Such restrictions may have the obverse effect, harming rather than helping these groups. This has been particularly true with psychology's concept of victimology, a view that certain groups have suffered so much that they cannot be held accountable for their actions should these have negative consequences.

Oftentimes we are responding to what happened in history, even though we are getting farther and farther away from that history. The Civil Rights march in Selma, Alabama, took place on March 7, 1965. It spawned a number of civil rights leaders who deserve their status as heroes but, like the leadership in psychology, are of the boomer generation that remains mired in the past. Suddenly a fresh new generation of outspoken leaders is emerging, rejecting psychology's curse of victimology and calling for the so-called victims to shake off that crippling self-image and take positive charge of their futures and their destinies. These leaders are indigenous, and it is time for psychology to heed their message and abandon the psychology of victimhood.

Historically, the late Daniel Patrick Moynihan (D-NY), one of the most intelligent senators ever to have served our nation, warned during President Johnson's administration that the misguided compassion that led to the enactment of the new welfare system would destroy the fabric of the black family. Finally repealed under another Democratic president, William Clinton, this prediction had become all too painfully true. We have seen the rise of a new African American leadership that rejects victimhood (and its psychological counterpart victimology) and is calling for the community to effectively address its ills. Speaking in Selma, Alabama, at the 42nd anniversary of the famous march, Barack Obama called himself the educated offspring of that movement, expressed gratitude for the hard-fought educational opportunities that he inherited, and challenged his black audience to renew the educational values it had somehow come to reject.[5]

Bill Cosby is remarkably candid, and his invitation to address the American Psychological Association at its New Orleans convention in 2006 may have signaled that the APA's romance with victimology is on the wane. He is blunt when talking about the poor speech, fatherless children of teenage girls, teenage gang clothing among black youth, and the general ignorance typical of school dropouts. Though first igniting a firestorm, he is now receiving wide attention in the black community, which is alarmed by the 50% school dropout rate of black youth, its escalating rate of violence, and the 75% birthrate among young, single mothers who are thus condemned to a life of poverty. He admonishes black youth that fatherhood does not end with insemination, and proffers a four-point life course to end poverty: (1) finish school, (2) get a job, any job, (3) get married and do not have kids until you are 21 and married, and (4) stay married. Cosby also has just written a book, *Come on, People*, with Harvard psychiatrist Alvin Poussaint (also an African American), which speaks to the issues confronting black youth.[6]

Bill Cosby makes much of the peculiar names black mothers dream up for their children, stating that they are branding them for poverty. This is underscored by the two economists Levitt and Dubner in their best-selling book *Freakonomics*.[7] They point out the paradox of the civil rights movement fighting for years to remove race from job applications, only to have the black community now naming their children in such a way that they are immediately identified as black. Certainly there have been blacks with these names who rose above the bias they could have evoked; Oprah Winfrey and Condoleezza Rice are two notable examples. But for the overwhelming majority of black applicants this is a severe handicap when filling out an employment application in situations where there may be subtle hiring bias.

U.S. Housing and Urban Development secretary Alphonso Jackson is even more candid.[8] A participant of the Selma march where, as he crossed the Edmund Pettus Bridge, the state troopers unleashed tear gas and dogs on the marchers, he nonetheless criticizes the traditional African American leadership as having "created an industry. If we don't become victims they have no income. They have no podium" from which to speak. He is not shy about naming such national figures as Julian Bond, Rev. Jesse Jackson, and Rev. Al Sharpton.

In his 2007 book *Enough*, TV commentator Juan Williams[9] excoriates black leadership and decries a self-defeating black culture of victimhood that says doing well in school is a cop-out. Bill Cosby is seen as a prophet whose boldness in clashing with those who have made an industry out of African American poverty is beginning to have an impact. He points out that blacks who come to America from Africa and the Caribbean are more successful than blacks born in the United States. Agreeing with Jackson, Williams says, "All you have to do is look at Miami's Little Haiti. Average income of a Haitian in Miami is the same as his white counterpart. They work very hard, but they have not been conditioned that the government owes them something." Not only does he remind us that the ancestors of these Haitians were also slaves, he goes on to state that Africans from such countries as Ghana, Nigeria, Gabon, and Senegal come to the United States with "one attitude; that they're going to get an education and make as much money as they can."

Psychology, through well-intentioned victimology, has undoubtedly fueled this attitude of victimhood, giving it ostensible scientific/professional credibility. Psychology's own political correctness prevented it from critically examining the destructive elements of victimhood, even to curtailing research on resiliency and the striving for success that was so characteristic of the early civil rights movement. Psychological credence fostered the idea that blacks were owed something because of slavery: Since their ancestors experienced the brutality of that era, their offspring should not have to struggle. Thus, psychotherapy failed the very people whom we intended to help.

## Runaway Multiculturalism Is Not Diversity

The foregoing is not the diversity for which psychology should be lauded. Rather, it is more an example of runaway multiculturalism that strives not to be all-inclusive, but rather to perpetuate differences that create a kind of tribalism. It fosters a form of separateness that in some obscure manner has come to be regarded as part of inclusiveness, a contradiction that is bound to result in failure.

I was born in the first quarter of the 20th century of Greek immigrant parents in the era of the "melting pot." Greeks, Irish, Italians, Jews, and Poles all tended to cluster in neighborhoods, but we all attended the same schools. My parents never felt their cultural heritage was in any way threatened; they had the freedom and encouragement to celebrate all of the Greek festivals and religious holidays. My friends celebrated with me, and I took part in their ethnic festivals. I remember as a child how much I loved joining my friends as we all ate delicious steaks at the annual Portuguese picnic and barbeque, did Celtic dancing on St. Patrick's Day, stuffed ourselves with red-hot chili on Cinco de Mayo, were introduced to blintzes and other delicacies at Jewish feasts (I will not mention inedible matzos), savored baklava at my own Greek festivals, and participated in parades and ate lotsa pasta on Columbus Day. I was fortunate to have grown up in California where—before southerners migrated after the Dust Bowl, bringing their prejudices with them—black and white kids went to classes together and played together after school. "Integration" was so much a part of our lives that even sociologist Carey McWilliams commented on the lack of color line in his widely read book, *California, the Notable Exception.*

Naomi, my first date when I was in the seventh grade, was black, and no one, including my parents or my friends, thought anything of it. It was a wonderful, multicultural time in which to grow up. We respected each other's diversity, while at the same time we all strove to become part of the American culture and the American dream. Oh, yes, we would tease each other about one another's ethnicity, but it was jocular. On the rare occasions when it went too far it was met by a swift fist to the jaw of the offender, all with the approval of bystanders who served unofficially as our juvenile league of nations. No one ever had to go to the teacher, the authorities, or their parents; we settled our own differences in a remarkable fashion. As in time immemorial, there were boys who were bullies and there were mean girls, but these were ethnically nonspecific and amazingly cross-cultural.

## Runaway Multiculturalism Fosters Separateness and Tribalism

What constitutes the difference between this past multicultural era and today's runaway multiculturalism? It can be stated in one word: assimilation, once known as the melting pot. Everyone had a common goal, the striving to become one thing: an American. While appreciating our own and each other's cultural heritage, we were all new Americans. In fact, look around you: The Irish have made St. Patrick's Day a celebration in which all of us wish we were Irish. Hundreds of thousands enjoy Greek dancing and wolfing down spanakopita and tyropita while sipping terrible bitter coffee at the Greek festivals. Nearly every police and firefighter funeral is attended by many dignitaries of all races and ethnicities and is graced by an honor corps of Scottish bagpipes and kilts.

Columbus Day was a time everyone wished to be Italian, but that holiday is now regarded as politically incorrect—ostensibly because if it were not for Columbus, Native Americans would still own the New World. This smacks of pitting one tribe (Italian Americans) against another tribe (Native Americans) 500 years after the fact. Why, then, should not Greeks hate the Italians for the Roman invasion 2,000 years ago, or the Iranians for the Persian invasion of Greece 2,500 years ago? In fact, Iran's Ahmadinejad, upon the release of the movie *300*, in which that number of Greek soldiers held off the large Persian army thousands of years ago, condemned the movie as prejudice toward Iran, a Farsi culture that traces its heritage to Ancient Persia. Where does this nonsense stop? Are we fostering tribalism rather than a multicultural but unified society by pitting one group against the other?

In addressing his fellow psychologists, Martinez called attention to the inherent dangers in well-intentioned, but runaway, multiculturalism. He states, "The stereotypic ethnic vacuum refers to the implication that, by identifying a cultural reason for the existence of a behavior, the behavior is understood as being inherent to the culture and therefore dismissed or minimized. This sometimes prevents intervention or preempts change." Thus, sexism and the oppression of women are dismissed or glossed over in cultures in which women have little or no rights, clitoral circumcision is practiced on little girls, a husband has the right to murder a disobedient wife, and if a woman arouses a man by appearing in public without her headdress, he has the right to rape her. The same psychologists who are so adamant in the defense of women turn their eyes away from egregious behavior by excusing it as cultural.

The epitome of runaway multiculturalism is found in psychology's approval of Muslim separateness, a refusal to assimilate that is stronger in Europe than in the United States. This separateness is so fierce that it meets all the definitions of aggressive tribalism, spawning attitudes and behaviors that include waiting to be offended, followed by a lashing out in which Western freedom and tolerance are used aggressively against the so-called offender. Beheadings of Westerners are cheered, while cartoons of Mohammed provoke riots. Denmark, one of the most liberal nations on earth, has had enough, and one wishing to migrate there must first pass a cultural acceptance test. Interestingly, in this decision there is a clash between two politically correct dictums: freedom not to assimilate versus the hostile rejection of gay and lesbian rights. The latter is an important cultural right in Denmark and takes precedence over the right to hate or disapprove of another's rights. The conclusion in Denmark, and one beginning to fester in other countries, is: If you cannot accept our culture, stay home.

### You Have to Be One to Treat One

Not too long ago psychotherapy was lily white and there were no African American, Latino, Asian, and openly gay therapists.

Doubtlessly many cultural misunderstandings occurred, and the current drive for cultural understanding and sensitivity is an important component of today's psychotherapy training. Unfortunately, it has gone too far, with standards to qualify as culturally sensitive escalating exponentially. The indigenous proponents of cultural diversity stand to gain as they become the trainers in an endless cycle of ever-increasing requirements. To be on the safe side, it is better to be one if you are going to treat one. This, too, increases the coffers of the proponents.

Overreaching in this regard can also inadvertently create bias in reverse. Consider the remarks of two patients who quit with their original therapists because the interventions were hampering rather than helping. An 18-year-old black youth who had dropped out of high school and was having trouble getting a job complained to his new psychologist about his previous therapist, "The brother kept saying it was racism that was keeping me down." As a result of his new therapy he went back and finished high school, and was employed soon after his graduation. A woman in her early 20s abandoned her openly lesbian therapist, saying, "I'm having enough trouble with men without the doctor telling me men are no damn good."

What did psychotherapists do during the 50 years preceding cultural competence? They were trained to be alert and sensitive to where the patient was, culturally as well as psychologically. The "third ear" was tuned to the patient in all his or her aspects. If you did not understand some cultural behavior, attitude, or custom, you simply asked. Whether it was psychologically or culturally, you never clashed with where the patient was. All of the cues and clues came from the patient; if you did not comprehend any, the patient was more than willing to explain to a therapist in whom a neutral attitude was discerned. Not all therapists were able to do this, of course, and this is why cultural competency is imperative. But if it goes too far, it is a hindrance to psychotherapy, as in accepting a patient's victimhood at face value and depriving him or her of the resiliency to overcome.

During the 1960s and 1970s, San Francisco was rapidly becoming a gay mecca as thousands of lesbians and gay men moved there from all parts of America. There were no openly gay therapists, and I became one of the therapists of choice by word of mouth because my fairness, acceptance, and competence were legendary in the community. When it became possible, I hired the first openly gay therapists, which encouraged other psychologists to come out of the closet.

San Francisco was also known for its ethnic diversity. I recall a scheduled visit to a Filipino home to assess an elderly woman's mental status. I was surprised that the event called for the presence of the entire extended family, numbering over two dozen people. I was expected to conduct my evaluation before this audience, which I did, adjusting my procedures to inform them of what I was doing in each step of the process. I also learned that the family had prepared an elaborate lunch in appreciation, and quickly realizing that to refuse would be a severe insult, I called my office and cancelled the next three hours of appointments. Several referrals from the Filipino community came in rapid succession shortly thereafter, even though I remained a neophyte about the culture of the Philippines.

Cultural competency constitutes an important contribution to psychotherapy, but it can in itself be overly restrictive and can even become a fetish. No amount of training can create sensitivity in an insensitive trainee, and the importance of fine-tuning one's neutral third ear and letting the patient educate us is still irreplaceable.

## What of Cultural Competency Without a Profession?

Our stellar success in diversity and cultural competency has allowed psychology to rest on its laurels and be distracted from the realization that our practice ship is listing and may even be sinking. It goes even farther, since criticizing any failings of diversity, cultural competency, or multiculturalism has become taboo. Most psychologists tread as if in the presence of the Holy Grail, reminding us of the dangers of making anything sacrosanct and above criticism. Again, we are reminded of the admonition by Professor Watson that to be above criticism is to be denied the ability to change constructively, which will eventually lead to obsolescence and even corruption.

If one peruses a broad swath of APA journals, including the *Monitor on Psychology*, there is a surprisingly large number of articles in which diversity is tangential or even irrelevant, yet still is included. Recently I was invited to write an article for one of the leading APA practice journals on where reimbursement mechanisms and patterns for psychotherapy were going. This, I was told, would be of prime interest since the APA wished to provide a heads-up for practitioners. I worked very hard on the article, predicting that pay for performance (abbreviated P4P) was to be the future system for reimbursing psychological services. It was submitted in a timely fashion so colleagues in practice would be forewarned. One of three reviewers lauded the article, calling it important enough to be published immediately so that colleagues could plan effectively. The other two reviewers scolded the article for not solving the problem of how third-party payers would pay for diversity.

Insurance companies, HMOs, and managed behavioral health organizations have no intention in the near or even distant future to address the topic of pay for diversity. However, the industry does not seem to regard it as an issue, and therefore has no plans to resolve it. My attempts to apprise the editor of this were of no avail. Finally, a compromise was attained: I indicated that the APA would have to set aside its hostility toward the industry and enter into a period of constructive engagement to address and resolve this and other problems. The editor accepted this, but during the two and a half years of delay in publication there emerged almost 100 pay-for-performance initiatives in the private sector and several in Medicare and Medicaid. The ability of the article to serve as a heads-up for those struggling to make a living in psychological practice had long passed. The fetish that commands the address of diversity, no matter how tangential or irrelevant, once again trumped the importance of practice issues.

The sad fact is that our associations do not know how to pull practice out of the doldrums. As previously stated, parity legislation has not helped, the unbridled proliferation of specialty standards has not convinced the public that we do something master's-level therapists are unable to do, and our continued inability to define a core curriculum perpetuates the stagnation. Practice reimbursement fees have remained static, and some have even declined while overhead costs steadily increase. HIPPA requirements, increased paperwork, and declining referrals resulting in suppressed income have created a sense of futility. Practitioners have been numbed to the importance of association leadership to their practices, and contributions to practice initiatives have diminished. Our APA needs an accomplishment that can be touted, and diversity and multiculturalism as a stellar success (if one overlooks the limitations) provide a ready and visible banner.

## A Mask for Failure

Psychology could be extremely proud of its track record in diversity were it not for the fact that (1) it has become a fetish, with diversity for diversity's sake, and (2) it serves as a mask for failure in effectively responding to the myriad challenges confronting practice. As it has with political correctness, psychology is in danger of becoming healthcare's most diverse and culturally sensitive, but extinct, profession. Mental health professionals' efforts are to be commended, but there must be the freedom to critique the excesses. Currently, to question whether multiculturalism has gone too far and is doing more harm than good is to invoke accusations of racism, homophobia, insensitivity, and lack of compassion. On this subject the status quo does not tolerate even the slightest degree of questioning, and since no one wants to be called a bigot, it will take the kind of boldness within psychology that is being demonstrated by the new breed of African American leadership. To eschew the old guard, younger psychologists must challenge and eventually replace the current entrenched power elite in our associations. Do such contrarians exist, or have we picked successors that are mesmerized by platitudes as a substitute for action? As one philosopher (A. J. P. Taylor)[10] put it more than half a century ago, "There is nothing more agreeable than to make peace with the establishment—and nothing more corrupting."

## Unblundering

Yes, diversity is one of psychology's achievements. But it also has become a banner behind which to hide many of our failings, especially our inability to define a firm economic base for our profession or to address the many problems confronting society that should be the province of a psychology unhampered by political correctness.

## DIVERSITY SHOULD NOT BE DOGMA: A PROPOSAL TO ARTICULATE THE WARRANT FOR, AND TO EVALUATE, DIVERSITY AND DIVERSITY PROGRAMS

Philosophers have pointed out, and psychotherapists can often see in their patients, that values at times compete against one another. It can be challenging to decide which value is super-ordinate. If someone has a total of $1,000 to give to a charity, the diverse values represented by the different charities compete against one another for the dollar. All might be desirable, but which is the best? Does one help hungry children in Africa or in India? Does one contribute to malaria eradication and treatment in Africa, or breast cancer research? Are reading programs in the United States more important? One has to determine a hierarchy of values to make these decisions. Even two "good" values can clash with each other.

It appears that organized psychology has placed a very high value on diversity of outcomes along certain ethnic and sexual dimensions over other values, for example, procedural justice in hiring and admission decisions, or in valuing merit. We think this is wrong and does not serve our patients or the public well.

Discrimination certainly exists and psychologists should oppose this, study it, and develop programs to combat it. However, from the proposition that discrimination exists, it does not follow that diversity programs should be rigorously instituted. There are many missing propositions needed to complete this argument. Most of the existing propositions are dubious or at least in need of further justification, as are the following:

- There are no viable alternatives to combat discrimination. Diversity programs are the only, or at least the most effective, way of combating discrimination and problems in opportunity for certain groups.

- Diversity programs have been shown by the scientific standards of the field to actually achieve the beneficial effects that they are purported to deliver by their proponents.

- Diversity programs do not have any known negative effects, including negative effects on those hired through them.

- Diversity programs are just.

- Diversity programs are not inconsistent with other important values. If they are, there is a good way to mediate this value conflict.

- Diversity programs are legal.

- All the correct groups are appropriately represented in the diversity program.

Many of these propositions just lead to other questions. For example, one might ask: How does it feel and what are other psychological consequences of being hired as a token representative of some group versus being hired entirely on merit? How do others react to such hires? Should Catholics, Jews, Mormons, Persians, Arabs, or dwarfs be formally included among the groups represented?

There was a cartoon in a recent issue of the *Wall Street Journal* illustrating that diversity is not an unmitigated good. The cartoon shows two Native Americans in traditional dress looking at the arrival of what obviously are the first Europeans on their sailing ships. One Native American says to the other, "Not to worry. Diversity can only enrich our culture."

We need to recognize as a field that diversity and its cognates have been neither argued nor analyzed in any deep, systematic fashion. In addition, they seem to escape the empirical scrutiny to which we generally hold "solutions" to problems. Diversity should be held to a higher standard. We should ask proponents of diversity to make the conceptual and empirical case instead of treating diversity and diversity programs as some sort of self-evident good. Diversity does not deserve to be exempt from the normal scrutiny that any ameliorative proposals have been subject to in our profession. The fact is that to date diversity is treated as dogma and not as an exemplar of rational belief and practice. We all know, and the case of Larry Summers is an example, that speaking or behaving in a manner that others deem inconsistent with dogma is a dangerous practice that can lead to various forms of punishment. This dogmatic quality associated with diversity prohibits necessary discussion. Our clients would be better served with open debate, analysis, criticism, and evaluation.

## A PROPOSAL TO STOP THE NONSENSE OF THE DIVERSITY "IN-GROUPS"

There has been a shifting rationale for groups that have been included in the ameliorating efforts of diversity programs. In the 1960s the programs in President Johnson's Great Society initially focused on the poor. Then social welfare programs tended to focus on African Americans, particularly because they were over-represented in the poor and because of their noble struggle for civil rights in the later 1960s. Programs also started to focus on other ethnic groups (e.g., Hispanics, Asians, Native Americans). Soon programs included smaller groups (e.g., Aleutian Island-ers). Finally, gays and lesbians were included. Most recently, this morphed into GLB (gays, lesbians, and bisexuals), and even to GLBT (gays, lesbians, bisexuals, and transsexuals). What is next, GLBTFF (gays, lesbians, bisexuals, transsexuals, and foot fetishists)? The diversity movement must constantly worry about whom it is leaving out.

For example, there has only been one African American APA president (Kenneth B. Clark, over 35 years ago) and one Asian American APA president (Richard Suinn, about 7 years ago). No Hispanic, Aleutian Islander, or Pacific Islander has ever been president of a mental health association. There has never been a transsexual or openly gay psychologist in that office. Should psy-chology show its commitment to diversity and racial and sexual quotas by asking no Caucasians (especially heterosexual ones) to run for presidency in any of its associations until these historical imbalances have been corrected? Or should it just sidestep its internal lack of diversity and show its commitment by altering the admissions and jobs offered to 20-year-olds in the job market totally outside of psychology?

The historical progression of diversity encompassing more and more groups (and even shifting dimensions, from poverty to race to sexual orientation) is never given any intellectual justification. Thus, there is the question of what principles are utilized to determine what groups should be included in diversity programs:

- Are these groups chosen because of evidence of a certain kind and certain level of prejudice or discrimination that they have historically experienced? Apparently not, since Jews have and continue to experience significant prejudice, yet they are never in diversity programs. Paradoxically, however, if one wants proportional representation to the American population, in some cases Jews would have to be fired even though as a group they experienced terrible prejudice in the 20th century. Such "ameliorating" firings to achieve balance would include finance and our own field of psychology. Arabs are never included in diversity programs, even though a strong case can be made, especially given recent events, that this group experiences prejudice and is grossly underrepresented in psychology.

- Are these groups chosen because of demonstrated socioeconomic advantage? Homosexuals, for example, earn

more on average than heterosexual males. Yet GLBT
tends to be inside the diversity tent.

- Are these groups chosen by their abilities to lobby, march,
  protest, and cajole to achieve the economic advantages of
  diversity programs? Does diversity reward histrionics? Is
  it an example of what Charles Murray calls the law of
  unintended reward that is unfortunately contained in
  many social reengineering programs? While certainly
  part of the rhetoric of achieving the status of a group to
  be benefited are claims about discrimination and economic disadvantage, the counterexamples above show
  that it is not the entire case. It seems like the ability to
  claim what George Will has called "the coveted status of
  victim" is key in gaining the economic advantages that
  diversity programs can dole out.

However, this is an unhealthy game to play. We should recognize this as psychologists. One has to paint a history and current experience of victimhood to gain the financial advantages of
diversity programs. Not painting such a picture ostensibly makes
one less competitive in the marketplace. Some discriminated and
initially economically deprived groups have not done this, preferring to take constructive advantage of the opportunities accorded
by American freedom. Thus, recently arrived Haitians in New
York earn as much as whites, and far above the median income
of American-born African Americans of several generations.

The groups who eagerly adopt this route do so even in the context of racism, sexism, and so on, showing much better outcomes than those groups that move toward the victimhood/special diversity programs alternative. America has had wave after wave of minorities coming to its shores, mostly poor and despised, that have lived the American dream. The eminent economist Thomas Sowell has shown that racial and economic groups do not perform in the same way when confronted with hostility and prejudice.[11] Unfortunately, there has been (and continues to be, although we think significantly less) hostility and prejudice toward Asians, Hispanics, Blacks, Jews, and the Irish in the United States. Certainly, the historical circumstances differ greatly (e.g., a legacy of slavery is a severe historical circumstance).

However, Sowell points out that groups with certain values—that is, the importance of education, family, hard work, and delay of gratification—have been rewarded with substantial economic and social advancement. Another critical variable, according to Sowell, is taking responsibility for one's own fate instead of developing a victim mentality and waiting for some ameliorative government program. We believe that another corrective would be for psychology to more thoroughly examine this analysis, instead of solely and uncritically focusing on racial, gender, and sexual quotas, known as diversity programming.

## A Proposal to Focus on Merit

It would be interesting to see what the composition of the field would look like should the practice of psychology become primarily committed to merit and quality rather than diversity and its attendant racial and sexual quota systems. There is little evidence of payoff for all the efforts and rhetoric of the diversity programs over the last few decades. The U.S. military focuses on merit, and it is one of the most diverse contemporary institutions. See the following sections for military diversity composition, according to a 2003 report on the military.[12]

### African Americans

In FY 2003, African Americans were equitably represented in the military overall. In the enlisted force, African Americans were slightly overrepresented among non-professional service (NPS) active-duty enlisted accessions at 15%, relative to 14% of 18- to 24-year-olds in the civilian population. African American officer accessions are fairly representational at just under 9%, compared to just over 8% in the civilian comparison group.

### Hispanics

Hispanics continue to be underrepresented, with just under 12% among NPS accessions, compared to just over 17% for 18- to 24-year-old civilians. Hispanics make up 5% of officer accessions, compared to a 7% ratio among 21- to 35-year-old college graduates in the noninstitutional civilian population.

6. B. Cosby & A. F. Poussaint (2007), *Come On, People*, Cambridge, MA: Cambridge Press.

7. See S. D. Levitt & S. J. Dubner (2005), *Freakonomics*, New York: William Morrow (an imprint of HarperCollins).

8. HUD secretary Alphonso Jackson's comments are included in a candid article by Ronald Kessler, "Victimhood," *NewsMax*, March 2007, p. 29.

9. See Juan Williams (2007), "Enough: The Phony Leaders, Dead-End Movements, and Culture of Failure That Are Undermining Black America—and What We Can Do About It," New York: Three Rivers Press (Random House).

10. The quote from A. J. P. Taylor was originally found in *The New Statesman*, August 29, 1953, and was reprinted in the article by S. Vogel-Scibilla (2006, summer), *NAMI Advocate*, p. 29.

11. See Thomas Sowell (1985), *The Economics and Politics of Race*, New York: Harper. See also Thomas Sowell (2003), *Applied Economics*, New York: Basic Books.

12. Figures for ethnic representation in the military can be found at http://www.defenselink.mil/prhome/poprep2003.

# 11 RxP:

## *Is This Our Sole Economic Thrust?*

> It is not the strongest of the species that survive, nor the most intelligent, but the one most responsive to change.
>
> —**Charles Darwin (1809–1882)**, *Origin of the Species* **and**
> *The Descent of Man*

If it is possible, the volatile debate over pursuing prescription authority has become even more contentious than the battle for evidence-based psychotherapy practice. Both arguments have pitted the scientific and professional sides of psychology's house against each other with increasing bitterness. Uneasy that professional psychologists were now in control, academic psychology bolted the APA in the 1980s to form the American Psychological Society. Shortly after the turn of the 21st century, the name was changed to Association for Psychological Science, still with the initials APS, but almost as if to slap the APA in the face as not being scientific.

Slowly, the push for evidence-based therapy is winning,[1] especially since the publication of the Institute of Medicine's insistence upon such evidence in medicine. Payers are beginning one by one to announce that they will not pay for psychological treatment unless it is grounded in evidence. Equally slowly, the drive for prescription authority is moving forward with the enactment of such laws in Louisiana and New Mexico, and their near enactment in several other states. This chapter addresses psychology's drive to obtain prescription authority, and the several missteps along the way.

## Historical Perspective

Few psychologists remember that the concept of prescription authority, now known as RxP, was first considered by the APA in the early 1970s. This was the era of the new professional school movement, the Vail conference, and the resurgence of optimism for practicing psychologists. As founding president of CSPP, I had been busy drastically updating the professional psychology curriculum, and the thought of limited prescription authority to expand the scope of psychology practice seemed obvious. I was able to persuade the APA to form a task force to study the matter, and the late Karl Pottharst, a prominent faculty member on the Los Angeles campus of CSPP, was appointed chair. The task force deliberated for a year and decided that psychology had become the preeminent psychotherapy profession, was successfully innovating behavioral approaches, and to begin prescribing would detract and even dilute these efforts. It went on to add that there were already too many professions prescribing medications, and only psychology was actively innovating in psychotherapy. Accordingly, it concluded that psychology should not seek prescription authority at that time.

The idea remained dormant until the 1990s when Senator Daniel Inouye (D-HI), in a speech to the Hawaii Psychological Association, proposed that psychologists there seek RxP. Dr. Patrick H. DeLeon, his executive aide, a psychologist/lawyer, and soon-to-become president of the APA, played a seminal role and has continued to be a national champion for RxP. As of this writing there have been a number of RxP bills that have failed in the Hawaii legislature, but with each legislative session the Hawaii Psychological Association gets one step closer. In the meantime, the Department of Defense has had successful prescribing psychologists for well over a decade and, in contrast to dire predictions, without any untoward results.

In the early 1950s the mental health services of Kaiser Permanente in California, with several million covered lives and several hundred psychotherapists, embarked on a plan in which the treating psychologist evaluated a patient's need for medication. Although trained in psychopharmacology, the psychologist did not prescribe; however, once it was determined there was a need for a psychotropic medication, the psychologist presented his or her evaluation in a five-minute consultation with a psychiatrist, who then issued a prescription. To preserve the importance of the patient's trust and transference to the treating psychotherapist, it was the psychologist who handed the prescription to the patient, explained its use and possible side effects, and monitored its course.

Dire predictions spread across California, heralding that Kaiser Permanente would be hit with a spate of lawsuits resulting from medication mismanagement. In the 20 years in which I was with Kaiser we did not have a single untoward incident. This procedure was continued long after I left Kaiser Permanente in 1980, and there was no difficulty until the mid-1980s, when a disgruntled physician who did not make the cut for permanent staff and concomitant ownership filed a complaint. He accused Kaiser psychiatrists of being remiss in their responsibility, and further accused the psychologists of practicing medicine. By the time he filed his complaint the procedure had been going on successfully for 40 years without a single incident, so his charges gained no traction.

## Why RxP Now?

There are several reasons why after the first idea for RxP was abandoned in the early 1970s it resurfaced with vigor 25 years later, and is now the most important legislative thrust for psychologist providers.

- Psychotherapy practice is suffering. The medical revolution in mental health has resulted in a steep decline in referrals for psychotherapy, as most patients with depression, anxiety, and a variety of other psychological problems are prescribed the new psychotropic medications instead. It is startling that referrals for outpatient psychotherapy following discharge from psychiatric hospitals have dropped by more than 90% in one decade. Patients are put on a medication regimen instead.

- Psychiatry remedicalized and has become essentially a prescribing and hospitalizing profession. Psychiatric residencies either do not offer psychotherapy training, or it is deemphasized. Primary care physicians prescribe 80 to 85% of all psychotropic medications, and refer to psychiatry those patients who do not respond, have troublesome side effects, or need inpatient treatment.

- Most psychotherapy in the United States is performed by subdoctoral therapists inasmuch as doctoral psychologist practitioners have failed to persuade third-party payers and the American public that their services are superior or different.

- Since mental health has become, more than anyone thought possible a few years ago, a medication-oriented field, psychologists see RxP as saving psychological practice. Some providers are bold enough to admit this, while others are cagey.

- As psychiatry has abrogated its leadership role as a combined psychotherapy and medication profession, there is a need for psychologists who are well trained in behavioral interventions to assume that role. Without this balance between behavioral interventions and medication, psychiatry is overly prescribing drugs as its sole armamentarium.

- Society is pushing knowledge downward. Nurse practitioners are performing services that were heretofore physician practice, while primary care physicians are performing the first tier of specialty services. This trend is also seen in the steady gain of prescription authority by a number of non-MD health professions (e.g., podiatry, optometry, nursing). Psychology can be the next.

- Americans prefer one-stop shopping. In many instances today, a patient who is in psychotherapy is also being prescribed medication. Seeing one provider for psychotherapy and another for medication evaluation is cumbersome.

- On the distinctly positive side it is hoped that prescribing psychologists will restore an appropriate and much-needed balance between psychotherapy and medication.

## Public Sabotage

For well over a decade, the campaign by professional psychologists to obtain prescription authority has fueled the greatest schism in the history of psychology. Our discipline is marred by a long series of contentious struggles and turbulent disagreements in which one side of the house divided has been pitted against the other side with little peace since the mid-20th century. There has been a succession of differences in this internecine warfare that long preceded the current RxP issue.[2] When the APS, formed by academic/scientific psychologists who bolted from the APA in the 1980s, finally made it policy to pursue prescription authority for psychologists, it was erroneously thought the battle was over. But no longer able to influence the APA internally, the APS and its American Association for Applied and Preventive Psychology (AAAPP), which has never amounted to a strong organization, embarked on a campaign of public sabotage.

In 2007 the legislature of Missouri was considering HB 1147, a bill to enact prescription authority for psychologists, which was endorsed by the APA and the Missouri Psychological Association. The bill had a good chance of passage when out of the blue a letter in opposition was sent to the Missouri legislature by the AAAPP. It was signed by its president, Lee Sechrest,[3] who claimed concurrence to the AAAPP opposition not only from the APS, but also Section III of APA's Clinical Division (12), the National Council of University Directors of Clinical Psychology Programs, and the Council of Graduate Departments of Psychology. The letter began, "We are psychologists writing against the HB 1147...." Anyone acquainted with the legislative process knows that the fastest way to kill legislation is to confront the legislature by a house divided. In such cases the legislators direct the principals to go home and get together in some kind of agreement before they bother the state legislature again.

Sechrest quoted past opposition to RxP and phrased it in such a way that it appeared all these other organizations had signed on to his letter, which they had not. Later, in response to complaints, he removed the letter from the AAAPP website; however, its opposition and implied support had already been communicated to the Missouri legislature.

This type of public sabotage would never happen in medicine, nursing, dentistry, podiatry, osteopathic medicine, optometry, or any other health provider discipline. Only in psychology, and it occurs because after all these years we are still fighting the scientist versus practitioner war. It is unimaginable that the American Medical Association, the American Dental Association, the American Nursing Association, just as examples, would ever allow such public sabotage to occur within its own ranks. The APA, however, appears impotent in these matters and does not want to offend the APS, even though it wages continuous open opposition to the policies of the APA. Left alone, the APS and the AAAPP have the ability to stab in the back the overwhelming majority of practicing psychologists who are struggling to make a living, and lack the security of tenure—the academic equivalent of post office civil service.

The letter is too long to reproduce, but it is worth noting its several points of opposition (the language is exactly as in the letter's headings):

1. Psychologists are divided over the policy of APA to radically change the profession from a biopsychosocial one to a medical one by seeking prescription privileges.

2. There is risk to the consumer because of inadequate medical training.

3. We urge you to evaluate the effects of the laws in New Mexico and Louisiana before conducting this same experiment on your citizens.

4. There is no societal need for psychologists to practice medicine. Psychologists can collaborate with physicians.

5. Training psychologists to prescribe would be costly to the taxpayer and consumers and duplicates the current costs of training medical providers.

6. Psychologists who wish to prescribe may currently do so by completing nursing or medical school and utilizing the training and regulatory resources already provided by the taxpayer.

7. Psychology is an identified health profession that allows the consumer choices of treatment that does not include psychoactive drugs.

The American Psychiatric Association, in its own opposition to RxP, cannot rival the destructiveness represented by this back-stabbing by one side of psychology against the other. It is not the intent of this chapter to refute these points, even though the letter did not state the facts accurately. For example, number 4, which purports that there is no societal need, is completely wrong. Surveys have reported the shortage of psychiatrists, and in many metropolitan areas an eight-week wait for an initial medical evaluation is median. The scarcity of psychiatrists in rural areas has resulted in patients traveling long distances for an initial medication evaluation, incurring an average cost of more than $400, with some at $600. The California Department of Corrections is in federal district court receivership because it has not been able to provide medication treatment for its inmates, even though California has more psychiatrists than any other state.[4] Much of the shortage of psychiatrists stems from the disinterest of medical school graduates to enter a profession that perpetually spends its time in one 15-minute drug evaluation after another, with little else. It behooves the APS and the AAAPP to check the facts before attempting an assassination within its own family.

### Psychology's Perpetual Blunder: Uncivil War

The public sabotage by the academic side of psychology should come as no surprise, since the war between science and profession has a 70-year history.[5] The current opposition to RxP is but the latest in a long line of battles precipitated by providers' efforts to control their own practice destiny. For 15 years academics strenuously opposed the drive for statutory regulation, whether it be licensure or certification—which constitutes the very minimum required before any profession can engage in respected, viable practice before the public. Time after time academic psychologists have testified against licensure bills in various state legislatures. When the tide began to turn against their opposition, they made a last-ditch stand to be exempted from needing licensing, saying they were qualified to practice by virtue of being college and university psychology professors. Before the reader bursts into incredulous laughter, let us fast-reverse five centuries.

The great philosopher and early biologist Rene Descartes at one point in his career decided to take a leave from his university faculty chair to practice medicine for three years. In that era there were no medical schools and no licensure, and medicine was not as much a profession as it was a practice. By virtue of being a philosopher and biologist, Descartes was considered eligible to practice medicine with no additional training. In more modern terms, we might say he was an "applied biologist," a seemingly ridiculous term until we fast-forward to the 20th century, in which psychotherapy was not a profession but regarded as one aspect of "applied psychology," open to any scientific psychologist who believed she or he possessed the knowledge. Clinical psychology was subsumed under applied psychology, and when clinical psychologists broke away from the APA in the 1930s they formed the short-lived Association of Applied Psychology, an early counterpart to today's Association for Psychological Science.

A couple of centuries after Descartes practiced, medicine began to define itself as a profession. By the early 20th century it had its own schools, was firmly independent of mainstream academia, and began to build the foundations of professional practice: licensure and other regulation, a core curriculum, a training sequence, an enforceable code of ethics, a defined scope of practice, and total control of its own professional destiny. These are practice minimums, features that are the very antithesis of academia that flourishes on theory, endless scientific debate, letting a thousand flowers bloom with no core curriculum, and, above all, tenure and academic freedom. These are all foundations of science, necessary and imperative for discovery, but practice simply cannot operate in the same ambiguous fashion that is required for scientific inquiry to flourish.

The APA has never been able to prevent the two legitimate aspects of its house from warring, and until professional psychology is in control of its own education, training, and destiny, the APA will stand impotently by as the war between its science and profession flares up time and time again. Science that thrives on debate, theory, and discovery will never understand the need for structure and regulation of practice, and providers, recoiling from decades of academia's sabotage, have only nominal respect for the need for strong scientific underpinnings. Medicine resolved its science versus practice problems decades ago. It regularly incorporates scientific advances and discoveries, while the biological scientists making these discoveries do not meddle in practice issues.

Ask any successful practitioner of my generation who attended an APA-approved doctoral program what he or she most remembers about the faculty members, and the response will surprise you. They sneered every time psychotherapy was mentioned, and the fastest way to get kicked out of doctoral candidacy was to let the faculty learn you were contemplating future private practice. Far-fetched? Consider that on psychology faculties today one's prestige goes up by degrees the farther she or he is from direct service to clients.

## Failure to Put Our Psychotherapy House in Order

Given the animosity between science and profession, is it any wonder that we have failed to put our practice house in order? Lack of respect for the scientific side of the house has led to our disregard for scientific grounding of practice. The often flimsy evidence bases upon which many of our highly touted interventions rest have resulted in failures, reaping the public's distrust and belief that psychotherapy does not work. After 50 years as a psycho-religion, psychoanalysis collapsed with a thud. The wildly narcissistic "therapeutic self-explorations" of the 1960s and 1970s made us a laughingstock. We rush to champion crisis counseling, repressed incest memories, and multiple personalities before there is adequate evidence, and when the evidence starts to come in, the very concepts are called into question and the interventions themselves are often found to be deleterious. Eye movement desensitization has garnered many adherents, but the research corroborating it has all been done by enthusiastic proponents. When empirical research breaks EMDR into its components, it seems that the therapeutic effect is what the patient said before the actual eye movements. The APA has been remiss in not denouncing these deleterious interventions, even after innocent fathers were incarcerated following faulty psychological testimony, and a child suffocated in a rebirthing simulation with tight blankets.

Given this history of less-than-stellar research evidence for our behavioral interventions, there are critics who believe psychology cannot be trusted with prescription authority until it has put its psychotherapy house in order. Behavioral interventions can harm, but medications can kill. This objection is understandable, but it is not supported by facts. Numbers of untoward prescribing effects by psychiatrists have been documented, but to date there has not been a single one involving a prescribing psychologist. In reviewing the curriculum adopted for qualifying a doctoral psychologist as a prescribing psychologist, even Lee Sechrest, the author of the unfortunate letter to the Missouri State Legislature, admitted it was more than impressive. Still, he hastened to add in the published symposium in the *Journal of Clinical Psychology* that he still opposes RxP.

Enactment of prescription authority and opposition to it reflect two conflicting parochial interests:

1. It can rejuvenate a declining psychotherapy profession for practitioners. It took the biomedical revolution's usurping of the field of mental health to jar economically illiterate psychologists into the realization that their practices were fighting for survival. It is the first widespread, viable economic thrust by psychology providers since the era of the economically savvy Dirty Dozen.

2. RxP poses a threat to academic psychologists inasmuch as it requires a sea change in their orientation, and a massive shift in both teaching and research endeavors. Lee Sechrest and many scientific psychologists refer to psychology in its present state as a biopsychosocial discipline, but the fact remains that where most academic psychologists are long on psych and social, they are essentially ignorant about biology. This ignorance of biology is prevalent throughout our graduate psychology faculties. One tenured faculty member indignantly replied to my contention that psychologists should have a basic knowledge of biology by saying, "We have enough to study, and now you want us to study biology?" I replied that if she insisted in calling us a *bio*psychosocial profession, then "where is the beef?" Including the teaching of psychopharmacology along with prescriptive privileges would sharply move clinical psychology into biology.

## Some Academics Climb Aboard

There are some academics and graduate programs that have quickly grasped the teaching opportunities accorded by the sudden surge of interest in qualifying for the day RxP will be the law of the land. For example, Alliant University has established a postdoctoral master's degree in psychopharmacology and is teaching it not only on its campuses in California but also in enclaves across the nation. This is only one example of the academic programs that have climbed aboard the bandwagon.

In the meantime, several hundred psychologists have been trained in psychopharmacology in extensive APA-approved continuing education programs, and the National Alliance of Professional Psychology Providers (NAPPP) has established an online program for busy professionals who want to qualify but cannot take the necessary time off to participate in on-campus programs. From these another contentious battle has erupted, this time among RxP advocates themselves. On one side are those academics that are teaching the MA degree programs in psychopharmacology, and on the other are those who have completed CE programs or contemplate doing so in the near future.

For many RxP advocates the differences go beyond that of a mere jurisdictional dispute. Since academia, the APS, and other groups involved in scientific psychology overwhelmingly opposed and attempted to sabotage RxP efforts, providers are loathe to turn over control of psychopharmacology education to its avowed enemy. If the war between science and practice on this matter had subsided by now, this would not be such a contentious issue. If anything, the battle has heated up in spite of a few academic programs having gotten aboard. In a recent egregious display of bias, a member of the selection committee for one of psychology's most prestigious awards was able to prevent by filibuster the award going to the overwhelmingly most qualified candidate because this nominee has been prominent in bringing psychopharmacology training to academia.

## Hell Hath No Fury Like a Bureaucrat Scorned

When the Dirty Dozen a couple of decades ago was able to wrest the APA from the stranglehold of academia, little did it anticipate that the now largely practitioner-controlled APA would itself evolve into another oligarchy. It has become a bureaucracy that is long on deliberation and debate, but short on any innovative and effective economic action that would arrest practice decline. For decades the state psychological associations were the grassroots vitality of practice, setting the pace and direction that the APA would eventually follow. The last thing the Dirty Dozen anticipated was that so many of our state associations would morph into boutique bureaucracies, emulating the giant APA and marching to its drummer. Providers' impatience with the APA is reflected in the establishment and rapid ascendance of the NAPPP.

Many practitioners who were delighted by the passage of prescription authority for psychologists in Louisiana and New

Mexico were also alarmed by some of the provisions that gave medicine or academia too much control. One is reminded that the Dirty Dozen's fight to obtain licensure was delayed by as much as 10 and 15 years in some states because it would not settle for bills requiring physician referral before a psychologist could treat a patient, or exemptions from licensure for academics. Better to have no license at all than a token one.

There is currently expressed dissatisfaction between rank-and-file practitioners in such states as California, Kentucky, and Missouri and the bureaucracies that have replaced our once grassroots militant state associations, which appear to be co-opted by the APA. Two examples with which I have been directly involved are illustrative. In California the Department of Corrections was placed under federal circuit court receivership because it could not provide psychiatric medication services. The time was ripe, and several minority inmates filed a lawsuit—*Walker v. Department of Corrections*—to address this grievance. It asked that the director of corrections request the California legislature to take appropriate steps to relieve this shortage by licensing psychologists to prescribe. Neither the APA nor the CPA would sign on to this suit, giving strong credence to the rumor that the APA and the American Psychiatric Association have an undisclosed agreement to settle their differences legislatively, not in the courts. The NAPPP sees the problems with the Department of Corrections as a prime opportunity to push RxP in the bellwether state of California, and has gone it alone with the help of grassroots solicitations to finance this suit.

In early 2007 the NAPPP received signals from political circles in Sacramento that indicated the time was ripe for an RxP bill in California. The CPA was kept completely informed but demurred, saying it was beginning to collect resources for a bill to be introduced in 2012. Right after NAPPP introduced SB993,[6] the CPA, without warning or quid pro quo for NAPPP's keeping CPA completely informed, introduced its own bill. Anyone acquainted with political process knows that two competing bills are almost guaranteed to kill proposed legislation. If NAPPP withdrew SB993 and the CPA bill were to succeed, it would have been worse than no bill. Fortunately, the legislature directed the two parties to agree on one bill; the CPA bill was subsequently withdrawn, and with a few good modifications, SB993 became the one bill.

However, the bill was later voted down in the Business and Professions Committee of the California Senate because the one psychologist member of that committee stated he was stunned by the actions of CPA in putting forth a second bill and would not vote for any proposed measure backed by CPA. At its 2007 convention CPA cynically passed out campaign buttons reading "RxP in 2012," even as the membership remained ignorant of the fact CPA had just introduced a bill. A full account of the unfortunate sequence of events can be found in the archival postings on the NAPPP website.

## The Biopsychological Model of Medication

Even with primary care physicians prescribing 80 to 85% of all psychotropic drugs, and with psychiatry having become essentially a prescribing/hospitalization profession, there seems no doubt that many people who are given medication might do better with behavioral interventions, or a combination of medication plus psychotherapy.

At the 2006 APA convention in New Orleans I was on a panel in which prescribing psychologists described their daily practice. It became apparent that I could be listening to psychiatrists who knew nothing about psychotherapy and were merely doing drug evaluations with subsequent prescribing. There was not one word about psychotherapy. One of the presenters went through a series of typical patient complaints and enumerated when he would prescribe what for each. For insomnia he rattled off the names of various drugs, never referring to behavioral interventions; he seemed oblivious to the FDA guidelines stating that psychotherapy works much better for sleep disorders, calling sleep medications largely ineffective and a last resort.

It would be sad if psychologists gain prescription authority only to be seduced by the expediency and greater remuneration of the prescription pad and abandon the hard work of psychotherapy. In what we might term a truly biopsychological model, a patient might receive only behavioral intervention, and one who receives a prescription would also receive behavioral intervention and even assigned appropriate behavioral homework.

Properly practicing this model, psychology would become the only profession that balances psychotherapy and medication in accordance with need and best practices—an effective step to regaining public confidence and attracting patients.

## Unblundering

Recent surveys are hopeful in revealing that early prescribing psychologists take more patients off medication than they put on it. This is a pattern of practice that needs to be imbedded in the training, which is already being done in some programs. For example, Dr. Morgan Sammons,[7] a graduate of the first Department of Defense class of prescribing psychologists, states in his classes at Alliant University that no one leaves his office with a prescription who does not also have a cognitive behavior therapy (CBT) assignment or similar relevant therapy work to do. "We teach that the authority to prescribe also gives us the authority to unprescribe," and to begin the psychotherapy that the patient should have received in the first place.

If prescribing psychologists as a group reject the siren song of prescription pad expediency, there could be three remarkable outcomes:

- Patients with psychological disorders can rely on receiving medication only when actually needed and receiving appropriate behavioral interventions, either alone or in combination with psychotropic drugs.

- The wholesale overmedication of psychological disorders would diminish.
- Psychotherapy practice could be restored once again to respect and prominence within healthcare.

## PUTTING OUR PSYCHOTHERAPY HOUSE IN ORDER

A narrow window exists in which we can put our psychotherapy house in order. If we do not do this before RxP, it will be next to impossible to accomplish it afterward. The continuing fault lines of psychotherapy practice would drive more and more psychologists into a lucrative prescription practice, thus avoiding patient and societal dissatisfaction with less-than-effective psychotherapy.

Just a few long-overdue cleanups would include that we:

- Ensure that psychological treatment in healthcare is evidence based and effective. Those wishing to practice other forms of psychotherapy could do so outside the health system and without healthcare third-party reimbursement. It will be the responsibility of these psychotherapists to develop a financial base, such as out-of-pocket fee for service. This would require that they demonstrate the value of their services to the public.
- Stop rewarding ineffective treatment. Pay for performance (P4P) is one very probable avenue since this has already begun to take place in Medicare, Medicaid, and some private healthcare plans.

- Gain control of the destiny of practice. Practicing professionals themselves need to shape the future of psychology. This includes the delineation of core competencies, education and training, and evolution in the scope of psychological practice.

## PUTTING OUR ECONOMIC HOUSE IN ORDER

If we do not put our economic house in order during the next decade or two while RxP is being enacted, psychotherapy may decline so steeply as a sought-after health product that it would be left as a prescribing practice, sadly replicating the current state of psychiatry. If all that is accomplished by RxP is rescuing psychology by making it the new psychiatry, we will have failed miserably.

Some say that it is not possible for a prominent endeavor like psychotherapy to diminish so greatly that it virtually ceases to be part of healthcare. These optimists say that no well-established health endeavor has ever disappeared. Furthermore, no healthcare endeavor has sprung from virtually nothing to become the standard of the land. Before jumping to these two erroneous conclusions, let us look at homeopathic medicine and acupuncture.

### Homeopathy

Few people are aware that in the 1800s homeopathic medicine was the overwhelmingly dominant mode of healthcare. Allopathic medicine, the current form of healthcare that dominates throughout the world, was a distant second. By the 1900s this had reversed itself; as allopathic medicine ascended, homeopathy descended—and fast. The last homeopathic medical school closed its doors in 1939, and homeopathic physicians all but disappeared. With the current interest in alternative medicine, homeopathy has made a partial comeback, and there are now homeopathic medical schools once again.

During its rapid decline, homeopathy blamed attacks from allopathic medicine that were successful in passing various laws overseeing medical practice, much to the discredit of homeopathic practice. In the typical blame game played by losers, homeopathy cites unfair, restrictive tactics by allopathic physicians. But without a societal shift of acceptance, allopathic medicine could not have passed those laws. The fact is that homeopathy could not demonstrate its effectiveness as did allopathic medicine, and it lost favor. If homeopathy is now somewhat rejuvenated in this era of alternative medicine, it is because it has gotten its act together, while allopathic medicine has made some missteps.

### Acupuncture

Acupuncture, although practiced in China for centuries, came to the United States recently. Acupuncturists opened offices and began to enjoy considerable favor from certain sectors of American society. Of enormous help was the publication, with subsequent replications, of research showing the effectiveness of acupuncture for a surprising number of physical and emotional conditions. Suddenly, a brand new profession with no statutory regulation or societal recognition obtained both, then made another crucial economic decision.

Learning from the failure of psychology to vanquish managed care, the acupuncture society entered into constructive dialog with it. It was able to negotiate a fee comparable to psychology, which is low by mental health standards, and thus delighted the managed care companies. Acupuncturists were relying on the fact that they could see four patients an hour rather than one, as is true in psychology. Acupuncturists have a number of small treatment rooms, and after "pinning" the first patient, the practitioner goes to the next room, doing the same with the second patient, then the third, and finally the fourth. Thus, four patients are in treatment in the one hour, with the pinning and unpinning requiring a total of 15 minutes each from the practitioner. Consider the economics: Where a $70 fee (for example) would generate just $70 for the psychologist, it generates $280 for the acupuncturist.

It seems acupuncture, the new kid on the block, has run economic circles around psychology. The economics developed by acupuncture, other than its constructive engagement and successful negotiations with managed care, which the APA might well emulate, are not transferable to psychotherapy. But it would seem that giant APA—with its bevy of high-priced lawyers, its cadres of ostensibly expert psychologists, and its plethora of endless committees—would be able to come up with an innovative, economically viable solution during the few years in which the tiny acupuncture society established itself economically. We are talking about economics, not rocket science. Are acupuncturists more practice savvy, innovative, and intelligent than doctoral-level psychologists?

## BEYOND SYMPTOMS TO PSYCHOPATHOLOGY

Psychiatry is in the descriptive stages, and its propensity to go by symptoms alone rather than a solid grounding in psychopathology has led to a long trail of prescription blunders. The DSM creates diagnostic categories by filling a basket with a collection of symptoms for each. Although signs and symptoms are indispensable in diagnosis, alone and without grounding in pathology they are descriptive at best, limiting at the least, and misleading at the worst. Let us first consider an analogy. Presenting symptoms alone involve a large number of serious illnesses that can resemble the flu, such as polio, infection in the colon, valley fever, meningitis, and on and on. How many deaths would occur if these were misdiagnosed from presenting symptoms alone to be influenza, and not treated appropriately?

How does this apply to psychopharmacology? Failure to recognize latent schizophrenia, a mistake made easy by the DSM description of schizophrenia, has often led to the erroneous prescribing of antidepressants, inasmuch as the symptoms of withdrawal have a remarkable resemblance to depression. Antidepressants can drive a latent schizophrenic into full-blown psychosis, and a latent catatonic schizophrenic in particular into violent behavior. The man that shot up the McDonald's restaurant in

San Diego, Andrea Yates, who drowned her five children, and the Virginia Tech shooter who murdered 32 students, as just three examples, were all misdiagnosed as depressed.

Psychopathology, seldom taught as such anymore, has a simple test to differentiate the depressive from the latent schizophrenic. When asked, "Do your thoughts feel like you are swimming through molasses, or do they race so fast you can't keep up with them?" in spite of seemingly identical exterior symptoms, the depressive will recognize the first, the schizophrenic the latter.

Even with true depression an antidepressant is not always the best answer. Bipolar and unipolar depressions need medication, along with supportive therapy. Reactive depression is best treated with psychotherapy, while depressions with underlying biological issues (e.g., hypothyroidism, medication side effects) are best managed medically, with supportive psychotherapy. Psychotic depression requires antipsychotic medication, sometimes along with and sometimes without an antidepressant. Bereavement is a natural healing process, and the antidepressants frequently given retard healing and prolong grieving.

In short, prescribing psychologists should dump the DSM and use it for what it was really intended: statistical reporting and reimbursement.

## WE ARE BIOLOGICALLY CHALLENGED

Our uncivil war is not merely psychological science versus its profession. Our soft science itself is absent knowledge and appreciation of hard science, and it is especially biologically challenged. Fearing they would be too difficult, most psychologists avoided the hard sciences in high school and college, and now find themselves without even a rudimentary understanding of anatomy/physiology, biochemistry, cellular biology, and genetics. How one can make mental differential diagnoses without training in neurology and neuroscience is mind boggling. A course in embryology can open vistas with the appreciation that ontology recapitulates phylogeny, and vice versa. This could be corrected by appropriately designed courses as part of the undergraduate psychology major. However, the problem is even more pervasive: Psychology fears the hard sciences because they might refute some of our most cherished beliefs. This is extensively discussed by Dr. Janet L. Cummings.[8] Let us look at just a few taboos:

- The belief that homosexuality is always inbred flies in the face of available evidence that genetics, childhood environment, and personal choice are all factors. Granted, some may be more salient than others, but from the genetic standpoint alone, the genes responsible would have disappeared throughout the millennia from lack of reproductive activity.

- The belief that all people are equal is contrary to the bell curve that is present in all biological traits, as well as in all nature. We accept this truism in physical appearance, and even produce movies such as *White Men Can't Jump*, but we cannot accept that there are cognitive differences beyond those that result from opportunity or lack thereof.

- Every problem can be remediated. We cannot accept the fact that children born to drug-addicted mothers will never be normal, no matter how much remedial therapy is given.

- There is a belief that addicts can be reformed through cognitive therapy into controlled, or "social," users. We are not willing to accept the cellular and other permanent biological changes that occur with prolonged use of addictive drugs.

- We overlook obvious determinants of behavior such as the messenger hormone oxytocin, which is the basis of mother-child bonding, as well as a factor in all attachments, and is released with sexual activity. Oxytocin can be conditioned, and psychologists should be studying it. Are psychologists afraid to admit that in some activities women may be different than men? Biologists do not hesitate to warn women that they are more susceptible to lung cancer from smoking than men, and that they are more ravaged by excessive alcohol than men.

Psychology needs to close its challenged gap in biology, which may also challenge some of the politically correct beliefs it professes in the absence of—and sometimes despite—scientific evidence. This step, along with overcoming its economics illiteracy, would help psychology regain the viable path from which it has strayed.

## Endnotes

1. The contentious debate in psychology over evidence-based psychotherapies is discussed by the author in *Universal Healthcare: Readings for Mental Health Professionals* (Vol. 9), Cummings Foundation for Behavioral Health: Healthcare Utilization and Cost Series, Reno, NV: Context Press, and especially by S. O. Lilienfeld, S. J. Lynn, & J. M. Lohr (Eds.) (2003), *Science and Pseudoscience in Clinical Psychology*, New York: Guilford.

2. An extensive discussion of the evolution of psychology practice and its internecine warfare is found in N. A. Cummings (2005), "Resolving the Dilemmas in Mental Health Delivery: Access, Stigma, Fragmentation, Conflicting Research, Politics, and More," in N. A. Cummings, W. T. O'Donohue, & M. A. Cucciare (Eds.), *Universal Healthcare: Readings for Mental Health Professionals* (Vol. 9, pp. 47–74), Cummings Foundation for Behavioral Health: Healthcare Utilization and Cost Series, Reno, NV: Context Press.

3. The letter from Professor Lee Sechrest to the Missouri legislature was posted on the American Association of Applied and Preventive Psychology website (www.AAAPP.org), but it was withdrawn when the Association for Psychological Science and other organizations objected to the implication that they were part of the letter. The Sechrest letter has been available through the Missouri Psychological Association.

4. Information regarding the shortage of psychiatrists in California, the federal receivership of the Department of Corrections, and the fate of the RxP bill SB993 is available through the National Alliance of Professional Psychology Providers: www.NAPPP.org.

5. Much of the history of the contentiousness between academic and professional psychology was lived by the author during his career, which began in 1948 and continues as of the writing of

this book. It is also documented in R. H. Wright & N. A. Cummings (Eds.) (2001), *The Practice of Psychology: The Battle for Professionalism*, Phoenix: Zeig, Tucker & Theisen.

6. The full text of the California psychology prescribing bill SB993 can be found at www.NAPPP.org, along with a posting of the sequence of events leading to the bill being voted down in the California Senate's Business and Professions Committee.

7. The statements of Morgan Sammons, PhD, were conveyed in a personal communication from Dr. Steve Tulkin, head of the Alliant University's postdoctoral psychopharmacology master's degree.

8. For an extensive address of the changes in the undergraduate psychology curriculum to introduce hard science into psychology, see Janet L. Cummings (1996), "The New Undergraduate Education Required of the Future Prescribing Behavioral Psychologist," in N. A. Cummings, M. S. Pallak, & J. L. Cummings (Eds.) *Surviving the Demise of Solo Practice: Mental Health Practitioners Prospering in the Era of Managed Care* (pp. 81–92), Madison, CT: Psychosocial Press (International Universities Press).

# *Afterword: Hope for a Profession of Endearing Losers*

After interviewing the head of the campus psychological services at Virginia Tech—and observing the well-meaning but feckless, politically correct, and soft-spoken staff—former speechwriter and master wordsmith Peggy Noonan had a phrase for psychology: "endearing losers." It was Noonan who crafted President Reagan's indelible exhortation at his historic Berlin speech, "Mr. Gorbachev, tear down this wall." With equal incisiveness and candor, noting and appreciating the lovable, do-gooder characteristics of a profession that is both altruistic and impotent in the face of disasters such as the campus shooter who killed 32, she captured in this phrase the status of psychological service delivery in its present iteration. The appellation is at once sympathetic and pathetic, and ultimately devastating.

It was not always this way. As related in the Foreword, the founders of professional psychology were compassionate, but they were compassionate with balls. In other words, their dedication to service was balanced by the bluntness of reality. In my own case, this happened early in my career when as part of a team I went to the California State Hospital at Mendocino following the riot in the building housing the so-called criminally insane. It was there I learned there are no limits to mentally deranged psychopaths bent on violence. Several doctors and nurses were taken hostage, and they were tethered by having their tongues nailed to the floor. Of course they all died of shock.[1]

So the rampage of Seung-Hui Cho, who killed 32 fellow students at Virginia Tech, was no surprise in its disregard for life. What was surprising was the sequence of impotent interventions that led up to the massacre. Sprinkled throughout were feeble descriptions of Cho as "troubled" and "disturbed" and even "misunderstood," all words that are totally inappropriate in describing deranged psychopaths. In 2005 the courts remanded Cho to the mental health system, which not atypically failed to follow through.

Having interviewed extensively several convicted serial killers, shuddering inside at their total absence of empathy or regard for others, I think the word *evil* is more appropriate. And in spite of wishful thinking and compassion from well-intentioned colleagues, we simply do not have an effective treatment for psychopaths. So if as psychologists we also take seriously the obligation to protect the sane and the innocent, it is time we stop using endearing terms and face the bluntness of reality. We do not hesitate to quarantine ebola virus, meningitis outbreaks, and even severe cases of flesh-destroying staphylococcus. It is unfortunate that we do not have cures for psychopaths, but until we do, is it time for our endearing profession to devise some kind of psychological intervention that protects society, even if it is only humane quarantine as the best we can do currently? And would breaking away from political correctness enable us to conduct realistic research that might contribute to something beyond that?

Half a century ago it was commonly touted that the mentally ill were not violent. Although this is true of most such individuals, the basis of the perception came from the fact that mentally ill psychopaths were populating our state hospitals along with thousands of schizophrenics and regressed, cognitively impaired addicts who could not care for themselves. This was before deinstitutionalization. Now schizophrenics and hapless addicts populate the streets, and civil libertarians prevent the restraint of violence before it strikes.

Fifty years ago even "chronic inebriates" who fit specific criteria, such as landing in the "drunk tank" of the city jail several times a week, could be committed to the state hospital for 60 days of treatment. This saved many lives. Then came the era of misguided civil liberties; state hospitals were emptied, and our urban centers became populated by unfortunate, TB-infested street people. A practicing constitutional lawyer friend, himself a recovering alcoholic, pointed to all those already passed out as we drove by Lafayette Square in Washington, DC, early one evening, and said, "Last week two street people died there of malnutrition and alcoholism while exercising their civil liberties." It is not enough to empathize with street people or to assuage our guilt by giving them our loose change as we walk by. Realistic compassion is long overdue.

## Hope for the Little Time Left

Public trust of psychology is fading, and the clock is ticking on any remaining confidence that psychology might have solutions to some of our many societal issues. The appellation "endearing losers" is devastating, but it resonates with much of the American public. Society has lost much of its confidence in our testimony during sanity hearings, as psychologists line up to make unsubstantiated and often outrageous statements on both sides. There are predictions that if psychology does not significantly change course it will be eclipsed within two decades. Yet if we were to make a significant contribution toward understanding and managing the kind of violence that occurred at Columbine and Virginia Tech, along with its lesser copycats and proliferating serial killers and child predators, society would embrace psychology with the enthusiasm it had for it in the post–World War II era. Our discipline at that time was regarded as having great promise. We currently have little to offer society in this regard, and perhaps admitting that we do not know how to predict, manage, and treat psychopathic violence is the beginning of a departure from soft-spoken political correctness that hampers the realistic research that might lead to new discoveries.

I see some hope in a number of recent events. I earnestly wish that the hope is real and not a by-product of my eternally optimistic nature and my deep love for the profession of psychology and the practice of psychotherapy. Let us look at some of these glimmers of salvation.

## THE SEXUALIZATION OF GIRLS

In 2007 the APA Council of Representatives adopted the report of the six-member task force that for two years had been studying the effects of early sexualization of girls. Such examples of sexualization included marketing scantily clad dolls for six-year-olds, selling thongs sized for grade-schoolers, and teens turning to heiress Paris Hilton or pop star Britney Spears as role models. According to Dr. Eileen Zurbriggen, the chair of the task force, sexualization has a range of negative consequences for young women. "Studies show when you begin to see yourself as a sex object, it leaves you with fewer cognitive resources to do things like math…, and it can also lead to body shame, depression, eating disorders, and low self-esteem."[2]

This is a sea change from the APA's insistence in the 1970s that girls had a right (and even an obligation) to be as sexually free as boys. Though hedged with some political correctness, the task force report is a significant departure from the view that men and women are not different in various characteristics, and that any apparent differences are the result of biased cultural upbringing. Undoubtedly the APA's previous stance inadvertently contributed to the explosion in teenage pregnancy, as well as to many problems now seen as caused by the early sexualization of girls that it once fostered and now decries.

This is an important, widespread societal problem that is within the expertise of psychology, and does not squander our credibility by making pronouncements on such previous issues as athletic team mascots. There are a host of other issues that are within the province of psychology and are crying out to be addressed with equal vigor and candor, as opposed to pronouncements on boxing, Zionism, intelligent design, and, still reigning as the most gratuitous of them all, athletic team mascots. The report of this task force provides glimmer of hope number 1 that psychology might yet be saved.

## POSITIVE PSYCHOLOGY, RESILIENCE, AND THE DECLINE OF VICTIMOLOGY

In a recent interview Harvard University psychologist Daniel Gilbert declared: "Human resilience is astonishing. People are not the fragile flowers that a century of psychologists have made us out to be. People who suffer real tragedy and trauma typically recover more quickly than they expect to and often return to their original levels of happiness, or something close to it." In his recent book *Stumbling on Happiness*, Gilbert points out that the previous view of people as fragile beings had made it next to impossible during the past several decades for psychologists to predict happiness and well-being.[3]

For years victimology masked resilience, resulting in a kind of pessimistic view that deprived our research of nature's own healing propensity. Victimology was (and still largely is) politically correct, and to question it was (and still is, to a lesser extent) a sure sign of a lack of compassion. Science can be wrong, even to something as simple but monumental an error as failing for years to see the importance of magnetic resonance imaging (MRI), discounting its importance as nonevasive imagery, and creating an unnecessary lag in its final implementation in healthcare. In 1971 Paul Lauterbur, father of the MRI, sent a paper to *Nature* that was promptly rejected because the editors were unimpressed with the fuzzy quality of the pictures. They completely overlooked its noninvasive qualities, and did not even consider how rapidly technology would improve the image definition. Belatedly, 32 years later Lauterbur shared the 2003 Nobel Prize in Medicine for his discovery of the MRI.

As short-sighted as the scientific community was in this and perhaps other instances, it is even more baffling how a legion of psychologist researchers and psychotherapists failed for a century to see, measure, and understand resilience. Within psychology it eventually led to promoting victimhood, constantly barraging Americans with exaggerated reports of how stressed out and unhappy they were. It also gave an aura of scientific credibility to well-meaning but faulty social legislation that has created and perpetuates our permanent underclass.

For the past 30 years Martin Seligman has published his research on positive psychology, which was sidelined as marginal or just an interesting curiosity, until recently. Currently, positive psychology occupies much journal space, has Internet sites, and is being discovered by the popular press. Although gloom and doom still permeate the media, positive psychology is receiving more attention and may even become part of the pop culture. For the editors of this volume it signals the eventual decline of victimology and points psychology in a new direction that provides glimmer of hope number 2 for psychology.

## CLEANING UP OUR PSYCHOTHERAPY ACT

The cognitive revolution, aided by managed care when it introduced accountability into our practices, has dramatically changed the psychotherapeutic landscape. It first cast serious doubt over psychoanalysis, and as this was picked up by third-party payers who refused to reimburse for psychoanalytic treatment, decades of Freudian dominance came to a remarkably abrupt halt. Psychotherapy became almost synonymous with psychoanalysis, an orthodoxy that was akin to psycho-religion. In the 1960s and 1970s psychotherapy took a disgraceful plunge into runaway humanism and romanticism, eventually pulling out of its nosedive in the 1980s when cognitive behaviorism began to take a significant hold on the psychotherapy landscape. Pioneers who were using cognition in their therapy and teaching more than a half century ago were not taken seriously. But those such as Albert Ellis, who died in 2007 at age 95, and Aaron "Tim" Beck, now in his late 80s, lived long enough to see their techniques move from the shadows to their current prominence.[4]

Cognitive behavioral therapy has emerged from academic theory to mainstream practice. Thanks to its roots in scientific psychology, it is readily quantified and easily subjected to randomized prospective research, replacing nearly a century of dogma based solely on the writings of psychoanalyst gurus whose word was psychotherapeutic gospel. The healthcare industry, after decades of skepticism, now has tangible benchmarks upon which to base reimbursement. With the cognitive revolution has come evidence-based treatment, and the roster of such therapies is growing steadily.[5] In spite of opposition, or at least very little help from practitioners, third-party payers (1) are requiring evidence-based treatments and (2) are moving toward pay-for-performance reimbursement mechanisms, both of which will eventually lead to (3) quality performance measures that will revolutionize psychotherapy practice. These will cast a new public light on psychotherapy practice, increasing psychology's credibility and restoring confidence that psychotherapy works. This is our glimmer of hope number 3.

## FINALLY A HEALTHCARE PROFESSION?

Seemingly kicking and screaming all the way, psychotherapy is finally moving toward becoming a healthcare treatment. The spur has been largely economic, and it is interesting to trace how it happened.

Whenever mental health is asked what it needs to improve its services to the public, two clichés immediately resound: more money and more manpower. This is also true to a lesser extent in all healthcare. However, medicine has the ability to innovate solutions beyond the chant for more money and manpower that is the sole response of mental health. The integration of behavioral health into primary care is a mental health solution that leaps beyond the "give me more" mantra. It began with Kaiser Permanente in 1963, the world's first co-location of psychologists in the primary care setting. This integration has become standard at Kaiser Permanente, the U.S. Air Force, Cherokee Healthcare, and a number of healthcare systems to a greater or lesser degree. It now characterizes the direction for large healthcare companies that are beginning the process of integrating behavioral health into primary care.

Co-locating behavioral care providers (BCPs) alongside primary care physicians (PCPs) not only gives more bang for the buck, but also provides the necessary treatment for the 60 to 70% of primary care visits that involve significant psychological problems. Without increasing the number of providers, its efficiency multiplies the number of patients receiving significant behavioral interventions by 10-fold. In addition, it leverages the physicians' time, releasing them to address critical medical issues instead of struggling with psychological issues they only partially understand. Thus, integration of behavioral health into primary care has become the main impetus to catapult psychotherapy into healthcare itself.

David Barlow has come up with a solution for the myriad psychotherapists who do not want to be a part of the healthcare system. When delivered as healthcare, our services would be called *psychological treatment*, while traditional practice would retain the name *psychotherapy*. Because it would not be part of healthcare reimbursement, what remains as psychotherapy would have to define its own economic base, as either out-of-pocket payment or reimbursement from a yet-to-be-established psychosocial insurance benefit. Psychological treatment, however, would become part of the house of healthcare, not a separate silo begging for an increase in its relatively meager budget.

In the Kaiser Permanente health system, each department (medicine, surgery, dermatology, etc.) paid a percentage of the total cost of providing healthcare (e.g., hospital beds, emergency rooms, cafeterias, x-ray units, operating and recovery rooms). These were all expenses that psychotherapy did not need and initially was not charged for. However, when psychotherapy became a covered benefit, I insisted that we pay our share of costs from which the courtesy psychotherapy service had been excused. My colleagues thought I was foolhardy and told me as much. But I prevailed; having fought to become an integral part of healthcare, psychotherapy needed to step up to the plate. Of concern was our need to demonstrate that psychotherapy was cost effective to justify our becoming a covered benefit. Experience exceeded my fondest expectations, as psychotherapy, by becoming part of the healthcare system, saved so many medical and surgical dollars that the rest of the system became our strongest advocates.

Through integrated behavioral/primary care, psychotherapy is on the verge of becoming an integral part of healthcare, which provides glimmer of hope number 4 that psychology may yet be saved.

## PRESCRIPTION AUTHORITY

For a number of reasons, not least of which is that society is pushing knowledge downward, prescription authority for psychologists eventually will go far beyond the two states where it now exists. It will undoubtedly shore up the economic base of psychology and eliminate competition from subdoctoral psychotherapists, who will not be able to prescribe medication. However, we are less sanguine about this glimmer of hope than the preceding ones. It remains to be seen whether psychology goes the way of psychiatry, yielding to the expediency and financial rewards of the prescription pad over the hard work and lesser remuneration of psychotherapy.

The template for integrating psychopharmacology and psychotherapy into a best practices system was written in 1991, paradoxically by the psychiatrist who as head of the Alcohol, Drug Abuse and Mental Health Administration (ADAMHA) presided over the remedicalization of psychiatry and the National Institute of Mental Health. Gerald Klerman championed the dismantling of the psychosocial thrust of the government in favor of a more medical pharmacology/behavioral model.[6] Too late he saw the pendulum swing way beyond his intent, while both the government and psychiatry devalued psychotherapy (disdainfully renamed "talk therapy") in favor of medication. Belatedly, he and a colleague wrote a book describing how best medication and psychotherapy would be melded into a system in which one or the other was used in accordance with what was most effective in each particular condition. Klerman was the first to recognize the existence in psychiatry of two opposing camps, medication versus psychotherapy, that were hampering progress. These two conflicting ideologies have now become a contentious debate within psychology, and the authors question whether psychology will be able to form the treatment consolidation that psychiatry failed to accomplish.

Prescription authority has the advantage of catapulting psychology into a health profession once and for all. Given that psychologists do what psychiatrists failed to do, patients would have an effective treatment system that balances psychotherapy and medication as needed. To that end we have glimmer of hope number 5 that psychology will survive.

## Benediction

If these five glimmers of hope are successful, psychology and psychotherapy may not only survive, but also prosper, so that we can shed our appellation of "endearing losers."

## Endnotes

1. The events at Mendocino State Hospital in California occurred in 1951 and 1952. By late 1955 the criminally insane section at the hospital and the sexual psychopath unit were transferred to the newly built Atascadero State Hospital. Mendocino State Hospital was closed entirely, along with several other state hospitals, during the deinstitutionalization in California that took place in the late 1950s and early 1960s. The author served for a year as chief psychologist of the unique sexual psychopath program and elected not to follow the program to Atascadero.

2. For the APA's report on the sexualization of girls, see T. Angelis, "APA Task Force Report Decries Culture's Sexualization of Girls," *Monitor on Psychology*, April 2007, p. 51. A full task force report is available online at www.apa.org/pi/wpo/sexualization.html.

3. Harvard professor Daniel Gilbert's recent interview was published as follows: E. Jaffe (2007), *Smithsonian*, May, p. 47. His book was published shortly before this interview: D. Gilbert (2007), *Stumbling on Happiness*, Cambridge: Harvard University Press.

4. For a detailed historical account of the evolution of psychotherapy from Freudian psychoanalysis to integrated behavioral/primary care, see N. A. Cummings (2005), "Resolving the Dilemmas of Access, Stigma, Fragmentation, Conflicting Research, Politics and More," in N. A. Cummings, W. T. O'Donohue, & M. A. Cucciare, *Universal Healthcare: Readings for Mental Health Professionals* (Vol. 9, pp. 47–74), Cummings Foundation for Behavioral Health: Healthcare Utilization and Cost Series, Reno, NV: Context Press.

5. For the criteria of evidence-based treatments see the Chambless Report: D. Chambless (1996), "In Defense of Dissemination of Empirically Supported Psychology Interventions," *Clinical Psychology: Science and Practice*, *3*, 230–235. For a resource of such treatments see J. E. Fisher & W. T. O'Donohue (2006), *Practitioner's Guide to Evidence-Based Psychotherapy*, New York: Springer.

6. The blueprint for integrating medication and behavioral interventions was proposed almost two decades ago by Bernard D. Beitman & Gerald L. Klerman (1991), *Integrating Pharmacotherapy*

*and Psychotherapy*, Washington, DC. Alcohol, Drug Abuse, and Mental Health Administration. Dr. Klerman was head of the Alcohol, Drug Abuse, and Mental Health Administration (ADAMHA) in the late 1970s. He was the architect of what later became known as the remedicalization of psychiatry (and the National Institute of Mental Health). ADAMHA was succeeded by the current Substance Abuse and Mental Health Services Administration (SAMHSA).

# Bibliography

Adelson, J. (2001). Politically correct psychology. *American Scholar, 60*, 580–583.

Amentia, C. (2005). *The Lourdes of psychotherapy*. Phoenix, AZ: Milton H. Erickson Foundation Press.

American Psychiatric Association. (2000). *Diagnostic and statistical manual IV*. Washington, DC: Author.

American Psychological Association. (1996). *Template for developing guidelines: Interventions for mental disorders and psychosocial aspects of physical disorders*. Policy document: The Chambless Report. Washington, DC: Author.

American Psychological Association. (2007). The national survey of 2007 psychologists' salaries. *Monitor on Psychology* website: http://swz.salary.com/salarywizard/layouthhtlms/swazl_com-presult_national_HCO7000044.html.

Angelis, T. (2007). APA task force report decries culture's sexualization of girls. *Monitor on Psychology, 38*, 13–14.

Anonymous MD. (2006). *Unprotected*. New York: Penguin.

AP-Ipsos Poll. (2007, March). http://www.outsidethebeltway.com/archives/2007/03. New York: McGraw-Hill.

Barlow, D. H. (2004). Psychological treatments. *American Psychologist, 59*, 869–878.

Begley, S. (2003, September 12). Is trauma debriefing worse than letting victims heal naturally? *Wall Street Journal*, B1.

Beitman, B. D., & Klerman, G. L. (1991). *Integrating pharmacotherapy and psychotherapy*. Washington, DC: Alcohol, Drug Abuse, and Mental Health Administration.

Bickman, L. (1996). A consortium of care: More is not always better. *American Psychologist, 51,* 689–701.

Blank, L. (2005). *Chinese papers.* New York: Author.

Cantor, D. (1997). A bill of rights for patients: 625,000 practitioners can't be wrong. *Independent Practitioner, 17,* 5–7.

Carson, R. (1962). *Silent spring.* New York: Houghton-Mifflin.

Chambless, D. (1996). In defense of dissemination of empirically supported psychology interventions. *Clinical Psychology: Science and Practice, 3,* 230–235.

Corner, C. (2007, August 22). *Hot jobs for 2007.* CareerBuilders.com.

Cosby, B. (2006, August). Opening keynote address. American Psychological Association Meetings, New Orleans.

Cosby, B., & Poussaint, A. F. (2007). *Come on, people.* Cambridge, MA: Cambridge Press.

Cummings, J. L. (1996). The new undergraduate education required of the future prescribing behavioral psychologist. In N. A. Cummings, M. S. Pallak, & J. L. Cummings (Eds.), *Surviving the demise of solo practice: Mental health practitioners prospering in the era of managed care* (pp. 81–92). Madison, CT: Psychosocial Press (International Universities Press).

Cummings, N. A. (1986). The dismantling of our health system: Strategies for the survival of psychological practice. *American Psychologist, 41,* 426–431.

Cummings, N. A. (2003). Just one more time: Competencies as a refrain. *Register Report, 29,* 24–25.

Cummings, N. A. (2005). Resolving the dilemmas in mental health delivery: Access, stigma, fragmentation, conflicting research, politics, and more. In N. A. Cummings, W. T. O'Donohue, & M. A. Cucciare (Eds.), *Universal healthcare: Readings for mental health professions* (Vol. 9, pp. 47–74). Cummings Foundation for Behavioral Health: Healthcare Utilization and Cost Series. Reno, NV: Context Press.

Cummings, N. A. (2005, December 9). My sixty years as a psychotherapist: Triumphs, disappointments, and future challenges. Keynote address delivered in Anaheim, CA: Evolution in Psychotherapy Conference. DVD available, Milton H. Erickson Foundation, 3696 N. 24th St., Phoenix, AZ 86020.

Cummings, N. A. (2006, August). *Psychology needs reform: APA presidents debate the 10 amendments.* New Orleans: American Psychological Association Meetings.

Cummings, N. A., Cummings, J. L., & Johnson, J. N. (1995). *Behavioral health in primary care: A guide for clinical integration.* Madison, CT: Psychosocial Press (International Universities Press).

Cummings, N. A., Dorken, H., Pallak, M. S., & Henke, C. J. (1993). The impact of psychological interventions on healthcare costs and utilization. The Hawaii Project. HCFA Contract Report 11-C-98334419.

Cummings, N. A., O'Donohue, W. T., & Ferguson, K. E. (Eds.). (2003). *Behavioral health as primary care: Beyond efficacy to effectiveness* (Vol. 6). Cummings Foundation for Behavioral Health: Healthcare Utilization and Cost Series. Reno, NV: Context Press.

Cummings, N. A., & Wiggins, J. G. (2001). A collaborative primary care/behavioral health model for the use of psychotropic medication with children and adolescents. *Issues in Interdisciplinary Care, 3,* 121–128.

Deming, W. E. (1986). *Out of crisis.* Cambridge, MA: Massachusetts Institute of Technology.

Dohrenwend, B. P., Blake, J. B., Turse, N. A., Adams, R. G., Koenan, K. C., & Marshall, R. (2006, August 18). The psychological risks of Vietnam for U.S. veterans: A revisit with new data and methods. *Science, 31,* 57–89.

Dranove, D. (2000). *The economic revolution of American health care: From Marcus Welby to managed care.* Princeton, NJ: Princeton University Press.

Duhl, L. J., & Cummings, N. A. (Eds.). (1987). *The future of mental health services: Coping with crisis.* New York: Springer.

Ehrlich, P. R. (1968). *The population bomb.* New York: Sierra Club–Ballantine.

Ellis, A. (1993). The advantages and disadvantages of self-help groups. *Professional Psychology: Research and Practice, 24,* 334–339.

Enthoven, A. C. (2002). *Health plan: The practical solution to soaring costs of medical care.* Stanford, CA: Stanford University Press.

Farberman, R. K. (1997). Public attitudes about psychology and mental health care: Research to guide the American Psychological Association public education campaign. *Professional Psychology: Research and Practice, 28,* 128–136.

Federal Reserve Bank. (2001, December 14). *FCRB SF Economic Newsletter.* Number 2001-36. San Francisco: Author.

Fisher, J. E., & O'Donohue, W. T. (Eds.). (2006). *Practitioner's guide to evidence-based psychotherapy.* New York: Springer.

Follette, W. C., & Houts, A. C. (1996). Models of scientific progress and the role of theory in taxonomy development: A case study of the DSM. *Journal of Consulting and Clinical Psychology, 64,* 1120–1132.

Frank, P. (2002). *Einstein, his life and times* (George Rosen, Trans.). New York: Da Capo Press. (Original work published 1947)

Friedman, T. L. (2005). *The world is flat.* New York: Farrar, Strauss and Giroux.

Fromm-Reichman, F. (1950). *Principles of intensive psychotherapy.* Chicago: University of Chicago Press.

Gaylin, W. M., Meister, J. S., & Neville, R. C. (Eds.). (1975). *Operating on the mind: The psychosurgery conflict.* New York: Basic Books.

Gilbert, D. (2007). *Stumbling on happiness.* Cambridge: Harvard University Press.

Goldberg, H. (2006). *Reframing the identity of psychologists.* Retrieved May 14, 2006, from Drherbgoldberg@aol.com.

Goodheart, C. D., Kazdin, A. E., & Sternberg, R. J. (Eds.). (2006). *Evidence-based practice: Where practice and research meet.* Washington, DC: APA Books.

Gottfredson, L. (2005). Suppressing intelligence research: Hurting those we intend to help. In R. H. Wright & N. A. Cummings (Eds.), *Destructive trends in mental health: The well-intentioned path to harm* (pp. 155–186). New York: Routledge (Taylor & Francis).

Greenberg, J., & Jonas, E. (2003). Psychological motives and political orientation—The left, the right, and the rigid: Comments on Jost et al. *Psychological Bulletin, 129,* 376–382.

Grossman, M. (2006). *Unprotected.* New York: Penguin.

Hayes, S. C. (2005). *Get out of your mind and into your life.* Reno, NV: Context Press.

Isaacson, W. (2007). *Einstein, his life and universe.* New York: Simon and Schuster.

Jaffe, E. (2007, May). Stumbling on happiness: An interview with David Gilbert. *Smithsonian Magazine,* 47.

Jost, J. T., Glaser, J., Kruglanski, A. W., & Sulloway, F. J. (2003). Political conservatism as motivated social cognition. *Psychological Bulletin, 129,* 329–375.

Kennedy, J. F. (2007, March 12). Inaugural address (January 1961). Quoted in *Forbes,* 26.

Kessler, R. (2007, March). Victimhood. *NewsMax,* 29.

Kingsbury, K. (2006, November). Pressures on your health benefits. *Time,* 53–54.

Koocher, G. P. (2006, October). Psychological science is not politically correct. *Monitor on Psychology, 37,* 5.

Kuehn, B. M. (2007). Men face barriers to mental health care. *Journal of the American Medical Association, 296,* 807–815.

Kuhn, T. S. (1962). *The structure of scientific revolutions* (1st ed.). Chicago: University of Chicago Press.

Landro, L. (2006, July 26). The informed patient. *Wall Street Journal,* D1.

Langreth, R. (2007, April). Patient: Fix thyself. *Forbes,* 80–86.

Lebow, J. (2003, September/October). War of the worlds: Researchers and practitioners collide on EMDR and CISD. *Psychotherapy Networker,* 79–83.

Levitt, S. D., & Dubner, S. J. (2005). *Freakonomics.* New York: William Morrow (Harper Collins).

Lilienfeld, S. O., & Lynn, S. J. (2002). Dissociative identity disorder: Multiple personalities, multiple controversies. In S. O. Lilienfeld, S. J. Lynn, & J. M. Lohr (Eds.), *Science and pseudoscience in clinical psychology* (pp. 109–142). New York: Guilford.

Lilienfeld, S. O., & O'Donohue, W. T. (Eds.). (2006). *17 great ideas of clinical science.* New York: Routledge (Taylor & Francis).

Ludwig, A. M., Brandsma, J. M., Wilbur, C. B., Bendefeldt, F., & Jameson, D. H. (1972). The objective study of multiple personality: Are four heads better than one? *Archives of General Psychiatry, 26,* 298–310.

Marinez, R. (1994). Cultural sensitivity in family therapy gone awry. *Hispanic Journal of Behavioral Sciences, 16,* 75–89.

McHugh, B. (2006, November). Top 10 medical breakthroughs. *NewsMax*, 80–81.

McKinnon, S. (2006, November 17). Proposed pollution to cool the planet. *Arizona Republic*, 2, 6.

Meyers, L. (2006, March). Mastering behavioral health: A new online master's degree can enhance practitioners' business skills. *Monitor on Psychology*, *37*, 38–39.

Miller, S. (2004). Baloney watch: Barlowism. http://www.tlingcure.com/baloney.asp?id=97. Retrieved August 12, 2007.

*Newsweek* (1975, April 28). The coming ice age. Author, 11–53.

Obama, B. (2006). *The audacity of hope: Thoughts on reclaiming the American dream*. New York: Crown.

O'Donohue, W. T., Byrd, M. R., Cummings, N. A., & Henderson, D. A. (Eds.). (2005). *Behavioral integrative care: Treatments that work in the primary care setting*. New York: Brunner-Routledge (Taylor & Francis).

O'Donohue, W. T., Cummings, N. A., Cucciare, M. A., Runyan, C. R., & Cummings, J. L. (2006). *Integrated behavioral health care: A guide to effective intervention*. Amherst, NY: Humanity Books (Prometheus Books).

O'Donohue, W. T., & Fisher, J. E. (2007). The role of practice guidelines in systematic quality improvement. In J. E. Fisher & W. T. O'Donohue (Eds.), *Practitioners' evidence-based psychotherapy* (pp. 1–23). New York: Springer.

O'Donohue, W. T., & Geer, J. (Eds.). *The sexual abuse of children: Theory and research*. Hoboken, NJ: Erlbaum.

Patton, D. A. (2007, March). ADL takes aim at famed DNA scientist [James D. Watson]. *NewsMax*, 34.

Pirani, C. (2007, September 16). Medicare for mental health displaces counsellors. *The Australian*, B3–B4.

Pollock, W. (2000). *Real boys' voices*. New York: Random House.

Redding, R. E. (2005). Sociopolitical diversity in psychology: The case for pluralism. In R. H. Wright & N. A. Cummings (Eds.), *Destructive trends in mental health: The well-intentioned path to harm* (pp. 303–324). New York: Routledge (Taylor & Francis).

Schneider, K. (1998). The death of clinical romanticism. *Journal of Humanistic Psychology*, *8*, 42–62.

Schofield, W. (1960). *Psychotherapy: The purchase of friendship*. Washington, DC: American Psychological Association.

Sechrest, L. (2005). Letter to the Missouri State Legislature. American Association of Applied and Preventive Psychology, www. AAAPP. (Note: Letter was withdrawn from the website because of objection from the Association of Psychology Science but is still available by writing the Missouri Psychological Association.)

Solerno, S. (2005). *How the self-help movement has made America helpless.* New York: Crown.

Sommers, C. F. (2000). *The war against boys.* New York: Simon and Schuster.

Sowell, T. (1985). *The economics and politics of race.* New York: Harper.

Sowell, T. (2003). *Applied economics.* New York: Basic Books.

Sternlieb, J. (2006). Balint—An underutilized tool. *Independent Practitioner, 26,* 28–30.

Sullivan, H. S. (1947). *Conceptions of modern psychiatry.* Washington, DC: William Alanson White Psychiatric Foundation.

Sullivan, H. S. (1953). *Interpersonal theory of psychiatry.* New York: Norton.

Summers, L. (2005). The future of education at Harvard University. Retrieved May 16, 2006, http://www.president.harvard/edu/speeches/2005/inber.html.

Thigpen, C. H., & Cleckley, H. M. (1957). *The three faces of Eve.* New York: McGraw-Hill.

Thomas, J. L., & Cummings, J. L. (Eds.) (2000). *The value of psychological treatment: The collected papers of Nicholas A. Cummings* (Vol. 1). Phoenix, AZ: Zeig, Tucker & Theisen.

Thomas, J. L., Cummings, J. L., & O'Donohue, W. T. (Eds.). (2002). *The entrepreneur in psychology: The collected papers of Nicholas A. Cummings* (Vol. 2). Phoenix, AZ: Zeig, Tucker & Theisen.

Valenstein, E. S. (1968). *Great and desperate cures: The rise and decline of psychosurgery and other radical treatments for mental illness.* New York: Basic Books.

Vogel-Scibilla, S. (2006, Summer). From the president. *NAMI Advocate, 29.*

Whitehead, B. D., & Popenoe, D. (2005). *The state of our unions: The social health of marriage in America.* Retrieved April 26, 2006, from http://marriage,rutgers.edu/Publications/SOOU/TEXT SOOU2005.htm.

Williams, J. (2007). *Enough: The phony leaders, dead-end movements, and culture of failure that are undermining black America—and what we can do about it.* New York: Three Rivers Press (Random House).

Wright, R. H., & Cummings, N. A. (Eds.). (2001). *The practice of psychology: The battle for professionalism.* Phoenix, AZ: Zeig, Tucker & Theisen.

Wright, R. H., & Cummings, N. A. (Eds.). (2005). *Destructive trends in mental health: The well-intentioned path to harm.* New York: Routledge (Taylor & Francis).

# About the Authors

**Nicholas A. Cummings, PhD, ScD.** As stated in the citation that awarded him the 2003 APF Gold Medal for Lifetime Achievement in Practice, Dr. Cummings "not only consistently predicted the future of professional psychology for the past half century, he helped create it." Always the visionary, he joined the other fearless members of the legendary "Dirty Dozen" at the forefront of battles for licensure, third-party reimbursement, and psychological advocacy.

In the late 1950s, he wrote and implemented the first comprehensive prepaid psychotherapy benefit while at Kaiser Permanente in San Francisco. In addition, he conducted research demonstrating that the medical costs saved by psychological services more than offset the cost of the behavioral interventions. It was this research that persuaded insurers to recognize psychotherapy as an important benefit in health insurance. Within the first two years of becoming the first chair of the APA's Committee on Health Insurance, he wrote and implemented legislation in six states mandating reimbursement for psychological services if psychiatric services are covered.

In the drive to involve psychology in advocacy, Cummings co-founded with Rogers Wright and Ernest Lawrence the Council for the Psychological Professions and Sciences (CAPPS, not to be confused with CAPP, which came much later). The success of CAPPS led to the formation of the Association for the Advancement of Psychology, which subsequently superseded CAPPS and flourishes to this day.

As APA president, Cummings' ongoing commitment to civil rights was evident in his appointing the first Committee on Ethnic Minority Affairs and the first Task Force on Lesbian and Gay Issues. In addition, as president-elect he insisted that if contracts for the next three APA conventions, which were to be held in states that did not support the Equal Rights Amendment (ERA), were not rescinded, he would resign as president and lead a counterconvention. This ultimately resulted in the APA becoming the first national organization to cancel existing contracts in support of the ERA, and Gloria Steinem readily accepted Cummings' invitation to be a keynote speaker.

Anticipating the industrialization of healthcare—particularly behavioral healthcare—Cummings' founded American Biodyne as a model of ownership of managed care. He promised to limit American Biodyne to 500,000 covered lives. But after two years in which psychology continued to ignore his admonitions about the future, he took his foot off the brake. In the next five years, American Biodyne grew to 14.5 million covered lives in 39 states. To this day, it remains the only behavioral managed care company that uses effective interventions to achieve efficiency in lieu of session limits, precertification, case management, and other bean-counter cost-cutting techniques. In 1992, approaching 70 years of age and despairing that psychology had missed a great opportunity, Cummings sold American Biodyne, which quickly changed when it came under the ownership of business interests.

Unable to convince the APA's Education and Training Board to permit practicing clinicians to hold faculty rank, he founded in 1969 the California School of Professional Psychology (CSPP) and its subsequent four campuses, a move that launched the professional school movement. Before leaving CSPP in 1976, Cummings founded the National Council of Schools of Professional Psychology (NCSPP), which continues to thrive. Other organizations that Cummings founded include the National Academies of Practice (limited to 150 distinguished practitioners each in the fields of dentistry, medicine, nursing, optometry, osteopathic medicine, pharmacy, psychology, social work, and veterinary medicine) and the American Managed Behavioral Healthcare Association. He is also a co-founder of the California Psychological Association, the San Francisco Bay Area Psychological Association, and the San Joaquin County Psychological Association. In addition to serving as APA president in 1979, he has been president of APA Division 12 (Clinical Psychology) and Division 29 (Psychotherapy), as well as the California Psychological Association. He is a fellow of APA Divisions 1, 12, 13, 29, 31, and 42.

Cummings has served the government in a pro bono capacity and has testified before Congress 18 times. He was a consultant to President Kennedy's Mental Health Task Force and a member of President Carter's Mental Health Commission. For a number of years, he served as consultant to the Health Economics Branch of the then Department of Health, Education and Welfare (now Department of Health and Human Services), the U.S. Subcommittee on Health, and the U.S. Finance Committee.

Cummings has always prided himself on being a practicing psychologist in the trenches. Throughout his professional career, he has seen no fewer than 40 to 50 patients a week, despite all his other activities. He maintains a profound involvement in research and is the author or editor of 28 books (5 co-authored with his psychologist daughter, Janet) and more than 400 journal articles and book chapters. He is the recipient of numerous awards, involving not only psychology but also medicine, nursing, and the Greek classics, and has received five honorary doctorates. Currently he serves as distinguished professor at the University of Nevada, Reno, and as president of the Cummings Foundation for Behavioral Health. He chairs the boards of both the Nicholas & Dorothy Cummings Foundation and the University Alliance for Behavioral Care.

**William T. O'Donohue, PhD,** is a licensed clinical psychologist and a full professor of clinical psychology at the University of Nevada, Reno, where he also held the Nicholas Cummings Chair in Organized Behavioral Healthcare Delivery. He is also CEO of CareIntegra.

He received his PhD in clinical psychology from the State University of New York at Stony Brook in 1986 and his MA in philosophy from Indiana University in 1998. Dr. O'Donohue is widely recognized in the field for his proposed innovations in mental health service delivery, treatment design and evaluation, and knowledge of empirically supported cognitive behavioral therapies. He is a member of the Association for the Advancement of Behavior Therapy and served on the board of directors of this organization.

Dr. O'Donohue has an exemplary history of successful grant funding and government contracts. Since 1996, he has received more than $1,500,000 in federal grant monies from sources that include the National Institute of Mental Health and the National Institute of Justice. In addition, Dr. O'Donohue has published prolifically: He has edited more than 20 books, written 40 book chapters on various topics, published reviews for 7 books, and has published more than 75 articles in scholarly journals.

Dr. O'Donohue, a national expert in training clinicians and developing quality improvement projects in integrated care, is currently directing a major grant-funded treatment development/outcome evaluation project. The project incorporates behavioral health specialists into primary care medical settings, with the aim of improving patient and provider satisfaction, clinical outcomes, and functional change, and decreasing unnecessary healthcare utilization. His clinical interests also extend to treating post-traumatic stress reactions among victims of sexual assault/abuse and other crimes. Currently, he is the director of the Sexual Assault Prevention Program and the Victims of Crime Treatment Center housed in the Psychological Service Center at the University of Nevada, Reno.

Dr. O'Donohue has served on the following editorial boards: *Journal of Mind and Behavior, Journal of Clinical Gerontology, Journal of Behavior and Philosophy,* and *Journal of Family Psychology.* In addition, he has served as a manuscript reviewer for *Abnormal Psychology, American Psychologist, Behavior Assessment, Psychophysiology, Clinical Psychology Review, Criminal Justice and Behavior, New Ideas in Psychology, Violence and Victims, Psychological Assessment, Journal of Consulting and Clinical Psychology, Journal of Child Clinical Psychology, Psychological Bulletin, Sexual Abuse: A Journal of Research and Treatment, Sex Roles: A Journal of Research, Journal of Clinical Psychology,* and *Journal of Sex and Research.* In addition, he was a guest associate editor for *Behavioral Assessment,* Special Issue: Child Sexual Abuse. Dr. O'Donohue reviewed *Thinking Clearly About Psychology: Essays in Honor of Paul Meehl,* D. Cicchetti and W. M. Grove (Eds.), University of Minnesota Press.

His business experience includes serving as vice president of Psychological Health Associates, Inc.; vice president of Mausert, O'Donohue, Fisher, & Zdenkova, Inc., a consulting firm on sexual harassment and psychological research; and CEO of the University Alliance for Behavioral Care, Inc.

# Index